Podcast or Perish

Podcast or Perish

Peer Review and Knowledge Creation for the 21st Century

LORI BECKSTEAD,
IAN M. COOK AND
HANNAH MCGREGOR

BLOOMSBURY ACADEMIC
NEW YORK • LONDON • OXFORD • NEW DELHI • SYDNEY

BLOOMSBURY ACADEMIC
Bloomsbury Publishing Inc
1385 Broadway, New York, NY 10018, USA
50 Bedford Square, London, WC1B 3DP, UK
29 Earlsfort Terrace, Dublin 2, Ireland

BLOOMSBURY, BLOOMSBURY ACADEMIC and the Diana logo are trademarks of
Bloomsbury Publishing Plc

First published in the United States of America 2024

Cover design: Andrew Walker

Library of Congress Cataloging-in-Publication Data

Names: Beckstead, Lori, author. | Cook, Ian M., author. | McGregor, Hannah, author.
Title: Podcast or perish: peer review and knowledge creation for the 21st century /
Lori Beckstead, Ian M. Cook, and Hannah McGregor.
Description: New York: Bloomsbury Academic, 2024. | Series: Bloomsbury podcast studies |
Includes bibliographical references and index. | Summary: "A call to action for the scholarly
community- introducing the merger of podcasting and peer review to encourage academics to
think about the medium as an alternative outlet for research output"–Provided by publisher.
Identifiers: LCCN 2023031392 (print) | LCCN 2023031393 (ebook) | ISBN 9781501385216
(hardback) | ISBN 9781501385209 (paperback) | ISBN 9781501385193 (epub) |
ISBN 9781501385186 (pdf) | ISBN 9781501385179
Subjects: LCSH: Podcasting. | Communication in education–Technological innovations.
Classification: LCC LB1033.5 B47 2024 (print) | LCC LB1033.5 (ebook) |
DDC 371.102/2–dc23/eng/20230918
LC record available at https://lccn.loc.gov/2023031392
LC ebook record available at https://lccn.loc.gov/2023031393

ISBN: HB: 978-1-5013-8521-6
PB: 978-1-5013-8520-9
ePDF: 978-1-5013-8518-6
eBook: 978-1-5013-8519-3

Series: Bloomsbury Podcast Studies

Typeset by Deanta Global Publishing Services, Chennai, India

To find out more about our authors and books visit www.bloomsbury.com and
sign up for our newsletters.

The authors would like to dedicate this work to Dr Gigi Grayson,
Dr Marina Makandar and their butterflies.

CONTENTS

SERIES PREFACE

The Bloomsbury Podcast Studies Series sets out to establish Podcast Studies as its own distinct field which spans the Humanities and Social Sciences. It offers granular political, cultural, historical, economic, literary, and data-driven analyses of podcast genres, production practices, institutions and platforms, narratives and semiotics, and national and regional currents by leading scholars and practitioners. With commitments to both accessibility and rigor, the series promotes research and knowledge creation about, through and with podcasting, and offers insights to policy makers, academics, and creatives alike. Its underlying intention is to develop the practical yet sophisticated vocabularies, methodologies and critical tools needed to fully appreciate the depth and dynamism of our newest audio medium and what it contributes to the broader world.

Martin Spinelli & Lance Dann
Series Editors

PRELUDE: SHOULD YOU READ THIS BOOK?

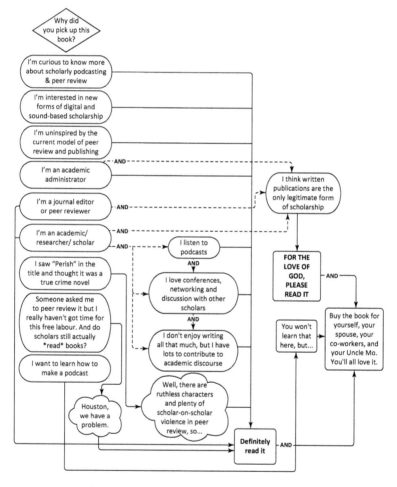

FIGURE 1 *A flowchart demonstrating the need to hire a graphic designer. And maybe an engineer or logistics consultant.*

ACKNOWLEDGEMENTS

Writing a book takes people away from their families, friends and loved ones for much longer than is either expected or reasonable. We would not have been able to work on this book even half as much as we did were it not for the support and love of Alexandra Szőke and Dave Rose, as well as the often welcome interference of Máté, Toby, Ernie, Lexie, Pancakes and Al Purrdy.

Thanks to series editor Martin Spinelli for his patience and editorial flexibility, and to the staff at Bloomsbury Academic who guided the manuscript from its inception.

We had an amazing peer review process in which wonderful people joined us on a number of peer review experiments, all of whom we have listed in the Gratitude section of the Afterword.

The study of podcasting is now 'a thing', due in large part to the enthusiastic engagement of the PodAcademics community of which we are grateful to be members.

A NOTE FROM THE AUTHORS

Co-authors Lori, Ian and Hannah love to talk. In fact, we talked a whole lot during the collaborative writing of this book. We also love to laugh. And as part of our writing process, we spent some time imagining what knowledge creation might look like if academia were more, let's say, amenable to talking and laughing – you know, the kinds of things you hear in a lot of podcasts. So here and there in this book you'll find things that might be a little surprising for a 'serious' work of academic writing: some short transcripts of our conversations, which are meant to illustrate, in many cases, how we co-created ideas and theoretical insights through conversation; some fictional 'alternate realities' featuring Dr Gigi Grayson and Dr Marina Makandar that help us imagine an intellectual world that we'd love/hate to live in; and flow charts – one of which you've met already – that may or may not 'flow' as expected. There are also things that make us laugh, like dad jokes and even the occasional devolution into juvenile humour, the inclusion of which we maybe should apologize in advance for, but have chosen not to.

1

Can Podcasting Save Knowledge Creation?

A Lift in Doha (Alternate Reality Break No. 1)

Dr Gigi Grayson and Dr Marina Makandar almost caught the same lift last year. They'd both been forced to spend the night at an airport hotel in Doha, having missed their connecting flights to and from their conferences (on butterflies and the Pannonian Avars,[1] respectively). Dr Gigi Grayson was busy sending an email to her students about the importance of checking footnotes[2] and saw the lift doors closing. As she ran towards the lift a pile of printed-off PDFs on butterflies fluttered out of her hands and over the floor of the hotel lobby. Dr Marina Makandar saw Dr Gigi Grayson flying

---

[1]Lori, co-author of this book, author of this footnote and Highly Food-Motivated Person, imagined a Pannonian Avar was probably a traditional pastry produced in some South American country. Ian, co-author of this book and Smarty-Pants Aficionado of Central European History, *apparently* knew that the Pannonian Avars are a group of nomadic Eurasians who established the Avar Khaganate, ruling from the late 6th to the early 9th century in the Pannonian Basin and large parts of Central and Eastern Europe, and decided to make this our fictional Dr Makandar's specialty. Hannah, co-author of this book and Very Busy and Important Person, was too busy and important to worry about it (or too lazy to google, one or the other).

[2]Like Dr Gigi Grayson, we believe in the power of footnotes and ask you to please go hunt for them like they're Bigfoot and you're an amateur cryptozoologist with a camera.

across the lobby, and shoved her foot across the lift threshold, her toes thrusting into the lobby like a horse-riding Avar entering Europe in the 6th century CE. Dr Gigi Grayson smiled apologetically and waved at Dr Marina Makandar to go on without her, but did so with some regret, wishing she'd had an opportunity to talk to this stranger with kind eyes and butterfly earrings.

Our Argument

This book is a response to a problem many scholars face: dissatisfaction with the way peer review of knowledge production is currently conducted. It's also about a promise: the promise scholarly podcasting holds for imagining how peer review might be done differently. This book, then, is a radically hopeful exploration into what might change if conventions of scholarly communication and the current system of peer review are dethroned, and, excitingly, what new forms of peer review might emerge.

Before things go too far, though, we should clarify: this book isn't an attack on writing as a form of knowledge production and dissemination. We have, after all, written this book. We love writing (well, mostly). And, crucially, while scholarly writing has become so entangled in the hyper-individualized competition that marks contemporary higher education that sometimes it feels impossible to pull ourselves free from instinctive performances of critical cruelty, writing is, nevertheless, not an inherently cruel mode of engagement. It's just that, with publications reduced to lines on a CV, peer review becomes another hurdle to get over, rather than a collaborative process of engaging with one another's ideas. The challenge that scholarly podcasting poses to traditional models of peer review is an opportunity to more widely reimagine how scholars engage with each other's ideas. And a different attitude towards peer review, we believe, can help reinvigorate scholarly communities' relationships with publics, many of whom are sceptical about the way scholarly knowledge is produced, as well as its purpose and reliability.

Many scholars who podcast are motivated by this challenge to conventional modes of knowledge production, and by the sense that they have become staid, intellectually stunted and are often driven by a motivation to tick boxes rather than unfolding along lines of curiosity, societal need or radical critique (Cook 2023). Podcasting in academia offers scholars the chance to experiment with different media and to decentralize textual knowledge production. It also allows for multiple modes of creating public, engaged, and accessible knowledge (Cook 2023). However, podcasting has, for the most part, sat outside structures of peer review. These important (if often problematic) checks that scholarship needs in order to build communities of intellectual consensus while also curbing overt forms of bias and misinformation are not inherent to podcasting's processes and forms.

Sitting in a somewhat liminal space, academic podcasting pushes in two directions – expanding what might be considered serious scholarly output, while changing the contours of peer review itself. That is to say, academic podcasting can not only be peer-reviewed, but in developing peer review processes for podcasting we can also, we hope, rework peer review itself and, as a welcome and desperately needed corollary, potentially transform wider structures of academic knowledge production and practice. Podcasting in this context forces us to ask 'who are the peers?', 'who are the listeners?' and 'who make up our scholarly communities?' What is the relationship between these emergent, shifting groups and the idea of scholarly knowledge? And how does the digital sonic medium of podcasting reconfigure these relationships?

A podcast is digital audio content that can be subscribed to and listened to on demand. We understand there is debate about whether videos can also be podcasts or whether podcasts that do not have RSS feeds are podcasts (see McGregor 2022a), but we have a political stake in the preservation of podcasting as an open medium, particularly in the context of Spotify working actively to close that medium down. A *scholarly* podcast[3] is distinguished from other forms of podcasts in that it is capable of being subjected to one of many possible forms of peer review. Such a conception means we do not limit our inquiry to those working in academia or with a PhD, but, rather, focus on those podcasts that have the *potential* for review. Scholarly podcasts, then, are podcasts that create new

---

[3]With thanks to our peer reviewers Anonymous, Kim Fox and Siobhan McHugh who pointed out in our original draft that we were using the phrase 'scholarly podcast' without parsing exactly what we meant by it.

knowledge; whose content is accountable to a community of peers, whether they be scholars or others; where it is possible for knowledge to be interrogated, cited and, in some disciplines, reproduced; and, crucially, where podcast series are able to respond to comments, critiques or suggestions either before publication or afterwards as part of a series or through additional material.

Our work builds on and differs from existing research into the phenomena, production style and sonic affordances of scholarly podcasting. In Ian's previous book, *Scholarly Podcasting: Why, What, How* (2023), he argues that i) scholars podcast, in part, as an 'insurgency' against anti-creative, anti-transformative and anti-generous academic structures; ii) scholarly podcasting feeds and generates curiosity in ways that change forms of knowledge production and creation; and iii) scholarly podcasting, if it is to realize its potential, should understand, appreciate and develop the craft of the medium. It is the craft, or, rather, the production style, that underpins Hagood's (2021) categorization of scholarly podcasts as 'hi-fi, mid-register' (polished radio-like programmes in which journalists help translate academics who appear as experts) and 'lo-fi, high-register' (conversations between academics, which may not have the high production values of the former). There is also a growing number of podcasts that fall into what Hagood calls the 'third space' between these categories: shows that feature expert knowledge produced by scholars but that are also interested in the affordances of sound, something also advocated for by Clevenger and Rick (2021) in their exploration of an arts-based style of podcasting that can help create a more affectively charged relationship between scholars and audiences. These three overlapping understandings of scholarly podcasting – as a phenomenon with differing roles for experts and use of the affordances of audio within different productions – all speak to the ways in which scholarly knowledge is being communicated and assessed by different groups.[4] Our focus, however, is explicitly how such knowledge might be reviewed.

The challenge, as we see it, is not merely to develop best practices for peer reviewing a medium that has become an increasingly

---

[4]Readers who want to know more about how and why scholars have taken up podcasting, what these podcasts are like and who exactly listens to scholarly podcasts should consult these works.

popular form of scholarly output, but also to explore how sound-based scholarship might offer an opportunity to rethink some of the fundamental questions of how and why we produce and communicate research. Post-secondary education and institutions are facing several simultaneous crises: the disintegration of academic freedom and tenure (Kezar, DePaola and Scott 2019), the precaritization of the workforce (Kezar and Maxy 2013; OECD 2021; Souleles 2021), the defunding of public institutions (e.g., Estermann et al. 2020; Statistics Canada 2022; Whitford 2020), the rise of under-resourced online courses and the related erosion of the traditional idea of university programmes (Morris, Rai and Littleton 2020), and neoliberal frameworks through which research value must be quantified (Feldman and Sandoval 2018), among others. It could be said that higher education is facing a moment of reckoning.

Part of this reckoning relates to how scholarly knowledge is produced, by whom, and how 'the university' or 'academe' is being (re)made by those who both seek to breach and uphold its boundaries. Following Bacevic (2019), we understand that there is a wide mix of different forms of expertise and knowledge, and that the university neither controls nor defines what constitutes expert knowledge, despite its ongoing attempts to do so. In an age when any scholar can say anything they want online, the boundaries of knowledge and expertise – and the judgement of that knowledge and expertise – are much more porous than the boundary-making project of the university would have us believe. Scholarly podcasting is playing a key role in these processes of boundary-making and -breaking in relation to 'the university', 'the scholar' and 'academic knowledge'. In part that's because it is deeply embedded in social media circulation, where anyone can say pretty much anything; and in part because it affords deep and lengthy engagement into a topic in a way other digital media often do not, thus highlighting the expertise of people who (gasp!) might not have PhDs. While some of that boundary-breaking may be distressing, with some academics becoming know-it-all pundits espousing hateful views through their online presence or unqualified former actors positioning themselves as authorities on public health, our response cannot be an attempt to reinforce hierarchical differences between expert and non-expert. That cat, as they say, is already out of the bag.

In fact, we are at pains to point out that we are not invested in understanding how scholarly podcasting might lead to the restoration of past processes and structures. There was no golden age of peer review and knowledge production; any nostalgia for a perceived golden age is simply a longing for a time when knowledge and access to it was proscribed by one particular type of privileged person.[5] Rather, we're interested in how scholarly podcasting might transform 'traditional' models of knowledge production. We ask: what radical potential lies in scholarly podcasting to rethink the work of scholarship, the frameworks of peer review and publication, the metrics of evaluation and, indeed, the entire relationship between scholarly knowledge and society as a whole? (Because if we're going to ask questions, why not go *big*?)

In this chapter, we will argue that peer review and the wider sphere of scholarly publishing is currently unsound. It's too slow, leaving important work languishing too long; it's too much work, drawing on exploitative labour practices; it's too mean, with some reviewers abusing anonymity to exercise cruelty and gatekeeping along the contours of real or imagined hierarchies; and it's too constrained, by both writing norms and the managerial demand for productivity to be measured and ranked. Scholarly podcasting, we suggest, promises new avenues for knowledge creation that could transform academia for the better; but these new forms of knowledge creation will need new structures to support them.

Podcasting isn't a medium we want to pull into the existing structures of academia, but, rather, podcasting is an intrusion into these structures – a site of slippage from which we might stage a larger resistance to the status quo of scholarly communication. As such, we should not unthinkingly transfer the norms of text-based scholarship (including writing conventions and peer review processes) onto scholarly podcasting. New peer review processes need to be developed, because the current norms of peer review are neither neutral nor free from historical peculiarities. Rather, they developed as forms of control, discipline and accountability in relation to particular historical moments, such as the formation of academies in Europe, the Cold War and the global neoliberalization of higher education. Moreover, not only were many norms put

---

[5]Hannah, co-author of this book and professional Feminist Killjoy, would like to point out that none of the co-authors of this book – being women, queer, lower middle-class or some combination of the three – fall into this 'type'.

in place relatively recently, but they were also never meant to be extended to all forms of scholarship. This invites the question: what types of peer review are needed for podcasting? To answer this, we argue that we first need to understand what scholarly podcasting is, and what affordances and challenges it offers in relation to possible forms of peer review.

In Chapter 2 we describe scholarly podcasting as a public and participatory sonic action. It's created by *voices,* which push us to think about intimacy, trust and authority as they play out through gender, class, ethnicity, age and other social structures. It's created by *conversation,* which pushes us to think about how meaning is created discursively, unfolding across episodes, through projects and within richly varied contexts. And it's created through the contours of *digital publishing,* which pushes us to think about how seriality creates expectation, anticipation and predictability; how it forms new and potentially shared rhythms; and how it calls for an interactivity with listeners through social media, listener segments, calls to action, fan communities and listeners turned podcasters.

Considering the spaces where voice, conversation and digital publishing overlap, we further argue that scholarly podcasting engenders *performances of authenticity* that create new and different ideas of expertise, challenging authority and asking fresh questions about how meaning is made and for whom; that it produces *rhythms of engagement* as spaces for interaction and co-production that emerge through open-ended patterns and invitational cadences; and that it facilitates the creation of *expansive micropublics* who understand themselves as being entwined within processes of knowledge creation. As such, we argue that scholarly podcasting as a public and participatory sonic action creates peer reviewers who are *aware* of what hearing a scholar's voice does to their ability to offer critical insights, as well as how peer reviewing a potentially unfinished and ongoing piece of scholarship changes their relationship to the scholar and their work.

In Chapter 3, we turn to the ways in which peer review is currently being transformed with an eye to being more equitable, useful, collaborative and open, divorced from academia's ever-increasing fixation on metrics and rankings. Analysing ongoing experiments and innovations in peer review (both within scholarly podcasting and beyond) leads us to identify particular attributes that begin the process of turning awareness into appreciation.

There are *public* reviews, wherein reviewer comments can be heard by all, leading to more respectful, attentive and explanatory styles of review; *conversational* reviews, wherein the dynamic back-and-forth of talking through ideas pushes both reviewer and reviewee to further their thinking; *media adaptive* reviews, in which the affordances of different media change the norms and forms of review; *'summiterative'* reviews that allow for work to be published, reviewed and improved in public and without long delays to its first appearance; *community accountable* reviews, in which scholarship is assessed by those whom it is for and/or about; and *recirculating* reviews, through which published scholarship goes through new cycles of review and reflection, keeping the knowledge creation process going.

Pulling these attributes together, we argue that these various experimental and appreciative approaches to peer review have a shared set of values, a kind of ethic that underpins them all: this is peer review as an activity that is *creative, communal* and *caring*. To be appreciative of podcast scholarship is to seek to understand both the scholarship *and* the scholar, and also to be grateful for the way its production suggests radical new ways of doing scholarship. Appreciative reviewing is *creative*, because it's ongoing, open to change and about working things out as they go along; it's *communal*, because it's developed through trusting relationships with an expansive concept of peers and publics for scholarship; and it's *caring*, because it's predicated on mutual vulnerabilities and a willingness to be generous with one another's work. Such a creative, communal, caring framework for doing peer review leads us to one final question: how might such a generous and generative form of review allow us to think beyond the status quo of scholarly communication, as we develop knowledge creation fit for the 21st century?

As we explain in Chapter 4, appreciative review motivates us to do away with a bunch of problematic aspects of academic knowledge creation processes. These include the following: daft measurements – we want to get rid of metrics and stop giving students grades, because knowledge is more than a number and students and scholars are more than their position on scale; scholarly publishing norms – we want to throw out the long turnarounds in academic publishing and the obsession with writing as the be-all and end-all of publishing, because no one wins in arms races except the weapons manufacturers;[6] and exclusivity, because disciplines that are beholden to a canon and universities that are beholden to class reproduction and that rely on precarious labour are destroying themselves.

At the same time, we want to hold onto, and, indeed, build more space for, those aspects of knowledge creation and universities in general that we love. We argue that we should celebrate the centrality of conversation in academia as a method for working things through, a non-measurable form of intellectual exchange, a site of resistance to the neoliberal fixation on constant productivity,[7] a means of immersing ourselves in the unpolished forms of knowledge creation, and a genuinely pleasurable activity. We believe teaching should be celebrated for being an open-ended discovery with and for students, always in conversation with our research in and beyond the classroom. And we argue that we should celebrate freedom: the freedom to conduct research not for lines on a CV, but as a vital and vitalizing process for our academic and other communities, a process that is steeped in experimentation and joyful discovery through failure and, like lots of good things in life, is best done slow.

Finally, we serve up a manifesto of sorts, arguing that there are (at least) three things we can do to revitalize knowledge creation. First, we can ensure that scholarship is pedagogical. This means that public education is not an afterthought, a bit of fluff done on the side of our 'real work', and that teaching, research and service are combined through activities like scholarly podcasting. Secondly, podcasting (like all forms of experimental and multimedia scholarship) needs to be citable. This entails making sure we properly index podcasts, consistently create thorough transcriptions and properly archive podcasts when they end. Thirdly, scholarship needs to be collaborative. This entails moving into new disciplines, evading 'the canon', and being generous and open to the joys of knowledge creation.

And how can we make all this happen? How can we build the structures of knowledge creation we need for the 21st century? As you might imagine, we think scholarly podcasting can help, though

---

[6]Elsevier is as bad as Lockheed Martin in this analogy. We might be overstretching.
[7]See also Clevenger's 'On Idleness and Podcasting' (forthcoming).

it's no silver bullet. The old saying in academia is 'publish or perish', but that's a very individualized way of thinking about being a scholar (and of perishing). We'd rather perish together than play that game alone. So when we say 'podcast or perish', we don't mean this as a warning to individual scholars, but, rather, as an invitation to the community of knowledge creators in and around academia: let's save knowledge creation from the vile clutches of neoliberal managers and prestige-seeking professors, and let it flow from the mouths of scholars.[8] But – and this is the point of this book – if we are to escape perishing, if we are to resist some of the structures that limit knowledge creation, then we need to build our own practices and structures, including making scholarly podcasting reviewable.

And so, because we believe in practising what we preach, we subjected this book to a set of experimental peer review processes in line with the values we identify in Chapter 3: we made the review *public* by inviting interested readers to engage with this very chapter in a Google Doc and to use the comments function to have open conversations with one another; we made it *conversational* by inviting series editor Martin Spinelli onto Lori's *Open Peer Review Podcast* to discuss the second chapter; we made it *community accountable* by inviting the creators of all of the case studies discussed in Chapter 3 to read and respond to our analysis of their work; and we made it *conversational* by inviting early career scholars to record audio journals of their responses to Chapter 4. The Afterword summarizes our approaches and what we learned from the process.

A Word on Method

It was hard, and kind of strange, to *write a book* about scholarly podcasting when the whole point, for us, is that making podcasts transforms the way we do our scholarship. In our weekly Zoom meetings we had a blast, laughing uproariously, fielding interruptions from pets and kids and spouses, navigating time zones (Hannah was often drinking her morning beer while Ian was unwinding with

---

[8]Who might also be babes.

a coffee) and external pressures, personal and professional. We got to know each other well over these months, despite never having met in person; we grew closer, more comfortable with each other, which made it easier to both build ideas together and challenge one another's assumptions. Coming from three different disciplinary backgrounds – Hannah is in publishing studies, Lori in media production and Ian in anthropology – we learned to articulate and question our unthinking assumptions, from how to use citations to what exactly we mean by the concept of 'sound'.

And then we would sit down to write, and all of those old academic orthodoxies would come rushing back in. What we were writing just didn't feel as interesting or *fun* as the actual conversations we were having. We began to ask: why are we writing a book at all, when the whole *point* is that sound lets us do things differently?

So we decided to get a little weird with it. We asked ourselves what we wanted to port over into this book from our podcasting experiences. As mentioned in the author's note, one thing was dialogue, so we've incorporated bits of our conversations throughout as a means of making transparent how collective knowledge can be created discursively (one of the affordances of podcasting that we'll touch on in Chapter 2). Another was the specificity of the anecdote, often emerging from individual lived experience, so we created a couple of fictional characters to help illustrate our points (Dr Gigi Grayson and Dr Marina Makandar, who opened the book and will reappear from time to time).

The arguments we make throughout this book emerged from personal experience, collaborative conversation and, of course, research. We've all made podcasts, we've all participated in experimental peer review processes and we've all spent at least some of our careers thinking about the nature of sound-based scholarship. We've also spoken to more than 100 scholars and intellectuals who podcast, and their reflections pepper the book. As we've written this book, though, something exciting has happened: we've learned from one another. The resulting ideas are more than the sum of their parts; this is the magical process of collaboration and conversation, in which, by thinking together, we come to understand things in a way none of us could have individually. At the same time, while we have written this book in a collective voice, we've tried to maintain space for difference and disagreement, both within our collaborative team and more generally between different understandings of podcasting and its relationship to peer review. Because, as it turns out, scholars are doing a lot of different things with podcasts, and a lot of the fun lies in the messiness.

But wait: isn't this a book about peer review? Is there anything that is fun or messy about that process? Let's pause here for a moment and consider a typical peer review experience.

How Peer Review Works (Alternate Reality Break No. 2)

Let us visit, fly-on-the-wall style, the imagined Professor Gigi Grayson in her office as she hovers her cursor over a new email. Subject line: '*Interdisciplinary Journal of Butterfly Studies* Decision Letter'. She sent her article off to *IJBS* almost a year ago, and between her work on a new grant application[9] and the grad seminar she just finished teaching, she can barely remember her argument. With a sigh, she clicks the message open to read the editor's covering letter. Skimming the opening platitudes, she looks for the decision: revise and resubmit. Heaving another huge sigh, she downloads the attached text documents, titled only 'Reviewer A' and 'Reviewer B', and starts reading.

Reviewer A's report is thoughtful, detailed – and *long*. Fifteen pages long, to be precise. 'This could be its own article', Dr Grayson mutters, skimming the contents. The critiques are substantive, but generous: there's some significant new scholarship in the field that she hasn't read yet but would help to tighten her argument and the reviewer has some suggestions for how she could restructure her literature review to make it more intuitive. Making a mental note to return to Reviewer A's extensive notes when she has more time to dig into them, she turns to Reviewer B. This document is much shorter – and much less encouraging. Reviewer B was shocked to see an article based in so little research (Dr Grayson has been researching the topic for a decade at least), assumes it must have been written by a graduate student (she finished her PhD eight years ago) and

---

[9]Earlier we promised you dad jokes, so here goes: What's the difference between a genie and an academic? One grants wishes while the other wishes for grants.

patronizingly points the author towards 'foundational' texts in the field – all written by white men, all outdated before Dr Grayson even began her PhD. Reviewer B goes on to accuse the author of having 'fallen into the trap of identity politics' and recommends that she engage with some of the more rigorous research on the topic, pointing to three recent articles all by the same author. Dr Grayson is willing to bet money that this illustrious researcher and Reviewer B are one and the same.

Our professor can feel a headache building. She won't be able to satisfy Reviewer B, not without fundamentally betraying her principles and her whole approach to her topic. She realizes that this will mean pulling her article and submitting it elsewhere. And while Reviewer A's feedback will help her strengthen the piece before resubmitting it, this setback means another year at least until the piece comes out. She wishes she could just write a blog post about her findings; there's new data in there and, based on how well received her recent conference papers have been, other scholars in her field want to know this stuff! But she needs the publication for her upcoming review process. Her Dean has been at her again about not publishing enough single-authored scholarship in high-impact journals. Heaving a sigh, Gigi shoos a languid fly off the wall next to her desk, and stares at the waste-paper bin.

What Is Peer Review *For*, Exactly?

When it comes to peer review, we think it's pretty uncontroversial to suggest that a lot of academics and organizations are dissatisfied with the status quo. As part of their November 2021 statement on Open Science, UNESCO called for a transformation in how peer review is practised, advocating for greater openness and community engagement in the process in order to help connect vital research with the public more readily. But this is hardly a new intervention. Richard Smith was editor for *The BMJ*, a high-impact British medical journal, for thirteen years; in his article 'Peer Review: A Flawed Process at the Heart of Science and Journals' (2006), he reflects on the role of peer review and the experiments he instigated to try to improve it. He concludes that the process was 'full of easily identified defects with little evidence that it works', leading him to suggest that academics continued to believe in peer review despite the evidence of its limitations, and that he found it 'odd that science should be rooted in belief' (182).

But before we get to the critiques, we should take a moment to ask what peer review purports to be for. This question is important because peer review as a process is poorly understood both outside and inside of academia. Recently a trade non-fiction book, Rosemary Sullivan's *The Betrayal of Anne Frank* (2022), made waves for its controversial claims; many readers have expressed shock that the book – based on rigorous archival research – was not reviewed by experts prior to its publication.[10] But in fact, trade non-fiction books are neither peer-reviewed nor even fact-checked, for the most part (Newman 2014). On the other hand, readers generally assume that anything published in a journal is peer-reviewed, a belief that oversimplifies the different kinds of scholarly knowledge production, which include book reviews (generally not peer-reviewed), editorials (sometimes peer-reviewed), as well as more conventional articles (usually peer-reviewed, though in different ways) and books (usually peer-reviewed, but differently again from articles). Arguably, understanding peer review – how it works, and what it says about the work you're engaging with – is a vital component of contemporary media literacy. But far from it being richly understood by the broader public, it's barely understood within academia, where it is often viewed as an ahistorical truism of how scholarship is created.

To start with relatively uncontroversial categorizations, peer review is practised in a range of ways that are defined, as Tennant et al. (2017) explain, drawing on the work of Ross-Hellauer (2017), by their 'different approaches to the relative timing of the review in the publication cycle, the reciprocal transparency of the process, and the contrasting and disciplinary practices' (para. 2). Most definitions focus on the review's level of anonymity, or 'blindness'.[11] As indicated in the types of peer review listed in what follows, the

---

[10]Various online discussions of the book's controversial withdrawal by its publisher have included expressions of surprise that the book was not peer-reviewed prior to its publication, a reminder that many readers are not aware of the lack of peer review or fact-checking required of trade non-fiction books.

[11]We'll use the term 'anonymous' throughout this volume, instead, to avoid the ableist associations of 'blindness' with lack of knowledge.

level of anonymity ranges from neither the author nor the reviewer knowing one another's identities, to everyone involved not only knowing each other but actively collaborating in the review process. Possible approaches include:

- Single Anonymized: The reviewer knows the author's identity but the author doesn't know the identity of the reviewer. This is generally the peer-review approach at university presses.

- Double Anonymized: Neither the author nor the reviewer know one another's identities. This is frequently the peer-review approach at journals.

- Open: The author and reviewer know one another's identities. The reviewer's identity may also be public.[12]

- Transparent: The review is published alongside the work of scholarship.

- Collaborative: The reviewers are known to each other, and collaborate on producing their review. Collaborative reviews may also be open, allowing the reviewers to collaborate with the author. ('Types of Peer Review', *Wiley Journals*)

The aforementioned typology and explanation all relate to peer review as a process (i.e., the various procedures and approaches used for reviewing). But we need to distinguish this from peer review as a paradigm or set of ideas (including how it has been mythologized or demonized within academia), and the different forms of media in which peer review can be done (audio, text and so on).[13] While it is useful to make this analytical distinction, it is also true that often the process, paradigm and medium of peer review can reinforce and mask one another in the creation of unsound peer review (e.g., anonymous text-based journal reviews that have led to the much reviled figure of 'Reviewer 2' who destroys submissions just for fun).

---

[12]As we discuss further later, open review is an umbrella term that can encapsulate various approaches (Ross-Hellauer 2017).
[13]We thank peer reviewer Ebrahim Bagheri for this useful suggestion.

But this doesn't tell us what peer review is *for*. In the review process for this book, a few of our peers suggested it might seem as if we were creating a straw man argument[14] by highlighting all that's wrong with the current system without engaging with the paradigm, processes and medium of peer review as publishers intend them to be. As such, it is worth quoting the academic journal and book publishers Taylor and Francis at length to understand how peer review is seen by those at the forefront of the current system. This is information for potential authors within their many publications:

> Peer review is the independent assessment of your research paper by experts in your field. The purpose of peer review is to evaluate the paper's quality and suitability for publication. As well as peer review acting as a form of quality control for academic journals, it is a very useful source of feedback for you. The feedback can be used to improve your paper before it is published. So at its best, peer review is a collaborative process, where authors engage in a dialogue with peers in their field, and receive constructive support to advance their work ... Peer review is vitally important to uphold the high standards of scholarly communications, and maintain the quality of individual journals. It is also an important support for the researchers who author the papers. Every journal depends on the hard work of reviewers who are the ones at the forefront of the peer review process. The reviewers are the ones who test and refine each article before publication. Even for very specialist journals, the editor can't be an expert in the topic of every article submitted. So, the feedback and comments of carefully selected reviewers are an essential guide to inform the editor's decision on a research paper. There are also practical reasons why peer review is beneficial to you, the author. The peer review process can alert you to any errors in your work, or gaps in the literature you may have overlooked. (Taylor and Francis n.d.)

So conceptualized, the peer-review process has two key elements: quality control and feedback. Editors also play an important role

---

[14]Thanks to peer reviewers Jessica McDonald, Kim Fox and Anonymous for the help here.

in the peer-review process. They or a member of the editorial board are responsible for both the initial quality assessment of a given piece and overseeing the feedback process (the sourcing of peer reviewers, checking whether or not authors respond to the reviews in an appropriate way, etc.). In terms of checks before any possible peer review, according to Taylor and Francis's guidelines (n.d.) an editor should consider:

- Is the manuscript of good enough quality to be sent for peer review?

- Does it conform to the aims and scope of the journal and has it followed the style guidelines and instructions for authors?[15]

- Does it make a significant contribution to the existing literature?

In some journals the editor-in-chief or a member of the editorial team gives an initial round of feedback, maybe suggesting changes to make it better fit with the journal's aims or scope, or highlighting areas where work needs to be done, but many simply issue curt desk rejects or pass it on to reviewers without a first round of feedback. Working structures, types of publication and more change an editor's role and approach. Many of the norms of peer review in journal publication have been developed around the needs of the STEM fields, whereas university presses, which often specialize in social sciences and humanities research, have developed different standards and processes. In the latter, peer reviewers will be carefully selected by editors to strengthen a manuscript, and incorporated into a robust editorial process that includes developmental editing as well as, generally, professional copy editing. Many editors of journals are scholars who are doing it as a form of service and so have minimal time and sometimes minimal expertise, while editors at presses are full-time employees with expertise in developmental

---

[15]Needless nitpicking about style guidelines is often a waste of an author's and a reviewer's time and should become important only once a piece is selected for publication. (Some people suggest that journals 'game' the system by rejecting manuscripts for stylistic reasons and asking the author to resubmit, thus creating an inflated illusion on how difficult it is to publish in a certain journal.)

editing and, as such, authors and peer reviewers can have widely differing experiences. Within that range of possible editorial approaches, the quality check that editors perform includes a host of possible considerations, some more easily grasped (e.g., plagiarism), but some that require more unpacking and may include methodology, age of sample/data, logical argumentation, fact checking and so on. We will return to a discussion about editors in Chapter 3, but for now let's turn to quality control and feedback in a little more depth to see if they live up to their promises.

Quality Control

As practised by scholarly journals and academic presses, as well as some academic conferences, peer review is a process whereby experts in a field evaluate the work of other scholars in their field. Peer reviewers should thus have a depth of expertise that enables them not only to understand and critique the subtleties and nuances of arguments and interpretation of data, but also to judge the soundness of the methodologies employed and conclusions drawn.

Quality control is important in the context of publishing, because abundance is a problem: how do we decide what to read and what to ignore, what's important and what is not? The answer to this question changes depending on the publishing ecosystem under consideration, but in academia the answer has been the implementation of various kinds of automated metrics, including impact and citations. Peer review is another way of managing the overabundance of scholarly publications, producing artificial scarcity in the marketplace of ideas, so to speak. Upholding double-anonymized peer review as a 'gold standard' of academic rigour is a relatively recent shift in the scholarly publishing landscape as we shall demonstrate in what follows, and one that reminds us that this so-called gold standard, in fact, has very little to do with understanding or appreciating scholarly work.

Throughout the COVID-19 pandemic, peer review has been a subject of more-public-than-usual attention as studies have been rushed through the process in an attempt to keep up with constantly evolving scientific knowledge about the virus (Else 2020). As pre-print articles show up in news coverage and rushed peer reviews are sometimes found to be unreliable and even dangerous, a somewhat traditional definition of peer review has been circulating: peer review is a process whereby expert knowledge is validated by other experts to ensure that it is accurate.

But that image of peer review as a kind of intellectual blue check mark,[16] verifying the reality of what's being published, both oversells and undersells what peer review really is. For one thing, peer review is *not* fact-checking, and it turns out it doesn't always do a great job of locating errors (Jefferson et al. 2006; Schroter et al. 2008). That's a disappointing revelation if we thought that was what peer review was meant to be doing – but if that *was* what peer review was supposed to be doing, then journals, like magazines, would hire professional fact checkers to review any confirmable information (citations, for example, or archival holdings, both sources of evidence that have been found to be unreliable in some academic publications [e.g., Pavlovic et al. 2020]). And some of those big journal publishers – Elsevier, Black & Wiley, Taylor & Francis, Springer Nature and SAGE – could probably afford to do so.

Feedback

Good scholarship is built on the back-and-forth of dialogue and discussion, but traditional review processes rarely facilitate this. The norms, particularly in journal publication, of double-anonymous review (in which both the author and the reviewer are unknown to each other) discourage both immediacy and a generative conception of dialogue. The isolation of reviewers from each other and from the author can lead to loss of clarity in communication or understanding intent. Reviews, nearly always text-based, will sometimes be directly contradictory, with journal editors often not helping resolve contradictions but, rather, passing on reviews with little comment. At other times reviewers will spend extensive time writing about issues that could have been cleared up with a simple conversation.

Anonymity does not mean equality between those who are reviewing and those who are being reviewed. While an adversarial approach to intellectual exchange may be fruitful in certain

---

[16]Ha. Just wait until Elon Musk starts buying up academic publishing houses.

settings, such a 'thinking against' or 'courtroom' approach is highly problematic when applied to anonymous peer review because it ignores the hierarchies and inequalities that exist within international academia (Brković 2022). Many of us have felt the cruelty of mean-spirited peer review, which can be exacerbated by a reviewer's assumptions or projections relating to gender, ethnicity, country of origin and use of non-western/non-northern or non-patriarchal theoretical framings or methods. One scholar described their first attempt at publishing as 'a traumatising one that could be called a form of academic hazing' (Docot 2022, 127). In response to calls for opening up peer review, critics often express a worry that signed reviews would lead to backlash, but according to a multi-author[17] collaborative study on open peer review (Tennant et al. 2017), the research does not support this general concern. In fact, several randomized control studies have shown that when they knew that their identities would be made known, peer reviewers gave more substantive feedback, which was furthermore regarded as more courteous and helpful by reviewees (Bastian 2015). Any potential backlash resulting from knowing the identity of the reviewer is likely not as bad as the way anonymity currently breeds critical cruelty.

In 'On Critical Humility' (2020), Métis scholar Warren Cariou points out that contemporary academia is 'extremely hierarchical, very focused on commodifiable forms of research, and frankly, very elitist' (6–7). He includes the jargon-filled language of academic writing in this critique, as well as the practice of anonymous peer review. Conventional academic publishing, he points out, is focused on building up the authority and perceived importance of the author rather than 'the quiet work of building relationships':

> Reviewers may feel the need to demonstrate their rank by providing needlessly pedantic requirements for revision. This is a gatekeeping mechanism which, as with all types of gatekeeping, can be informed by dynamics of power, gender, race, method, area of research inquiry, and so on. (9)

---

[17]Seriously, this thing has like thirty-eight co-authors. It's wild.

The gatekeeping function of peer review, in which peer reviewers often (intentionally or not) privilege work that resembles what they are already familiar with, is a disciplining process that encourages other scholars to produce more of the same and discourages experimentation and new approaches. Scholars working from the academic periphery or focusing on less established topics often face enormous hurdles when trying to convince western/northern journal editors that they have original, important research deserving of publication (Blagojević and Yair 2010). The closed system of peer review as it is currently practised 'protects the status quo and suppresses research viewed as radical, innovative, or contrary to the theoretical or established perspectives of referees' (Tennant et al. 2017). Among the many forms of innovation curbed by standard review is the creation of scholarship in forms other than writing.

We are not, of course, suggesting that all peer review experiences are bad or that peer review across the board fails to produce better scholarship by giving feedback and providing quality control. What we are suggesting is that we need to critique how peer review works currently so that we can produce better scholarship. A refusal to do so, we suggest, is unscholarly. But it's not only that current peer review practices can be critiqued on their own terms, as failing to embody their own paradigms; the structural issues with peer review extend into so much of the status quo of how knowledge is created in the 21st century.

Structural Problems: Unsound Review

Earlier we have shown how the two purposes of peer review (quality control and feedback) often fall short of their aims, but we also want to raise three further issues that scholars raise with us when discussing (complaining about?) current peer-review practices and the scholarly publishing ecosystem[18] in which they play a key role: time frames, labour and writing.

---

[18]Many of the arguments we make here apply to scholarly publishing (especially journal publishing) in general; we find it difficult to separate peer review from some of the wider issues plaguing scholarly publishing.

Time Frames (As Spinning Plates)

Because peer review is done voluntarily by scholars, it is a slow process: articles often come out years after their submission. It takes time to find willing reviewers and then even more time for them to complete and submit their reviews. This slowness can be especially problematic if the research itself is moving at a much faster rate. Indeed, many scholars 'now view traditional peer review as sub-optimal and detrimental to research because it causes publication delays, with repercussions on the dissemination of novel research' (Tenant et al. 2017).

Part of the problem clearly relates to workload and the temporal organization of work that academics must negotiate. Scholars often feel as if our working lives are speeding up to such a degree that it negatively impacts our work (Menzies and Newson 2007; Ylijoki and Mäntylä 2003). Cognitive and institutional times do not always align, and must be negotiated (Vostal, Benda and Virtová 2019). Additional balancing of the disjunctures between supposedly linear careers, timeless disciplines and clearly time-bound projects is required (Smith 2015). It's unsurprising that scholars often feel shame at being unable to realize aspirations of who and where they want to be in the future, or at being unable to fulfil commitments to others (Shahjahan 2020), that their lives become colonized by unrelenting work demands (Shahjahan 2015), or that they are unable to be present in the here and now because they are always working towards a future version of their scholarly self (Bunn and Bennett 2020). Finding time to review an article in and among all these temporal pressures can be truly difficult.

Such temporal concerns are felt acutely by those among the increasingly large number of precariously employed or unemployed academics. What happens to the paradigm of peer review when, for example, scholars on annual teaching contracts with zero research allowance or those between jobs are still asked to engage in the review process for journals they might consider publishing with one day in the future; or when the time-consuming process of writing responses needs to be balanced out against the need to find new work, write grants or undertake non-academic labour for immediate material needs?[19] Here we see the 'cruel optimism' (Berlant 2011) that sustains exploitative labour conditions by trading on the future desires of those living with academic precarity (Bone 2021).

---

[19]We thank peer reviewer Jessica McDonald for this useful point.

Academic Labour (As Exploitation)

The temporal organization of academic work is only part of the problem. It's also the case that for many scholars, including ourselves, it's hard to give our free labour into a business model which, in the case of large journal publishers, is undeniably exploitative: authors submit their work for free, complete unpaid peer review as an act of service to the discipline, and then journals sell this work back to academics via annual subscriptions from universities. Moreover, publishing companies like Elsevier have been steadily increasing the annual subscription fees they charge university libraries (Crowe 2019). These increases reduce the budget libraries have remaining to build their book collections, which in turn cuts into the primary customer base for university presses, thus undermining the financial viability of university presses (Fitzpatrick 2011). As UC Berkeley's University Librarian and economics professor Jeffrey MacKie-Mason – co-chair of UC's publisher negotiation team which recently brokered a new open access deal with Elsevier – explains, scholarly publishing at this scale certainly has costs associated with it, but 'Elsevier's prices are still too high, and it makes outrageous profits' (Kell 2021, para. 12).

While the predatory models of journal publishers like Elsevier[20] are part of the problem troubling academic publishing in the 21st century, they are in some ways symptomatic of a larger structural problem: we are all publishing too much and taking fewer risks in our work as a result (Burnard et al. 2022). At the root of this problem is the shift of universities around the world to a corporate model, using metrics to evaluate individual scholars, departments, faculties and even entire institutions. These metrics rely on automated measures of productivity, including the 'impact' of the journal, number of citations, total number of publications and so

---

[20]It might seem like we're picking on Elsevier here, but they really are the biggest fish in a small, algae-clogged pond. As Martin Hagve (2020) explains, 'The market is largely dominated by five large publishing houses: Elsevier, Black & Wiley, Taylor & Francis, Springer Nature and SAGE, which control more than 50% of the market between them. Elsevier is the largest, with approximately 16% of the total market and more than 3000 academic journals. As an industry, these publishing houses are unique in terms of their profitability, generating large net profits. Elsevier has a profit margin approaching 40%, which is higher than that of companies such as Microsoft, Google and Coca Cola, and the curve is pointing upwards.'

forth.[21] The number of articles published in peer-reviewed, English language journals has been increasing exponentially in recent decades (Fire and Guestrin 2019), with as many as 2.5 million new articles published in 2014 alone (Ware and Mabe 2015). In this same period, the expansion of the university system has led to a surge in PhDs: the number of doctorates conferred in America in the humanities is estimated to have increased by more than 40 per cent in the last 25 years (Carey 2020), flooding the previously relatively shallow market of scholarly texts while increasing competition for a shrinking number of secure positions, thus further motivating scholars to publish as much as possible.

Within this vast pool of production, peer review has become increasingly systematized, making it feel like a distanced and disengaged process. The depersonalization and non-urgency of the task can lead to us shoving it to the bottom of a long list of things to do. There's no real pressure to get to it because it doesn't always *feel* like the work we're reviewing was written by an actual living, breathing person. This is not to say that all reviewers are bad, or that all reviews lack compassion alongside their critiques,[22] nor is it even to place the blame on individual reviewers (except you, yes you, you know who you are and what you did!) but, rather, to point to the problematic conditions that create exasperation when scholars sit down to do review work, an exasperation that can lead to critical cruelty finding its way into our reviews.

Writing (As Measured Production and Standardized Knowledge)

We know how to write good. But does everyone? And what does writing good even mean? In the social sciences and humanities, 'good writing' mostly has to do with internalizing a set of communication norms – largely unspoken and, at many universities, untaught – that serve to amplify the hegemony of Anglo-American

---

[21]This problem is not unique to academia: new publishing technologies have long facilitated the massive expansion of publishing output across all fields, culminating in the internet's truly industry-breaking output of an endless stream of new content.
[22]#notallreviewers

scholarly structures within the English-language academy.[23] What's considered 'good' academic prose privileges native or near native English speakers or those who have been able to afford to study in English-speaking, western/northern countries from abroad, leading to 'cases of linguistic inequality and language-oriented research segregation, in a world where research is increasingly becoming more globally competitive' (Tennant et al. 2017).

There are, of course, different styles and tones of scholarly writing. The style and tone in which we have written this book would not be acceptable in most academic journals (and as one or two reviewers of this book told us, its style and tone may also be inappropriate and distracting for an academic book, lol). When we critique scholarly writing we are, for the most part, thinking about journal article writing, as writing journal articles is the most important demonstration of 'academic worth' to those who count a scholar's worth (disciplinary differences notwithstanding). And that writing tends to be pretty impenetrable. We aren't trying to claim here that there is no place for specialized terms or phrases in scholarship, or that every work of academic writing needs to be pitched to some illusory 'public' with a somehow identical level of understanding – though, with the low value many universities place on public scholarship (Alperin et al. 2019), there's little motivation to communicate to wider audiences, or even to experts in neighbouring disciplines. The point is, many of the conventions of scholarly communication are implicit and unquestioned, and academics are praised for the degree to which we indoctrinate ourselves to and thus reproduce them.

And we reproduce them *in writing*. Our primary output is published texts, vetted generally through an anonymized peer-review process. Ideas, innovations and discoveries must be fixed in written form, usually in journals, and passed along to experts in the subject matter to scrutinize the methodologies used and to check for sound reasoning and supporting evidence. Written feedback is returned to the author, who then proceeds to revise the written

---

[23]We focus primarily on the Anglo-American scholarly structures within the English-language academy as this is what we know best and because it is often seen as (and often problematically held up as) the 'international standard', especially within matrices of measurements used by university managers in other parts of the world.

text for publication. But the standardization of written journal scholarship as 'real' scholarship has nothing inherently to do with writing as a technology. In fact, much like the standardization of peer review, it's a remarkably recent shift that has more to do with the status of the modern university – a claim we'll unpack further in our account of the evolution of peer review, in what follows.

Suffice it to say, factors such as the codification of language and the incorporation of academia into late-stage capitalism with its focus on measurable and ever-increasing outputs have led to output and words becoming synonymous – not because scholarly ideas must be written-word-based, but because those are the forms of knowledge we're best at measuring, tracking and enumerating. If it feels like academic knowledge production has become overly fixated on the written word as essentially synonymous with information itself, that's less because of anything inherent about writing than it is because of how easily writing can be inventoried.

Writing can be creative, curiosity-driven, wondrous and free. Publishing books or chapters in edited volumes can offer more freedom than conventional journals, with editors or series editors playing important and active roles in shaping content; some academic-run journals not only allow but encourage different styles and tones; and many 'standard' journal articles can also be wonderful to read (and write). What we take issue with is the paradigm of written scholarship that has become entwined with unproblematized writing conventions and the unthinking application of processes of peer review.

*   *   *

With these issues around time frames, academic labour and writing coupled with less than ideal forms of quality control and feedback, no wonder so many academics feel dissatisfied with the current landscape of scholarly publication and peer review. Publishing is often framed by a demand to constantly produce more and more works so that they can be tracked and counted and added to our university's prestige markers, as well as ever more elaborate systems for ranking and managing the resulting overabundance that is itself a product of what our universities demand of us. Universities need us to be in competition with each other, much as they need to compete with one another for students and rankings (Fitzpatrick 2018).

While research communities still agree for the most part that peer review plays an important role, there is division around what exactly that role is, and how peer review actually ought to be practised. As digital publishing has transformed the landscape of scholarly publishing, it has opened up a wide range of new possible approaches to peer review. Part of that expansion of digital scholarship is, of course, the rise of scholarly podcasts and other forms of sound-based scholarship. These new models have been taken up slowly in many research communities, largely because of what Tennant et al. (2017) refer to as the cultural inertia of academic publishing, namely 'the tendency of communities to cling to a traditional trajectory' as driven by 'highly polarised motivations (i.e., capitalistic commercialism versus knowledge generation versus careerism versus output measurement)' (n.pag.). Whatever the reason behind cultural inertia, it is difficult to model the efficacy of innovative approaches to peer review in an environment that discourages experimentation and risk-taking in not only *what* is published but also *how* it is published. Much as open access digital journals have demanded new approaches to review, so too do podcasts invite us to question some of our core premises about how scholarship ought to be communicated, including the premise that scholarly communication and writing are synonymous.

This dissatisfaction with conventional peer review and scholarly publishing in general might seem to suggest that we're advocating to do away with peer review altogether, but that's not quite right. What we'd *quite* like to do away with are the current paradigmatic norms of how peer review fits into academia, the application of one-size-fits-all review processes in most journal publishing and the unspoken conventions of the written medium. And in our opinion, one of the most effective ways to denaturalize the status quo is to historicize it.

The Evolution of Peer Review

How did this kind of anonymous, slow-moving and often unproductive peer review become the norm? To answer this, we first need to explore the origins of peer review itself. In 'From Book Censorship to Academic Peer Review', Mario Biagioli (2002) questions why academics, so concerned with questions of disciplinarity and power, have historically had little to say about peer review as a form of discipline, drawing a hypothetical line between 'early modern book-burning (the public material destruction of the text as object)' and 'modern peer review (the internal disciplining of a text and its author)' (11). In historicizing the contemporary practice of peer review, Biagioli links it to the 17th-century emergence of royal academies as institutions with the right to publish their own works, 'an extraordinary exception from the licensing and censorship systems that since the 16th century had been established by political and religious authorities throughout Europe in response to the perceived political and religious threats posed by the printing press' (14). The shift he notes is not from complete openness to restriction, but, rather, from state or church censorship to internal review within academic systems, a development that parallels the Enlightenment's movement of scientific knowledge out of the domain of church or state. This was not so much a liberation of knowledge from the restrictions of licensing and censorship as it was an increase in the specialization of who licensed what, perhaps as a means of managing the ever-increasing production of printed texts (i.e., peer review as a management system).

Reflecting on such historical developments is particularly interesting in light of ongoing debates around the role of misinformation or 'dangerous knowledge' disseminated through podcasting (and digital publishing in general). Podcasting superstar Joe Rogan generated a lot of attention for featuring interviews with scientists who were sceptical of the vaccines being used to combat the COVID-19 pandemic. Because of the immense popularity of his podcast, some called for him to show more responsibility when selecting guests, to provide a contrasting range of viewpoints or to act less like a naive interviewer, doing more background research before interviewees make claims on the podcast. Rogan did concede he needs to consider a greater diversity of viewpoints on the vaccine topic, but also expressed a commitment to his style of podcasting as the inquisitive, occasionally critical, non-expert (Patten 2022). The debate, in part, is about the role of expertise: who gets to gate-keep expertise and who does not, and who, if anyone, should take responsibility for the thorough interrogation of knowledge when or if it is to be published.

Back to the 17th century. While that moment when a particular kind of peer review was invented did not mark the widespread adoption of peer review, let alone anonymized peer review, it does suggest a long history of peer review being connected to institutional control, the restriction of knowledge via licensing and the use of censorship to discipline potentially dangerous knowledge. The fact that review was delegated to royal academies is not, in Biagioli's argument, a sign of the sciences radically liberating themselves from the church and state, but, rather, a sign that scientific publication was not considered dangerous, particularly not in comparison with radical political and theological texts (15). Anyway, academics weren't sticking it to the man by taking control of peer review, since academics literally *were* the man (that is, members of the royal academies were often *also* state officials of some kind). What distinguished peer review from censorship, then, was that peer review was used for texts that were produced within the state apparatus – the royal academy – rather than external to the state; these texts didn't need to be censored because they were already disciplined by their proximity to the state, and thus lower risk. This early peer review was deliberately *not* anonymous: 'it was precisely by not being blind (that is, by being tied to specific authoritative institutions and their memberships) that peer review could emerge to begin with' (Biagioli 2002, 25).

The end of state censorship did not mark the end of peer review: while it no longer had a legal function (the right of academies to license scientific works), it persevered as a means of asserting the legitimacy of both the academies and the works they produced. As academic science expanded and dispersed, becoming decentralized from the royal academies, so too did the practices of peer review, such that they were no longer a form of institutional control but an internalized discipline (in the Foucauldian sense,[24] though also in the disciplinary knowledge sense). 'Peers' no longer meant members of the same royal academy, but, rather, other individuals who had been disciplined in the same way, that is, through acquiring a PhD (itself a highly disciplined process, in every sense of the word). Biagioli's history of the emergence of peer review in early modern Europe convincingly connects the practice to censorship and

---

[24]Foucauldian 'discipline' refers to a mechanism through which power is exercised, not through the external regulating of behaviour, but through the normalization of behaviours by which individuals discipline themselves.

discipline, an argument that aligns with how many academics *feel* about peer review: that it is a form of gatekeeping that disciplines unconventional knowledge as well as a form of quality assurance.

We have to jump *way* forward in history to get to the normalization of anonymized peer review being synonymous with scholarly rigour, but once again it has a lot to do with the relationship between scientific research and state control. Historian of science communication Melinda Baldwin (2018) sketches this history. She points out that the crucial context for the contemporary role of peer review in scientific publication is the Cold War, a period when the increase in public funding for science research was accompanied by a call for greater accountability: if the research was going to be publicly funded, shouldn't the public get a say in what was funded?

Scientists, writes Baldwin, 'balked at the suggestion that their methods or conclusions might be vetted by scientific laymen but did not want to surrender the public status or funding opportunities they had gained' (2018, 539). The compromise was the incorporation of peer review into the funding process – emphasis on the *peer* in peer review, a phrase that Baldwin demonstrates didn't emerge until this period (prior to this, the process was called 'refereeing' [548]). The goal of *peer* review was to distinguish between those who did and did not have the expertise to evaluate research: 'The new term established a narrow range of acceptable reviewers and implicitly deemed those without a scientific background unqualified to evaluate the work in question' (548). Peer review was less about the importance of review and more about the definition of *peer*.

The history that Baldwin outlines makes it clear that peer review was not developed as a foolproof system for determining scientific accuracy, but, rather, as a means of managing calls for public accountability in a landscape of increased public funding for research. Many of the contemporary critiques of peer review's limitations emerge from the overinflation of its utility following the cultural shifts of the Cold War. Perhaps more insidious has been the expansion of this scientific model of peer review into the social sciences and humanities, fields where it is arguably even less useful. Only after government funding bodies began to use anonymized peer review as a way to disperse funding did journals incorporate the same practice. Commercial journals drew on the professionalization of academics as a source of voluntary labour whose peer reviews gave the journals legitimacy (Fyfe et al. 2017), which changed review from being a more community-oriented affair into a commercial one, in which journals sold back research (usually via university library subscriptions) to the same scholars who both wrote and reviewed the work as part of their professional activities (Tennant et al. 2017).

Despite the elevation of double-anonymized peer review as the 'gold standard' of scholarly communication,[25] scholars across disciplines have persisted in experimenting with, critiquing, and otherwise seeking to overhaul standardized review practices. Perhaps the best example of this resistant ethos is the world of open review, which has often gone hand in hand with other movements towards openness, particularly open access publishing. 'Open review' is an umbrella term that could refer to a whole suite of interventions, including open identities (non-anonymity), open reports (published reviews), open participation (anyone can review) and open interaction (author and reviewer can communicate) (Ross-Hellauer 2017, 7). These different forms of openness seek to intervene into different critiques of standard review; the open identities approach, for example, eliminates anonymity to address issues such as 'reviewers stealing ideas and passing them off as their own, or intentional blocking or delaying publication of competitors' ideas through harsh reviews' (Ross-Hellauer 2017, 4), while open reports can address the lack of incentive in traditional review by publishing reports alongside articles. In his systematic review of definitions of open peer review, Tony Ross-Hellauer (2017) notes interesting differences between the kinds of openness prioritized within different disciplines, with STEM fields more likely to emphasize open identities while social sciences and humanities definitions demonstrate a greater focus on open participation (9). Open review as a cluster of approaches, then, seeks not only to intervene into how review is practised but also to make space for the differentiation of appropriate practices within different disciplines. In a historical moment when so much of academia is trending towards standardization, open review is a site of ongoing innovation and resistance.

---

[25]We place gold standard in quotations here as a marker of the ongoing critiques of the fully anonymized peer-review process as the highest quality, most rigorous and, thus, most effective model of evaluating scholarship.

Specifically, open review offers a point of resistance to the accelerating neoliberalization of academia through the late 20th century and into the 21st. Neoliberalism, or neoliberal capitalism, which 'reveres competition, promotes social Darwinism and valorises profit' (Feldman and Sandoval 2018, 216), takes a clear form in the modern university in the rise of productivity metrics that are always oriented towards the market. Different metrics have been introduced in different locations, as informed by the political understandings of education and scholarship dominant in those areas. In the UK, for example, the Research Excellence Framework has become a terror for many scholars (O'Regan and Gray 2018), while conservative governments in Canada are working to introduce metrics that will attach funding for universities to the employment rates of graduates (Canadian Press 2019). At the same time neoliberal capitalism has spawned a growing disdain for the role of the 'expert':

> Such discursive attacks on knowledge and expertise sit neatly alongside neoliberal capitalism's reverence for profit-oriented individualism. While knowledge is decried, the tenets of economic competition are encouraged and reproduced. This situation bodes poorly for universities – especially publicly-funded universities – and the academics working in them. This is largely because cultural disregard for knowledge means that universities and academic staff are now required to defend their existence through an alternate language: one of cost-benefit accounting. In other words, knowledge for knowledge's sake is no longer sufficient justification for why we need universities. (Feldman and Sandoval 2018, 216)

Within this neoliberal framework, where knowledge has no inherent value and academics must prove their worth through the logics of the market, metrics have taken over. For instance, in some parts of (what was) the Hungarian Academy of Sciences, bonus pay – which tops up a staggeringly low wage – is linked to the number of points gained through various activities, the top of which is publication in top-ranked journals. However, because Journal Impact Factors (JIFs) change over time, and it can take years to get an article through the publishing process, academics can be left without enough points if they submitted to a journal that was downgraded in the time between submission and publication.

We are, of course, not the first scholars to bemoan the stranglehold that metrics, and all of the norms of publishing accompanying them, have come to have on scholarly knowledge creation. Since 2012 the San Francisco Declaration on Research Assessment (DORA) has been recommending changes that coalesce around the following themes:

> the need to eliminate the use of journal-based metrics, such as Journal Impact Factors, in funding, appointment, and promotion considerations; the need to assess research on its own merits rather than on the basis of the journal in which the research is published; and the need to capitalize on the opportunities provided by online publication (such as relaxing unnecessary limits on the number of words, figures, and references in articles, and exploring new indicators of significance and impact). (DORA 2013)[26]

The fixation on metrics affects the ways scholars think about and carry out our research and work in a real, material sense. In the contemporary university the most readily quantifiable output becomes the most important; Fire and Guestrin (2019) point out that this follows Goodhart's Law, which stipulates that 'When a measure becomes a target, it ceases to be a good measure' – and when this happens in academic publishing undesirable and even unethical behaviours can develop (para. 3). For researchers, the most important (i.e., readily quantifiable) output is written scholarship published in high-impact journals.

This reframing of knowledge in terms of measurability of written work not only discourages all kinds of not-readily-countable knowledge creation, but it also encourages an environment of scarcity-based thinking and competition within academia (Fitzpatrick 2018). As scholars are pitted against each other for increasingly limited resources, we may stop challenging the logic of metrics in favour of trying to win at a deeply rigged game, namely, publishing more journal articles, that in turn demand ever more anonymous peer reviews. Currently, there is a vast pool of floating

---

[26]Thanks to an anonymous peer reviewer for pointing us to DORA in the review process.

academic labour: scholars with PhDs, numerous publications and multiple postdocs, but without a permanent contract. These scholars are still asked to perform voluntary review work, even though they may no longer be working in academia by the time an article is published, and thus may no longer have access to academic journals (at least officially). We are collectively pouring hundreds of thousands of hours into writing, submitting, reviewing and revising one another's work, while universities get poorer and a handful of journal publishers get richer.

So is all lost? Is there hope?

The Promise: Forever Delayed?

And so here's the promise: academic podcasting. It's here, it's happening, just a few years behind the rest of the podcasting world.

Do you remember where you were when podcasting first got big? It wasn't all that long ago. In 2014, *This American Life* producer Ira Glass appeared as a guest on *The Tonight Show*, sharing a video in which his elderly neighbour taught viewers how to subscribe to the new podcast *Serial*. In no time, *Serial* became the first real podcast super hit across the globe. For a while podcasting's growth – and the buzz around that growth – was seemingly unbridled, with everyone from sad British royals to happy American talk show hosts starting podcasts and big money takeovers getting the full-press fanfare treatment, such as when independent-music-destroying, artist-royalty-cheapskates Spotify purchased podcast production house Gimlet Media for more than $200 million. A lot of the hype and money was concentrated at the top, and a lot of the most popular podcasts were made by those already working for established media (BBC, NPR) or those who were famous enough to already have access to various platforms.

Do you remember where you were the day podcasting died? In 2023, as we revise this manuscript, the venture capital money that drove prestigious studio podcast growth is drying up, and Spotify's celebrity podcast business model is failing (Nimmo 2023). There is a strong suggestion that the bubble might have burst. However, scholarly podcasting, by and large, was never going to bother the big boys and their money; the path it started and continues to tread is, in terms of its size and niche foci, similar to that of the early days of amateur podcasting. Indeed, the 'big name bubble' bursting might even be something of an opportunity for those concerned with 'less popular' topics.[27]

Some academics (perhaps a *lot* of academics – it's genuinely hard to tell) have podcasts. Even as academia starts to catch up to the rest of the world's excitement about podcasting, something of a lag remains; we can see this lag in the way some academics continue to question whether podcasts can be 'real' research outputs, despite ample evidence to support the medium's impact. Within the small but growing number of academics who podcast, some consider podcasting as part of their 'proper scholarly work', but many still think of their podcasts as hobbies, side hustles or a way to promote more conventional work (see Cook 2023). But we're getting there. Podcasts are getting peer-reviewed, published in journals, counted towards permanent contracts and promotion (at least in the places where indefinite contracts and tenure haven't been eliminated by market-worshipping governments), even celebrated by the very institutions that until recently ignored them entirely.

Good news, right? Well, maybe. There are many ways this could go. On the one hand, academia's embrace of podcasting might lead to the orthodoxies of text-based and metrics-obsessed peer review being transplanted into the new medium, hauling it back into the lagging timelines (Björk and Solomon 2013) and outdated conventions of scholarly communication. But there's also an exciting kernel of potential here. We might contemplate what audio does for and to knowledge, and how the introduction of a different medium can transform the concept of peer review alongside our ideas of who our peers, and our audiences, are. We can envision new processes through which sound-based scholarship might be rigorously and fairly assessed that are appropriate to the medium, and that as a result upset the inherited, and too often unquestioned, practices of scholarship.

These processes – responsive as they are to the categorical difference between podcasts and sound-based scholarship on the one hand and textual scholarship on the other – will need to be similarly

---

[27]Thanks to peer reviewers Siobhan McHugh and Gordon Katic who helped nuance this section during the review process.

nuanced about the internal diversity of podcasting as a medium. Not all podcasts are alike, not all podcasts should be reviewed and not all types of podcasts should be reviewed in the same way. These nuances might depend on the academic discipline in which the scholar is engaged as well as the form and content of the podcast itself. For example, an audio fiction podcast in which actors and sound designers bring a dramatic script to life might not be considered a peer-reviewable research output for, say, a molecular geneticist, but certainly might for a scholar of scriptwriting, performance or sound design. A current events podcast might successfully demonstrate the application of a particular cultural research lens or methodology to world events. A chatcast could enable discussion and collaboration among social scientists. There is no one way to 'do' scholarly podcasting. And if you speak with academics who podcast, as we have, you will come to realize that they have many different, and sometimes irreconcilable, interests in the medium.

What's clear is that we shouldn't just try to jam podcasting into existing structures of peer review. But don't just take our word for it or . . . , actually, do take our word for it – we hashed this out a bit during one of our conversational writing meetings:

> **Lori:** Some podcasts try to fit into existing peer review structures; we can draw a parallel between the evolution of media and the evolution of this. For example, we've got radio, then television comes along, and everybody's like, *Okay, so now we can just do radio on television.* In other words, early television was a bunch of dudes in front of a microphone at a desk, reading the news from a script, right? We always go through this period of just trying to make this new thing fit the existing structures until we've kind of blown our own minds figuring out how transformative it can be. I feel like we're still in that stage of trying to make peer review podcasting fit into existing structures. Even my own podcast experiments[28] do that, too; I'm experimenting with how we can do some peer review via podcast and then publish something out of it later.

---

[28]See *Open Peer Review Podcast* at oprpodcast.ca

Hannah: A big part of how publishing works is through the creation of an infrastructure that allows for the production of the published work. And that infrastructure has been created around a certain finite set of outputs. And so what we are struggling with right now is trying to jam a totally different medium into an infrastructure that was not designed for that medium. And trying to figure out like, *Okay, where is the infrastructure going to change? What do we actually have to transform about the way that we produce scholarship?* Publishing is famously conservative, because they have all of these locked down production processes. What so many journals and publishers are trying to do is like, have this new medium, but not actually change anything about how they do the rest of the stuff around the medium.

Ian: That should go in the introduction [of the book].

Podcasts are, of course, already being used in the academic context in a variety of different ways. Some scholars use them as data collection tools, recording oral histories, interviews and other ethnographic and/or anthropologic information. Others use them as tools for knowledge dissemination or mobilization, seeking to share expert knowledge beyond the traditional audiences for scholarship. Between those two approaches lies the use of podcasting for the working out of ideas in public, conversations through which scholars are figuring out something together – akin to a really good conversation over whisky at the conference bar, say, but made public. And there are multiple genres in which scholarly podcasting might dabble, from scripted narrative podcasts to book reviews to interviews with academics about their forthcoming and already published research, with different levels of production quality and attention to sound design.

As a reminder, we suggest that what makes a podcast *scholarly* is that it has the potential to be peer-reviewed. This is a book about podcasting and peer review, but we can't limit our case studies to podcasts that *have* been peer-reviewed, because it's still such a new phenomenon. Even this delineation excludes all kinds of fascinating podcasting work, which is why it's important for us to reassert that we are not attempting to create a hierarchy but, rather, to be as specific as possible about the kinds of podcasts we're talking about. Within our definition of scholarly podcasting, there is still a wide range of possible approaches: not all scholarly podcasts sound alike, which is part of the pleasure of them. They might be humorous (e.g., *What the If?*), serious (e.g., *The Maxwell Institute Podcast*) or whimsical (e.g., *Witch, Please*). They might take the form of narrative non-fiction (e.g., *How to Build a Stock Exchange: Making Finance Fit for the Future*) or documentary (e.g., *Preserves: Manitoba Food History Project*), interviews (e.g., *The Sources of the Nile*), roundtable conversations (e.g., *The Familiar Strange*) or something altogether more experimental (e.g., *Podlog*). They could employ affective sound design and score (e.g., *Somatic*) or rely largely on voice (e.g., *New Books Network*). They could be one-off episodes,[29] limited series or ongoing shows.

Even within this space we've carved out, there is such a huge variety that some scholarly podcasters struggle to see how their work could even be considered in the same category. What does a sparingly edited weekly chatcast between a few academics (e.g., *This Week in Virology*) have in common with a painstakingly produced and award-winning documentary (e.g., *Heart of Artness*)? How does one scholar's experiments in sound design and non-linear storytelling relate to another's attempt to make peer-reviewed science more accessible? By putting this range of work into one category, calling it scholarly podcasting, and arguing that it has some potential relationship to peer review, we are not neutrally observing an existing pattern but, rather, deliberately and tactically calling a collective into existence where one did not exist before. Because all the various approaches to podcasting and scholarship that might fall into this category have one key thing in common: *a belief that something exciting happens when you bring podcasting and scholarship together.*

---

[29]While we don't consider one-offs to be podcasts *per se* (they lack the ongoing seriality that is an important aspect of the medium), there do exist one-off scholarly audio pieces that are presented as podcasts. We consider these to be part of the scholarly podcast spectrum.

A World Free from Rankers
(Alternate Reality Break No. 3)

Dr Marina Makandar had spent two years researching the Pannonian Avars as part of a wider research group where she supervised three PhD students and a postdoc. Her research had gone brilliantly well; she'd developed groundbreaking work on the political structures of the Avar Khaganate and presented it to all of the leading researchers on the Pannonian Avars at a workshop organized to close the project. Her talk on her research was cited by her peers before she managed to get around to writing it up. She enjoyed speaking about her research to students. A few of them started a reading group about the Pannonian Avars that she attended weekly and this, coupled with the time she was dedicating to helping her students finish their dissertations, meant that she didn't have much time to write. When she did turn her talk into an article for a journal and, eventually, a monograph, it wasn't that highly cited; people just kept referring back to the talk where she first presented her ideas. She was a better talker than a writer in any case, but it was a little annoying because one of the reviewers from the journal had given her wonderful advice on how to reconceptualize the Avars' relationship with the Franks based on a line of scholarship in Czech, which she did not speak.

All of her PhD students produced excellent dissertations. Two of them decided not to work in academia, but she stayed in touch with them for years after and occasionally they came to research talks at the university. The third decided to pursue a career in academia and Marina was happy to see how they progressed even though they moved on to a very different field and did not use any of the ideas they developed in their common project.

At the age of 53, Dr Makandar took up roller skating as a way to get over the end of her fourth marriage. She got quite good, but one day she was going a little too fast, slipped and banged her head. While she was unconscious, she had a terrible nightmare – she was told her research counted for nothing because the journal article was not highly cited, she fell out with the students of the Pannonian Avars because they didn't advance her own career, she had no time to join the student reading group because she was too busy writing four journal articles on the same research with slightly different angles so as to increase her citation count . . .

Interlude

Is Peer Review Working Well for the Scholarship You Produce?

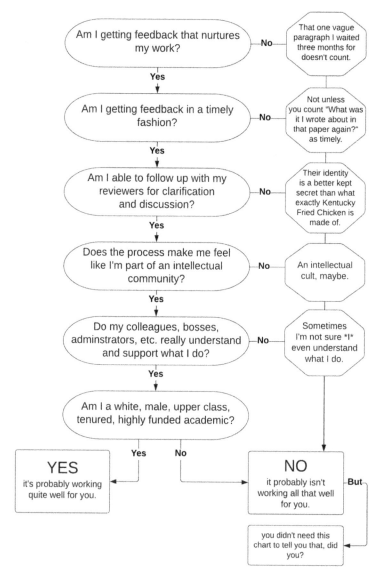

FIGURE 2 *Is peer review working well for the scholarship you produce?*

2

Sound Scholarship

Sound-based scholarship – in the sense of doing scholarly work out loud, via sound – is not a contemporary phenomenon. It's as old as academia, as old as knowledge itself. The dominance of print in academia is a more recent development than we often realize; memorization, oral lecturing, oral exams and formal debates all continue to be essential components of higher education. Sound-based scholarship is still deeply interwoven with the contemporary practices of academia, as well as the many forms of publicly or community-engaged knowledge creation that exceed the bounds of the university as an institution.

Take as an example the word 'lecture', which comes from the Latin word *lectura*, meaning reading. Modern definitions of 'lecturing' centre on the act of speaking to an audience, often in a unidirectional way (in pedagogical circles, the phrase is 'sage on the stage'). But the etymology of the word reminds us that reading and speaking used to be intimately entangled with each other: prior to the 16th century, reading and speaking aloud were all but indivisible. Historians of books and of reading cultures have pointed to the shift to silent reading as a pivotal moment in the development of a modern psychological understanding of interiority, the spread of literacy and contemporary understandings of reading as a private and intimate activity (Saenger 1997; Jajdelska 2007). Intellectual historians also link silent reading to the Enlightenment's focus on undisciplined thinking that pushed back against the intellectual hegemony of the church and state (Outram 2006). However, this misses the classed nature of libraries in the 19th and 20th centuries, when silent reading was a decidedly middle-class activity whereas working-class (and often union-funded) libraries were spaces for discussion and debate (Felsenstein and Connolly 2015).

The history of knowledge creation is one of collectivity and publicness. Whether we're looking at the many oral traditions that both predated and coextended with the rise of writing and then printing, or the cultures of public debate and group learning that span from the Athenian agora to the university oral defence, there is a long history of thinking through things together and out loud. Orality and writing have developed alongside one another, entangled and often symbiotic. We record what people say, and then talk about what we have read; we read aloud to one another, and then record our thoughts about what we've heard. The same holds true in modern academia. We might present our work at a conference, for example, or develop our ideas through a graduate seminar or simply by unpacking them over a glass of wine with a trusted colleague. But all roads lead back to the published text as the primary marker of institutional legitimacy.

Today, we see the tension between spoken and written forms of knowledge creation play out in a space like an academic conference, where in many disciplines presenters read from a typed presentation, rarely looking up to make eye contact.[1] Indeed, most calls for conference presenters invite academics to 'present a paper', prioritizing the written document over the in-person, spoken presentation. Even in those disciplines where more informal presentations are the norm, conferences are still conceived of as a way station on the journey to the 'real' scholarly output: the written

---

[1]The authors had differing thoughts about this. Lori indicated she would rather poke her own eye out with a dull spoon than listen to someone read a paper aloud. Ian indicated that he has done this (read a paper aloud, not poked his eye out), but assured us he is a very good reader. In discussing it further, we came to the conclusion that not only are our reactions discipline-specific (as a media and communications scholar Lori can't abide the idea of reading aloud a 'script' that only works for the print medium; Hannah, with her background in English literature indicated that the precision of language really matters in her discipline, so a pre-written paper read aloud might be the only way to attain that precision) but also that reading a paper aloud can be an anxiety-calming strategy for nervous presenters or scholars who are non-native speakers of the language in which they're presenting. Creating a culture in which more presenters are comfortable engaging with the audience directly has to go hand in hand with elevating norms of generous critique. Nonetheless, please do keep all dull spoons out of the vicinity of any conferences Lori is attending.

journal article, book chapter or monograph. Never mind how much more thrilling a lively Q&A is than a droning twenty-minute paper, or how much more exciting the conversation is later on over a lunch of soggy wraps.

It is not enough, however, to hark back to a golden age when Plato conversed in Academus' garden. We would not want our intellectual community to be limited by those we could meet in our local library, nor would it be practical to convert the classroom into a cafe. Rather, we need to be inspired by the ways in which spoken scholarship (and sound more generally) has enlivened and continues to enliven intellectual pursuits as we set out a path for scholarship in our digital times. To think seriously about scholarly podcasting and peer review, we need to turn our attention to the fundamental building blocks of podcasting: what they are and how they interact with each other, and how they invite and, indeed, preclude certain forms of review.

Scholarly Podcasting

Let's take a closer listen to scholarly podcasting and its various affordances. While some of the features we discuss are true of podcasting more generally, our goal is to focus on what podcast-based scholarship makes possible, with an ear to how its affordances might lead to the transformation of peer review. We argue that podcasting is a *public and participatory sonic action*, and we propose a framework for thinking about it via three main pillars: voice, conversation and digital publishing.

In what follows we're going to explore each of these pillars, where they overlap and what this means for peer review. But we can't start that yet, because a loud droning sound that's been coming in through one of our windows for a while is distracting us: a duct cleaning truck with all its engines and motors and suctioning mechanisms is parked across the street. The resulting niggling irritation has given way to a sudden awareness that this sound has been sneaking in the side doors of our collective brain for quite some time, all the while affecting us on a physiological and psychological level. Now, if only we could shut our earlids, we could get back to the flow of conversation and writing. But since earlids are nothing more than

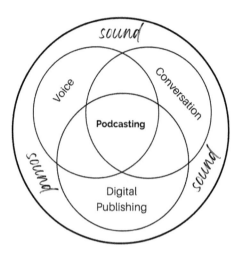

FIGURE 3 *Conceptualizing podcasting as the intersection of Voice, Conversation and Digital Publishing, rooted in sound.*

a concept serving to illustrate the human inability to consciously shut out sound (Schafer 1977), we're left to deal with our sonic environment as best we can.

What the annoying duct cleaning truck makes clear is that whether one is actively engaging with sound (listening) or passively exposed to it (hearing), sound will affect one whether one is aware of it or not. Sound is immersive. It moves around and through space, disrupting the very atoms of the air and setting them in motion in patterns that can be decoded from kinetic energy into electrical energy by our ears. This immersion is perhaps what makes us think of sound as having a direct link to not only our brain but also our emotions. Consider the emotions conjured by sound: joy from an uplifting song, dread from a sustained low-frequency note – a sure indication that the monster (Reviewer 2) is about to pounce on the unsuspecting character (scholar) on screen,[2] or the tranquillity imparted by the rhythmic swoosh of wind in the trees. Sound's

---

[2]It practically goes without saying that some of the best horror films of all time are really about peer review, at least subtextually (for example, *I Know What You Did Last Summer and It Wasn't a Proper Literature Review*).

affective qualities – the way it can drive us to respond emotionally, even before we perceive it intellectually – is part of what makes podcasts such a powerful medium (Scriven 2022).

Sound is also pervasive. As long as there are atoms there is the potential for them to conduct sound waves – waves that are created by movement and perceived by living bodies, which are also in motion, even when at rest. Silence is therefore impossible. Sound designers understand this. To depict silence in a film soundtrack, they insert the sound of air, crickets, a distant dog bark or the internal sound of blood circulating, but never no sound at all. They know the effect of no sound would be puzzling, even jarring to the listener. Podcasters also know this, often making sure to capture 'room tone', the 'silence' of a space when no one is speaking – which is, in fact, never actual silence. Sound, therefore, is not just something we hear, but something that surrounds us and moves us.

Despite the impossibility of silence, listening (unlike the more passive experience of hearing) is an active process. Listening for comprehension can be cognitively challenging; if you've listened to lots of intellectually inclined podcasts like we have, then you've probably had moments when you've zoned out of the conversation as your brain is happily distracted by something out the tram window – 'oh look that puddle is the exact same shape as Hungary prior to the Treaty of Trianon'. Listening asks for a concentrated type of attention in order to both hear and understand. This active participation challenges the consumer of media in a different way than reading text or watching visual media. Cognitive load, a measure of the level of effort required to process information, has been shown to be greater when engaging with sound alone versus sound combined with image (Mishra et al. 2013; Sommers and Phelps 2016). While the absence of visuals can pose a challenge, it also presents opportunities. There is a correlation between podcast listening and the listener's 'need for cognition', that is, 'the enjoyment of and engagement in effortful cognitive endeavours' (Tobin and Guadagno 2022, 3), suggesting that podcast listening can, indeed, be a cognitive challenge and that podcast listeners tend to enjoy that challenge. Visuals are a potential distraction from the substance of what's being said – 'oh, that's a cool shade of lipstick Hannah's wearing, but what exactly is going on with Ian's *hair*?' – and thus their absence may afford a more interactive engagement with arguments and ideas.

Thinking through some of the particularities of sound in relation to podcasting pushes us towards interrogating the relationship between listener and podcast. In this chapter, we will examine how this relationship is structured. The podcast–listener relationship is distinct from the relationship between text and reader, and is also distinct from other forms of audio media and digital media. We argue that podcasting, as a *public and participatory sonic action*, is a social act on the part of both the listener and the podcaster with important implications for peer-reviewed scholarship. Podcasting, we believe, creates a scholarly environment in which the performance of authority and expertise is decentred in favour of other qualities such as authenticity, intimacy, inclusion and open-endedness. This shift in priorities opens up possibilities for a reorientation of scholarly communication and peer review that encourages us to consider one another as people and to recognize the development of scholarly knowledge as a collective, public, accessible and ongoing activity.

This is why we prefer to think of podcasting not as something done by a podcast producer or producers, but, rather, as something done together with an audience of listeners. This echoes similar arguments made in respect to music, namely that

> [the] essence of music lies not in musical works but in taking part in performance, in social action. Music is thus not so much a noun as a verb, 'to music'. To music is to take part in any capacity in a musical performance, and the meaning of musicking lies in the relationships that are established between the participants by the performance. (Small 1999, 9)

In 'podcasting' – a word that is already often used as a verb – the participatory element is possibly even more pronounced than in music.

Podcasting as a public and participatory sonic action is central to how many scholars and podcasters discuss the heightened sense of parasocial intimacy that the medium engenders between hosts and listeners. Parasocial intimacy is, podcaster Glen Weldon (2018) asserts, 'unidirectional': 'You listen to [your favourite podcast hosts] talk to one another in exactly the same way you talk to your friends' but in truth 'they have absolutely no idea who you are.' Weldon may be slightly overstating the case here, or at least writing from the perspective of the host of a popular NPR podcast who doesn't know the vast majority of his own guests; in reality, many niche podcasters are familiar with at least some segment of our listenerships, if not all of them. Further, as scholar Alyn Euritt has argued, parasocial intimacy is not an accidental side effect of podcasting as a medium, but, rather, the result of a set of intentional choices podcast creators and listeners engage in, from hosts creating an informal and chatty tone to listeners contributing to call-in segments (Euritt 2020, 34–5).

The participatory nature of podcasting is evident when we think about voice: for instance, the triggering of the visual imagination that happens through listening to a voice without seeing a body; it is evident when we think about conversation: for instance, when a listener experiences a podcast as 'listening in' on two or more people speaking; and it is evident in digital publishing: for instance, when the serial nature of a podcast engenders community building. Similarly, the inclusive nature of podcasting is demonstrated in the intersections of voice, conversation and digital publishing, in that each affords opportunities for broad publics to engage.

In this chapter we will work through the implications for peer review when conceiving of podcasting as a public and participatory sonic action, first through the pillars of voice, conversation and digital publishing, and then through the intersections of each of these, i.e., voice+conversation, conversation+digital publishing, and digital publishing+voice.

Voice

Scholarly podcasting (as a public and participatory sonic action) primarily relies on the human voice to create meaning. Voices are personal, embodied and convey affective meaning. Voices can engender trust, intimacy, and express authenticity. Voices are subject to the political and cultural ideologies that are embedded in how we listen and how we perceive who has 'authority', which informs how we engage with sound-based scholarship.

Voices are what convey the information and emotion required to inform and entertain podcast listeners. While sound design and music alone might suffice, outside of 'sound nerd' circles experimental sound stories are not a format that attracts a wide listenership, and current copyright laws make it both complicated and financially challenging to use music in podcasts. This means that podcasting has come to rely on voice to do most of the heavy lifting. What is it about the human voice, then, that we need to understand in order to better understand podcasting and its potential for peer review?

One podcast pundit has gone so far as to argue that we tend to trust human voices inherently (Weiner 2014), while others have said that human voices can create intimacy (Llinares et al. 2018). Indeed, there is something about hearing a voice inside your head, in the case of listening with headphones or earbuds (see Lieberman, Schroeder and Amir 2022; Spinelli and Dann 2019) or hearing it in your own personal space such as your car, your bedroom or even in the shower, combined with the fact that the voice was likely recorded at a distance of just a few inches from the mic, that forges a feeling of closeness with the speaker. This can lead to greater empathy and openness to persuasion by the communicator (Lieberman, Schroeder and Amir 2022).

However, anyone who's listened to ads on a commercial radio station that feature inauthentic voices hyped up about a 2-for-1 burger special will know that voices are neither inherently intimate nor inherently trustworthy – and likewise we shouldn't assume scholars are inherently trustworthy when podcasting about their research (Cook 2020). Nonetheless, there is potential for the voice to generate trust within the listener–podcaster relationship, with research suggesting people are able to more effectively judge emotion in another person through voice-only communication than through face-to-face speaking (Krause 2017). If it's true that we're able to detect and identify emotion solely through the voice even better than we can when we both see and hear the speaker, voice must be a significant factor in emotional connection. It follows that the voice can indeed build trust, a perspective argued by podcast scholar Siobhan McHugh (2019) and further supported by data about podcast listeners' proclivity to trust the product recommendations of their favourite podcast hosts (Edison Research 2022).

The human body is central to this relationship-building, because voices are produced in the body, heard through the body, and express all kinds of information – emotions, physical sensations and states of mind – that are happening in the body, not in a mind divorced from the body. We can detect some of this information not only through the spoken words themselves but also through paralinguistic vocal cues. Pitch, volume, pace, timbre (the quality of the sound of the voice) and cadence provide the listener with semantic indicators about intended meaning – cues that are not nearly as easily conveyed through the written word. Prosody – the rhythms, intonations, emphases and pauses in speech that convey information beyond the literal meaning of a string of words – is largely absent in text.[3] It is not always as easy for writers to express, say, sarcasm, or uncertainty or any number of emotions, attitudes or affective states that most of us can manage through the spoken word. Thus, we can think of the voice as a significant conduit of interiority, a bridge from inside to outside that holds an 'almost unique position' at the boundary of interior and exterior (Anne Karpf as cited in Desson and Evans 2022), working as 'an index of interiority, consciousness, agency and self' (Kunreuther 2014, 36) that for many functions as 'the truest and surest marker of self' (Ong as cited in Goodale 2011, 92). For many listeners, the ability to enter the inner human domain is what allows human voices in podcasts to come across as personal, intimate and even trustworthy. As Evelyn Lamb, co-host of the *My Favorite Theorem* podcast explained to Ian,

> I like to help people have some kind of positive and humanising experience with math. And I think that's a huge amount of what *My Favorite Theorem* does. It gives people a human connection to abstract maths. Maybe when they learnt it, they did not feel some deep connection to the infinitude of primes or the Pythagorean theorem . . . But then [they hear] a mathematician talk about how powerful it is or how much they love it!

Hearing the voice without seeing the body does not mean, however, that the listener does not have a body in mind. Most of us have had the experience of seeing someone for the first time after hearing

---

[3]Although anthropologists, ethnographers and other scholars who rely on recorded speech as data use a system of annotations to attempt to include prosody, we can certainly agree this is a compromised abstraction of the spoken word. Also, poets would probably disagree with this whole premise, but that's a conversation for another day.

their voice on a podcast, on the radio or over the phone and being surprised that their actual face does not match the one we had created for them in our imagination. In podcasting, as in other acousmatic media – in which sound is heard without the origin of that sound being seen – listening is concentrated upon the source of the sound; when we listen we are most likely to be employing 'causal listening' wherein we question what the cause or the source of the sound is (Chion 1994, 25). This kind of listening stimulates the imagination of the listener as they create a 'sonic body' to go with the voice (Kane 2014).

The body that listeners create through imagination is structured by the often-unthinking ways in which we classify and label people, such as ethnicity, gender, sexuality, age and country of origin.[4] Radio scholars have noted how the ideal of the neutral, objective and authoritative voice is, in fact, deeply raced, classed and gendered (see, for example, Douglas 2013; Ehrick 2022; McEnaney 2019). Vocal difference, the audible sign of diversity, is often trained out of professional broadcasters in pursuit of an industry norm that is far from neutral. On top of that, the technologies of radio have a flattening effect on vocal differences; broadcasting technologies including microphones, compressors, de-essers and EQ filters are often used to remove dynamic range and emphasize certain frequency bands and attenuate others.

Podcasting, on the other hand, has opened out more space for markers of sonic diversity. The origins of the medium in independent and DIY production means that more untrained and undisciplined podcasters can take up the mic, while the production and distribution norms of podcasting – or lack thereof, perhaps – tend to have a less flattening effect. We're more likely to encounter vocal fry in podcasting, along with accented English, rampant use of slang and swearing, and other vocal tics that are frequently dismissed as 'unprofessional' or 'unpleasant' to listen to.

Perhaps unsurprisingly, there have been ongoing attempts to police and discipline the unruly sonic signatures of podcasting. Sound scholar Jennifer Lynn Stoever (2016) has argued that 'The listening ear . . . normalises the aural tastes and standards of white elite masculinity as the singular way to interpret sonic information' (13). We can see the

---

[4]The amazing podcast *The Vocal Fries* explores these issues.

listening ear in action in the barrage of complaints female podcasters often experience with respect to the sound of their voices and their modes of expression. *This American Life*, for example, revealed in episode 545 how much hate mail they receive from listeners complaining about vocal fry among the show's female producers. 'Listeners have always complained about young women reporting on our show. They used to complain about reporters using the word "like": and about upspeak . . . . But we don't get many emails like that anymore. People who don't like listening to young women on the radio have moved on to vocal fry' (Glass 2015, 31:20). The episode goes on to point out that host Ira Glass himself speaks with vocal fry, but has never heard complaints from those listeners who claim to find it excruciating. This suggests that the supposed problematic quality of the young female producers' voices is simply an excuse to complain about having to listen to young women at all.

While female voices might be perceived as shrill, or as talking too much or as not authoritative enough (Karpf 2007), racialized voices are subject to different kinds of scrutiny and judgement. 'Linguistic profiling' is used by many listeners to determine the linguistic subgroup to which the speaker belongs, including racial subgroups, and this profiling can, of course, be preferential or discriminatory depending on the listener's perception of race (Baugh 2000). However, extra-sonic information such as the appearance of a speaker also informs our perception of the voice, often more than sonic information, with people who believe they can detect race from a voice alone often being proven wrong (Eidsheim 2012). What this means, simply, is that some voices are perceived to convey markers of difference while others are perceived as 'normative' or adhering to western/northern cultural expectations of the ideal speaking voice, that is, white, masculine, educated and so forth.

The politics of voice play out differently in different disciplines, through the cultural contours of both national and regional contexts and through the peculiarities of certain systems of education. The internationalization of higher education in many parts of Europe makes it much harder to place scholars by region and class than, say, in the UK, where one's background is marked the moment one opens one's mouth, and some disciplines just seem much 'posher' than others. Historically, radio has rejected regional accents as well as racialized dialects in favour of a trained broadcasting voice, and while podcasting has expanded listeners' aural palettes, the perception of some voices as more neutral or more authoritative than others remains. Added to all this is the bias that many people have when they hear a particular person's voice; for instance, people often say that they can't stand someone's voice without being able to articulate exactly why this is so.

These ideologies of voice pose a fundamental challenge to the supposed fairness of anonymized peer review. Sound-based scholarship cannot be fully anonymized, since it is resolutely embedded in the voice of the scholar. Even the most distanced scholarship, once spoken aloud, has been stripped of one layer of anonymity, making it impossible to reconcile with the gold standard of fully anonymized peer review. This personalization of work can open the door to latent biases. Just as knowing that an author is, for example, a woman, an early career scholar, a non-native speaker or a person of colour may bias reviewers against their work in a non-anonymized peer-review process, so too can the politics embedded in how we listen to and attribute authority to different voices inform how we engage with sound-based scholarship.

Particular cultural formations allow for legibility to be granted to some forms of communication and not others and give agency to certain types of voice; such ideologies of voice set the stage for who is heard and to what degree (Weidman 2014). Thinking about voice requires reviewers to consider the language used alongside the dominant structures within which any given voice is heard, as well as how these structures are used, including by those marginalized, to not only be heard, but also legitimized (Lawy 2017). Within academia, this might mean that scholars whose voices are coded as differing from the default 'neutral' voice (white, male, cis, straight, upper class, non-disabled, etc.) via markers of class, gender, ethnicity or sexuality feel the need, consciously or not, to speak in ways that conform with dominant conceptions of how scholars speak.

Academic institutional norms and practices that devalue and problematize emotion in scholarship, viewing it as not only external to but also a distortion of knowledge, are a form of hegemonic control (Butterwick and Dawson 2005). Because women are 'always so emotional', it follows that they can't be trusted to Do Sciencey Things. Voice, with its ability to convey emotion, is a tool that can subvert the academic authority that has so long frowned upon the connection of mind and body and emotion.

At the same time, the ability to hear the human voice might, aside from some of the benefits mentioned earlier, reinscribe power relations through normative frames of what a scholar should sound like. An academic community, like any cultural formation, sets the boundaries of which types of speaking are considered acceptable or unacceptable, imbuing utterances with power or constraining them (Weidman 2014). Public radio in the United States, Canada and the UK, for example, 'strategically deploys a particular social voice that has been carefully crafted to convey authority but also a kind of intimacy' (Durrani, Gotkin and Laughlin 2015, 595), the latter quality being widely recognized as a salient characteristic of the podcasting medium. This voice – which has seeped into podcasting as surely as NPR is the progenitor of countless hit podcasts – presents a conundrum for academics who podcast: academics are used to writing with authority, but less often with intimacy or emotion. As Durrani, Gotkin and Laughlin (2015) observe, 'academic textual practice has been a process of concealing the body, of which the voice is an important part. Thus . . . the podcast form opens up what academics have tried to cover up' (595). In other words, podcasting places a rather different expectation of voice on academics than what they are used to employing in their scholarly writing.

In spite of the struggles those with 'problematic' voices have in being heard, we see a certain degree of positive potential in the plurality of voices heard in scholarly podcasting today. As Mert Kocak from the *Sexuality and Gender in Turkey Podcast* reflected when speaking to Ian,

> When I first started, I was really worried about my pronunciation. I was really worried about sounding – I wouldn't say as native as possible – but sounding at least understandable to people. Then after a while I realised that if I don't do this, it would mean that only native speakers could do podcasting, which is nonsense.

The range of voices in scholarly podcasting reveals the diversity of scholars, which might not be readily apparent to a general public conditioned to think of scholars as white men with beards. This plurality of voices has the potential to destabilize hierarchies within fields of research, where, in many of the social sciences, there is an assumption about who the 'we' is in most texts about 'others' (Chua and Mathur 2018). The possibility of hearing voices spoken by scholars of different backgrounds can hopefully undermine assumed ideas about who constitute the 'us' and the 'them' when scholars write about 'others' and themselves.

Voices in podcasts are not only solo affairs, however, but realized through conversations – and so it is to conversation that we now turn.

Conversation

Scholarly podcasting (as a public and participatory sonic action) is a process of meaning-making through conversation. Conversation begets story, and stories form the foundation of not only interpersonal relationships but also knowledge and understanding. Conversations are imprecise and messy but context-rich.

The second pillar of podcasting as a public and participatory sonic action is *conversation*. Podcasting and scholarly knowledge production are both conversational. Conversations (and good scholarship) do not begin with the ending predetermined; they unfold unexpectedly and via the process of exchange. In this sense, conversation is a process of collective meaning-making, in which multiple people participate in the social action of creating knowledge together (Lowe, Turner and Schaefer 2021). While podcasts are frequently conversations between two or more people, even single-voiced podcasts (like good scholarship) are conversational in the sense of unfolding unpredictably and collectively. After all, is a podcast really a podcast without a listener? And what is a listener but a silent (or not-so-silent, depending on whether you talk back to your favourite podcasts) participant in a conversation? If a podcaster falls in a forest and there's no one around to hear her, can she still sell merch?

Discourse is central to knowledge creation; in fact, we'd argue that most scholarship is created discursively even if the discursiveness is often hidden in scholarly writing (e.g., the conversations with colleagues, peers or students that helped develop an idea might appear in a footnote if at all). As Michaela Benson, sociologist and podcast producer (*Brexit Brits Abroad* and *Who do we think we are?*) pointed out when speaking to Ian:

> One of the things that gets lost, I think, in contemporary academic life is the idea of knowledge production as a dialogue. After your

average day, the idea that you're in conversation with anyone is slightly, I'm going to say farcical because, you know, you go to a conference, you present a paper, that's your 20 minutes done. And because everybody's so busy, we don't want to impose on our colleagues by asking them to comment on a paper or to give us feedback on things. I've remembered that through doing a podcast, through chatting with other members of my team on the podcast or through talking with other colleagues . . . that talking through ideas has been really generative of the analysis I've produced . . . whether that's in a traditional published form, or whether it's in blogs, whether it's on the podcast, whether it's an animation, whether it's on websites. It has definitely become part of the process rather than something that stands aside from the process of the project.

Acknowledging the role discourse plays in knowledge creation (both by the producer and the reviewer) is key because verbally articulating ideas draws on different processes than writing about them; as linguist Peter Auer puts it, 'writing is a private act; only the finished product of this act comes into contact with the addressee. Spoken language must (and can) reckon with interactive openness from the very outset' (Auer 2009, 1). Of course, this kind of binary construction of speaking versus writing is always going to be a bit of a straw man; the writing of this volume, for example, has certainly been collective, and through the review process, public. Nonetheless, the image of the academic as a lone genius penning obtuse volumes in isolation within their ivory tower endures, and in some disciplines (particularly the humanities) is still privileged via the focus on single-authored articles published in paywalled journals and monographs with prestigious publishers that may have price points in the hundreds.

So what happens to knowledge when we, instead, create it through conversation and preserve the conversational process in how it's presented? We suggest conversation creates knowledge that is often imprecise but richly contextual.

Let's start with the imprecision. Conversation has its own cadence and patterns; language used is usually simpler than that in written text and sentences are shorter (and, perhaps, a little less grammatically 'perfect'). Using language in this way can engender new ways of thinking about, and communicating, ideas, not only on the part of the scholar but also by opening those ideas up to a greater range of interlocutors. But it can also be difficult, via conversation, to actually arrive at a point. When we first sat down to articulate portions of this chapter out loud – we were thinking we might be able to 'write' the chapter by recording our discussion and using the transcript as the structural basis for the chapter – we quickly ended up having a meta-conversation about the nature of conversation itself:

> **Ian:** Well, I was honestly thinking maybe I'm the person who's least enthusiastic about this idea for the chapter . . . . I think especially if we're going to be talking about some theoretical stuff about sound, then I think precision is pretty important. And that's exactly when conversation doesn't work so well.
>
> **Lori:** That makes me think of something that Dan Misener[5] told me. One of his early mentors at CBC told him that audio media – radio in this case, but it could be extended to podcasting – is a medium that has very high emotional bandwidth and low informational bandwidth. So what you are getting at, Ian, is this idea that if we're doing a podcast about peer review, I can't really present you a table [of information] through conversation, right? So the informational capacity – the capacity for listeners to handle loads of information and numbers and statistics – is low, but emotional bandwidth is high. For me, there's something about podcasting, because of its high emotional bandwidth, because of its capacity for storytelling, that it really does add feeling and context back into scholarship.

Conversation is not a great way to precisely articulate an idea; if we thought a conversation *could* get exactly at ideas, we probably would have made this whole book into a podcast instead. But as much as we rely, in scholarship, on the beautiful precision of the written word, we also recognize how central conversation is to the development of ideas.

---

[5]Dan Misener is what you might call a Big Deal in the Canadian podcasting industry and also created the podcast *Grownups Read Things They Wrote as Kids*.

While articulating the complex details and nuances of an academic argument in the midst of a real-time conversation can be difficult, this challenge is also an opportunity: conversation insists on distilled, simplified, digestible information and explanation. Scholars know how easy it is to get bogged down in the details or lost within one's own argument. We may have experienced the dreaded questions at a family gathering or social event such as 'what are you doing your PhD on?' or 'what is your book about?' – questions that take significant consideration and distillation to answer in such contexts. While your Uncle Mo[6] and Auntie Radhika might not be listening to your academic podcast, the conversational aspect of the podcast still calls for a measure of distillation of complex ideas that, in turn, demands that the scholar comes to terms with the essence of their work in order to successfully talk it through via conversation. This process can not only improve the scholar's own understanding of their work but also the accessibility of the scholarship to a wider audience of scholars and non-scholars. Something about the messiness of conversation invites the listener – perhaps even Uncle Mo – to feel part of the production of knowledge, as Ian illustrates in this excerpt from one of our conversations:

> **Ian:** And I think there's probably something interesting there that I can't quite put my finger on right now, in terms of . . . when something is a bit more rough around the edges, you feel like you're, you know, like, wanting to jump in, and I think it's . . . do you get what I'm saying? Can someone finish my thought for me?

Scholars work things through via conversation: in classrooms and conferences, in the playground or over Zoom, in our marginal notes and discursive engagements with other scholarship in our fields. When we are first teaching students how to make their own arguments, we often tell them that disciplinary knowledge is like an ongoing conversation. You have to listen for a while before you can start contributing (it's rude, after all, to butt into a conversation

---

[6]Seems like bringing up your Uncle Mo is a good moment to tell another dad joke: What does a group of whales listen to to pass the time on a long journey? PODcasts, of course.

midway without any understanding of the context), and then when you do contribute, you need to both respond to what others are saying and add something of your own. The conversational model of scholarly meaning-making reminds us that we don't create new knowledge by tearing others down, just like we can't make conversation by shouting over one another. This is not to say that conversation cannot abide conflict. Indeed, conflicting views and diversity of thought strengthens scholarship. In their assessment of using podcasting for creating geographic knowledge, Kinkaid, Emard and Senanayake (2020) indicate that 'podcasts not only created opportunity for including diverse voices in polyvocal dialogue, but also for placing conflicting voices into conversation with one another. The ability to include conflict in the presentation of our data was critical for us in navigating our individual and collective positions as researchers' (84). But a conversation featuring conflicting voices is more likely to create space for complexity and indeterminacy rather than prioritizing the triumph of one voice over another.

Despite its tendency to be imprecise, conversation also brings new kinds of contextual information with it. Of course, context isn't always a benefit: conversation is subject to the same pitfalls pointed out earlier about voice. If disciplinary knowledge is a conversation, we must be careful to consider whose voice is dominating, and who is getting shut out or talked over. Conversation is neither inherently egalitarian nor inclusive. As Sarayu Natarajan, co-host of *Ganatantra* told Ian, even though she was co-hosting, male guests would often interrupt or talk over her when she tried to speak or ask questions.

Conversation is central to the making of knowledge, for all that it is frequently erased in the interest of positioning knowledge as static, absolute and authoritative, knowledge as something decontextualized. As Hannah ruminated during one of our conversations:

> **Hannah:** The word I keep thinking of is *context* . . . . The way that we practise scholarship right now is premised on various forms of decontextualization, including the privileging of double anonymized peer review, which is, in a way, about decontextualizing knowledge as much as possible, because context is considered to be a weakness. We

think of that context – scholars' identities – as information that can be used *against* people, to discriminate against them. But the feminist response to that for some time has been like, no, actually, you need to situate things, you need to insert context, you need to, like, *ritually* insert context. And sound-based scholarship brings context back into our work, all kinds of context: the context of our voice, and all of the things that that says, but also the context of the accidental sound that is picked up in the background, the context of the pause, the intonation, the silence, like all of those things.

This chimes with Walter Ong's arguments that cultures characterized by orality evidence thinking that is situational, contextual and centred in the human body, while cultures characterized by literacy evidence thinking that is abstract and centred around impersonal labelling and categorizing (as cited in Vitali 2016).[7] Indeed, Ong indicates that sound has 'unifying, holistic, harmonizing tendencies', while the written text isolates (Vitali 2016, 29).

An awareness of context and embodiment is demonstrated by Ted Riecken who, in one of the first examples we have come across of using podcast recording for peer review, recorded his thoughts on multimodal scholarship and layered underneath them a soundtrack of he and his dog walking in the forest. This audio bed highlights the situational, embodied and relational aspects of doing scholarship: 'much as we have foundational works that underlie our thinking as scholars as writers and authors, there's also foundational spaces that I think we occupy. . . . [O]ut there [I] occupy a space not digital but very real, very grounded, where I find myself connected to a much more physical web of life' (Riecken 2014, 02:58). Similarly, academic podcasters Sam Clevenger and Oliver Rick of *Somatic Podcast* – which, as the name suggests, emphasizes embodied aspects of experience – indicate that one of the goals of their podcast is 'to allow all of our everyday physical, embodied experiences to impact how we can then speak to their

[7]While we disagree with Ong's hierarchical placement of cultures of orality as 'pre-literate' or not yet evolved into the supposedly more sophisticated literate culture, we find his characterizations to be useful in understanding how voice and conversation are embodied and contextual.

various contexts and meanings' (Clevenger and Oliver 2016). These examples remind us that the capacity to reinsert the body and physical contexts into our scholarship is an exciting feature of podcasting.

Voices in conversation comprise two of the foundational pillars of podcasting. The third, digital publishing, is what enables those voices and conversations to not only reach an audience but also to disrupt the existing patterns of scholarly communication.

Digital Publishing

Scholarly podcasting (as a public and participatory sonic action) is a form of digital publishing, which opens out affordances of responsiveness and connection between podcaster and listener, as well as seriality which can disrupt the traditional rhythms of academic knowledge creation.

Podcasts – originally known as 'audioblogs' – emerged out of RSS or Really Simple Syndication technology, developed by programmers in the late 1990s and early 2000s as a tool for subscribing to blogs. Audioblogs became possible once audio files could be compressed enough to be delivered via the relatively slow data rates available at the time, though they weren't called 'podcasts' until journalist Ben Hammersley coined the term in 2004 (Hammersley 2004). We can't talk about podcasts, then, without talking about the publishing architecture of Web 2.0 – including the rhythms of serial publication, the act of subscription and the built-in opportunities for responsiveness and interactivity – and the impact this architecture has had on scholarly communication.

The qualities of digital publishing that excite us are all connected to the capacity of podcasting to transform the rhythms and patterns of relationality that characterize scholarly communication. Seriality, after all, is about the creation of rhythms that structure relationships between creator and audience – in this case, between the podcasting academic and their listeners, be they peer reviewers or a wider audience. Seriality invites responsiveness. Historically, fiction was serialized in magazines in order to create anticipation and conversation. Seriality reminds us that media is not just about the finished, perfect object but about the way it is moving in the world and how people are reacting to it. Podcasts are all about this kind of responsiveness. An episode is created, people respond to it, the producer incorporates that response into the subsequent episode, people respond and so on. Podcasters are always in dialogue with their listeners whether or not listener voices are actually present on the podcast; it's there in the texture of seriality. Podcasts are produced in implicit dialogue with the people who are listening. Podcasting's seriality brings something into scholarship that reminds us that knowledge is not just embodied in the creator, but it's also out there and circulating:

> **Hannah:** When I think about how I want my work to be peer reviewed, I don't want it to be peer reviewed as though it's this isolated piece of knowledge that exists by itself. I want part of the consideration of it to be how it moves through the world, and what people are doing with it, and what it makes possible and what conversations it opens up. That's what excites me. And that, I think, is something that peer review can contribute to, so it can be part of the way the work moves through the world and the conversations that emerge, and also it can capture something about the way our work moves and shifts and exists that like, isn't impact, quote unquote, but gets that research needs to *be in the world* somehow.

Seriality as a feature of publishing significantly predates podcasts and, indeed, the internet as a whole. Defined strictly, it is the quality of being serialized, which is to say, taking the form of a series. You could talk, for example, of a novel being serialized – as so many Victorian novels were – meaning they were released in multiple volumes and readers had to wait for the next instalment. Conversations about seriality have been popping up in the wake of streaming services' transformation of how we watch television; whereas early streaming series were released in a single batch, encouraging viewers to 'binge watch', newer prestige series like *Mare of Easttown*, *Yellowjackets*, *Succession* and *Severance* have returned to a more television-like weekly release schedule to drive anticipation and engagement, as viewers gather on social media to hypothesize about what will happen next.

Seriality is good at creating expectation and anticipation. It both satisfies the desire for more of something its audience likes while continuing to drive the appetite for future instalments. Periodical scholar James Mussell (2015) explains how serial media – he's writing about magazines – rely on a 'serial structure [that] is invoked through the repetition of certain formal features, issue after issue. It insists on formal continuity, repeated from the past and projected onwards into the future, providing a mediating framework whose purpose is to reconcile difference by presenting new content in a form already known' (347). What's key about seriality is the ability of the audience to recognize and predict these patterns of repetition and difference, giving pleasure and the desire to revisit (Rak 2013, 29). Matthew Levay (2018) notes than an equally central affect to consider when it comes to serial publication is boredom: 'not a simple emotion arising from a loss of interest, but rather a state of contentment in which expectations are so thoroughly met that the reader is soothed by that which might otherwise provoke anxiety (in this case, the narrative contingency on display in serial conventions like cliffhangers)' (x–xi). Seriality both invokes and then satisfies the desire for more, pulling us along from instalment to instalment as we're promised more of the same, but not quite.

But seriality is characterized not only by the promise of something more to come; it is also about the creation of rhythms that synthesize pasts and futures as they both confirm past beats and create anticipation of future ones (Abraham 1995). The first serialized medium may have been the newspaper, which generated a quotidian sense of structure and rhythm that came to characterize modern conceptions of time, in which our experiences of time are correlated without necessarily being completely contained or disciplined, allowing for experiences of synchronicity that still feel like they are deliberately chosen (Levay 2018; Mayer 2017).

While newspapers arguably created shared temporal regimes, contemporary serialized media are not always about shared rhythms – and when it comes to podcasts, the rhythms are, in fact, profoundly personal. That's because podcasts are not simply serialized, but also on-demand, a digital form of serial publishing that is distinct from broadcast. That distinction, simply, is about whether you have control over when you listen: if you want to tune into a favourite radio show, you have to turn on the radio when it's playing; if you want to listen to the new episode of a favourite podcast, you can download it at any point after its appearance on your RSS feed.

Podcast listening rhythms, then, are a relationship between listener and podcast, one built around expectation (e.g., this new episode will drop on Tuesday morning, it will be around 45 minutes long, it will open with familiar theme music and recognizable voices, etc.) and habit (I will listen to the new episode on my Tuesday walk home from work). For a podcast producer to be 'on time' or 'in time' means they must act in a way that does not only 'follow' the established rhythm, but also acts in expectation of it and, moreover, their act is not simply a marking of time, but also the making of it (Garfinkel and Rawls 2002). We know it must be Tuesday because our favourite podcast has a new episode; if, for some terrible reason no new episode appears on a Tuesday, then the whole tightly woven pattern of domestic, labour and listening routines that we have carefully established over time comes crumbling down – or at least is shaken.[8]

There are a number of ways to understand the intensity of podcast listeners' rhythmic attachments to particular shows, but certainly one of the contributing factors is that we don't passively *hear* podcasts, but, rather, actively choose to *listen* to them. And one of the key ways we choose to listen to podcasts is through the intentional act of subscription. Comparatively little of the media we consume in the 21st century operates according to subscription, but that's a relatively recent change. We tend, now, to either subscribe to services (like Netflix), to pay freemium rates for ad-free experiences (as with Spotify) or to pay with our data and attention for free platforms (like YouTube) that use corporately owned algorithms to drive content into our feeds, generally with the goal of keeping us on their sites for longer so we can watch more ads. Curiously, where subscription models for newspapers and magazines have for the most part struggled to make the leap into the digital publishing environment, podcasts have continued to thrive via the subscription-based model. In part that's because podcast subscription is free; when you hit 'subscribe' on your

---

[8]Frequent podcast listeners will have their own habits of consumption, including which shows they listen to as well as what app they use to subscribe, how often they listen and so forth. It's a compliment to dub a podcast a 'same day listen' – that is, a show that is consumed on the same day that a new episode is released – and extremely popular shows will even field listener complaints when the episode doesn't arrive exactly when listeners expect it. We might have other shows that linger in our queues for longer, perhaps because we prefer to let episodes pile up so we can binge listen, or because it's a show we feel we ought to be listening to but secretly don't like all that much.

podcasting app of choice, the only commitment you're making is to download new episodes of that show. You don't even need to listen!

What's important about the perseverance of the subscription model in the world of podcasting is that, low barrier though subscription may be, it is still a choice. When was the last time you accidentally overheard a podcast?[9] We overhear music all the time, playing too loudly through a fellow bus passenger's headphones or over a car radio, tinnily echoing over a corner shop speaker or filtering through a neighbour's wall. Podcasts, however, are something we are almost always *choosing* to listen to, whether that listening happens half-distractedly or not. Through the curation of a deliberate podcast feed and the structuring of domestic and personal routines around the rhythms of serialized listening, we don't simply say yes to podcasts once: we say yes again and again.

It is possible to subscribe to text-based academic content. Many academic journals allow readers to subscribe to receive content updates, Google Scholar allows users to subscribe to keywords or particular scholars and research aggregation sites like ResearchGate and Academia.edu allow tailored subscriptions. However, these subscriptions have neither the regularity nor the personal intimacy of podcasting, not least because of the purposes for which the content is consumed (i.e., scholars usually read journal articles to write their own journal articles). Getting a little closer to podcasting in terms of its relationship to audience is the academic blog. Often blogs will have a more personal tone, be published regularly and be free to access. They are usually not peer-reviewed and often do not count (or count for much) within measurement matrices. Many academics blog(ged) for reasons similar to many scholarly podcasters, not necessarily to reach wide public audiences (though some did/do), but, rather, to speak to their peers and create communities (Mewburn and Thomson 2013).

Scholarly blogging has somewhat waned, however, with the rise of social media platforms such as Facebook and Twitter. A scholar's Twitter thread (a collection of numbered tweets on a particular topic) has the potential to go viral in ways a blog does

---

[9]Lori's beloved better half listens to podcasts through the speaker on his phone, which he carries around the house in his pocket while he goes about his business. So she actually gets to overhear *WTF with Marc Maron*, *Freakonomics* and *Canadaland* quite often via this human mobile loudspeaker she shares a home with.

not, and allows for more immediate responses and discussion. Among those academics who use social media, most use it for the dissemination of research, or the development of networks, or for other personal reasons, such as career advancement (Chugh, Grose and Macht 2021). However, there is a difference between a social media follower and a podcast listener in that podcasts are a lean-in experience.[10] In contrast to a quick glance as part of an endless scroll of Twitter content, podcasts require the listener to *choose* to listen, and, as we have argued, listening is a commitment.

Much of the research on listener engagement with their favourite podcasts comes out of the world of advertising. Indeed, much of the success of the medium as a whole is linked to how well podcasters can sell things: host-read ads are significantly more effective than pre-recorded ads, giving listeners the impression that the hosts are personally vouching for the products they're selling (Brinson and Lemon 2022). And the reason they can sell things is because of the intensity of the parasocial relationship developed between host and listeners. What's crucial to note here is that subscription contributes to this feeling of investment, of being part of something – even of *participating* in the world of the podcast, despite its seemingly unidirectional flow. In fact, even though podcasts might appear to be as unidirectional as other broadcast media, fostering an ostensibly 'one-way intimacy' (Weldon 2018), podcasting is, in fact, a distinctly Web 2.0 publishing medium, meaning that, much like blogging, it has interaction built into it.

Web 2.0, also known as the participatory web or the social web, is all about building not just the possibility but also the *assumption* of interaction into new publishing platforms, and podcasting is no exception. There's a reason why podcasts feel so interactive, so live and present and immersive, despite the fact that they're a one-way and asynchronous medium. Podcasts also foster communities of interaction and response.[11,12] The shape

---

[10]Not in the Sheryl Sandberg sense of leaning in, mind you. We're not huge fans of capitalism's co-optation and neoliberal interpretation of feminism.

[11]García-Marín and Aparici (2020) specify that it is not a medium itself which is participatory, but, rather, that 'participatory ecosystems' exist around a medium.

[12]There is an ample body of scholarship on fan podcasts and the publics they generate. See, for example, Euritt (2020); McGregor (2019); Meserko (2014); Salvati (2015); Savit (2020); Wrather (2016); Yeates (2018).

of those communities vary by genre, listener demographic and sheer popularity. The community surrounding a tremendously popular comedy podcast like *My Dad Wrote a Porno*, for example, is international and actively engaged in a wide range of fandom activities, including listening groups and fan-created resources, while the listenership for British Columbia-based true crime podcast *Island Crime* is more modest and local but has actively participated in helping investigative journalist Laura Palmer solve the crimes and disappearances she investigates on the show. While shows with larger listenerships might prompt a broader range of fan responses, those with more intimate communities built around them might include more intensive forms of interaction, with listeners perhaps becoming guests in turn, for example. As we'll expand on in what follows, the dialogic nature of podcasts combined with their interactivity makes them an ideal medium to expand our sense of who constitutes the 'peer' in peer review.

Of course, the expansion of possible peers and publics for scholarship also comes at a potential cost: not all interactions with publics are positive, and the risks entailed in engaging publics through social media vary widely depending on the scholar in question and the nature of their research. As Alex Ketchum (2020) explains, 'Especially for scholars who engage with the public through social media accounts, a writer's ideas are not the only thing attacked; threats of death and sexual violence can fill a scholar's inbox' (75). The level of interactivity a scholarly podcaster builds into their work, then, may depend not only on their capacity to manage a social media feed but also on their vulnerability to online harassment and the supports their institution has (or doesn't have) in place to assist them should they experience harassment.[13]

It might be helpful here to break down some of the ways that interaction is or can be built into the digital publishing logics of podcasting, emphasizing the way podcasts move through the world and what people do with them.

---

[13]For more on universities' role in protecting scholars from harassment, see Alex Ketchum's 'Report on the State of Resources Provided to Support Scholars Against Harassment, Trolling, and Doxxing While Doing Public Media Work' (2020).

Social Media: While podcasts themselves are largely a unidirectional medium, they are shared, promoted, interacted with, replied to and discussed via social media where listeners ask questions, challenge episodes, contribute new ideas and so on. Often it is possible to see podcasters responding in real time, demonstrating their own sense of responsibility to their listeners.

Listener Segments: one or more segments that actively encourage listener participation via specific kinds of contributions.

Calls to Action: an explicit request for listeners to engage in some sort of activity that will support the show, for example, rating or reviewing the show on Apple Podcasts.

Fan Communities: listeners develop their own communities and fan practices that may or may not interact directly with podcast creators but that, nonetheless, emphasize the participatory dimensions of digital publishing.

Listeners turned Podcasters: the participatory nature of many digital platforms emphasizes the rise of 'prosumers' in modern media (Jenkins 2006), with podcast listeners often becoming podcast producers, sometimes as a form of response to a favourite show.

While not all of these forms of interaction are true of every podcast, they are all potentials of the medium, part of what Lisa Gitleman calls a medium's 'protocols', the 'vast clutter of normative rules and default conditions, which gather and adhere like a nebulous array around a technological nucleus' (7). Thus, when a scholar chooses to work in the medium of podcasting, they enter into this new set of protocols, bringing not simply new modes of expression but also new possibilities for audience engagement and interaction that differ quite fundamentally from the logic of older publishing forms like the journal article or the book.

Affordances at the Intersections

Having established the three pillars of how we're thinking about podcasting as a medium and as a set of activities, we can now consider where and how these pillars intersect and interact and how this affects the relationship between podcasting and peer review.

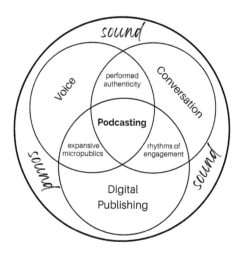

FIGURE 4 *Intersections of Voice, Conversation and Digital Publishing.*

Voice + Conversation = Performed Authenticity

Scholarly podcasting (as a public and participatory sonic action) facilitates performances of authenticity that decentre and distribute authority in a way that reimagines who the expert is, whom scholarship is for and how meaning is made.

Podcasters use voices in specific ways to project certain ideas about those who are speaking. Voice and conversation are culturally and historically constructed, and change over time in relation, in part, to how we perform our scholarly nature through a podcast. These performances – to our peers, our students and into a microphone for a podcast – are formed through pitch, volume, intonation and more (Eisenlohr 2007). We most probably all know what a 'direct' radio voice sounds like: cut through with liveliness and heavy use of the phatic function[14] (Kunreuther 2010). And while podcasting vocal performances do not, for the most part, mimic the direct liveness of

---

[14]Know what we mean? The phatic function, according to linguist Roman Jakobson (1981[1960]), refers to the elements of conversation that serve to build and sustain social connection without really sharing any meaningful information. Anyway, enjoy your day.

the radio host, they, nevertheless, are performances: performances of trust, integrity, authority, naivety and so on.

Scholars who are also teachers know that with every entry into a classroom one feels a little like an actor getting into character; from enormous lecture classes to intimate graduate seminars there is a measure of performance required. And often what we are performing is not only academic authority (i.e., there is a good reason I am being paid to lead you in your learning endeavours) but also, strangely, authenticity (i.e., I'm just a regular, approachable person who is keen to learn alongside you). Authenticity is known among podcast pundits as an 'inherent' part of the medium – it's thought that the often chatty nature of podcasts, as well as the expectation on the part of listeners that the hosts are *being* authentic, contributes to this perception – but it's a rare instance in which a chatcast is performed without something of a script, if only just talking points and background notes. A tension exists in podcasting between the expectation of authenticity and the fundamental requirement of performance, but that tension yields some interesting possibilities in the realm of *scholarly* podcasting.

The conventional scholarly voice is one characterized by authority and expertise; this voice is cultivated through the various disciplinary practices of academia, including peer review and certain approaches to copy editing, and it assumes an audience of other area experts. And this presumption is accurate for most disciplinary journals and many monographs. Some disciplines in the humanities and social sciences have inherited a tradition of writing *to* one another *about* communities who are not themselves addressed by the scholarship (see, for example, sociology and anthropology), while others write about topics of potentially widespread interest while actively excluding potential publics through paywalls, impenetrable jargon or both. As Kathleen Fitzpatrick (2018) argues, academics have historically understood those outside the university as objects of study or passive audiences, rather than 'a public, a self-activated and actualized group capable not only of participating in multidirectional exchanges both with the university and among its members, but also of acting on its own behalf' (8). Better yet, Fitzpatrick continues, we should understand them as 'a complex collection of communities' of which academics ourselves are, of course, members. It's no coincidence that the academics most concerned with publicly or community-engaged scholarship are often those who enter the university with a sense of accountability to communities beyond its walls.

Enter the podcasting voice, one that is characterized by authenticity, intimacy and transparency, even uncertainty. Add that vocal performance to the conversational dynamics of the medium, and we have ideal conditions for expanding who is addressed by scholarship, and how these new publics might feel invited to participate in scholarly conversations. The dialogic nature of knowledge produced through conversation further opens up its meaning-making processes, challenging the construction of the academic as an unquestionable authority in a way that invites more participants in ongoing scholarly conversations. We might even go so far as to say that scholarly podcasting invites a reconsideration of who the *peer* in peer review might be (more on this in Chapter 3).

But sound-based scholarship's capacity for including those who have traditionally been left out of academic discourse should not be underestimated. An enthusiastic research assistant recently told us that after describing to a friend the work she was doing on podcasting and peer review, her friend declared they might have gone on to graduate school if podcasting had been considered legitimate scholarship when they were at university. This friend, you see, had real trouble reading the complex and often inscrutable language used in written academic publications. While we are not against the use of expert language, particularly where specific terminology is crucial, we recognize the exclusionary and elitist nature of much writing in academia. (The number of times we referred to the thesaurus to find a more erudite [learned, bookish, high-brow, cerebral, egghead] word to replace a perfectly serviceable [useful, practical], unpretentious [simple, straightforward, plain, ordinary] word in the writing of this book[15] speaks to the connection between academic authority and exclusionary linguistic practices.) On the other hand, having a real-time *conversation* about scholarly work precludes the potential for most sesquipedalian (polysyllabic, affected, pompous) verbiage. Having to say things aloud often pushes one to articulate things in a more accessible way. (We return to this in the next chapter when discussing the *Open Peer Review Podcast* case study.)

---

[15]Ok, really it was only me who had to do this. – Lori

Before we go too far with proclamations of universal inclusion and the accessible nature of podcasts and podcasting, however, we note that the full experience of listening to a podcast is limited to those who are able to hear – at least in the traditional sense of the ears being the devices through which sound vibrations are turned into electrical signals that the brain interprets into meaningful information. In his book *Acoustic Justice: Listening, Performativity, and the Work of Reorientation* (2021), Brandon LaBelle reminds us that listening is much more than gathering sounds with our ears; d/Deaf[16] persons, for example, are capable listeners via alternate means. In terms of podcasting, transcripts are one alternate means of access for not only d/Deaf persons but also for anyone looking to find information in podcasts via keyword searches. We'll write more about the importance of transcripts in Chapter 4.

Digital Publishing + Conversation = Rhythms of Engagement

Scholarly podcasting (as a public and participatory sonic action) allows for ongoing and open-ended rhythms of scholarly communication that invite engagement in the co-production of knowledge by opening up gaps and spaces for response.

If vocal performances of authenticity alongside dialogic knowledge creation open up space for more people to participate in scholarly conversations, that openness is equally (though differently) manifested through the intersection of digital publishing and conversation. Podcasts, like conversations, are ongoing and process-based, unfolding in time and governed by internal as well as external rhythms. It may seem, at times, as if the interruptions and cross-talk produced by digital latency (e.g., a bad Zoom connection) is a good metaphor for digital media: everyone's talking, no one's listening. But podcasts, by and large, make a lot of space for conversation, both within episodes, as participants speak to one another (and edit

---

[16]The term d/Deaf is commonly used to designate both those who identify culturally as Deaf, and those who are legally or physically deaf.

out cross-talk in post wherever possible), and between episodes, as the seriality of the medium invites feedback and intervention.

Let's imagine our Professor Gigi Grayson has decided to make a podcast about her new area of research (cultural understandings of butterflies in Mediaeval Europe). In her first episode she invites an art historian who has been studying the iconography of butterflies in 13th-century Spanish churches. Rather than positioning herself as the expert, Gigi focuses on asking questions, gradually filling in gaps in her own knowledge while sharing her perspectives with her guests. They ask one another questions, and don't necessarily answer all of them, because their focus is on maintaining the pleasurable rhythm of conversation. Gigi publishes the episode on a Monday, and within the week has received feedback from a listener who is an amateur lepidopterist and has a theory about one of the historical butterflies that Gigi and her guest speculated might have been a fantastical invention by an obscure painter. While he isn't an expert in any of the ways a conventional journal would recognize (he's a landscaper by day; butterflies are just his passion), she decides to invite him onto her next episode to share his theory.

One of the primary affordances of digital publishing is its immediacy (Tenenboim-Weinblatt and Neiger 2018). Add in the fact that podcasts are published through (mostly) platform-agnostic, open RSS feeds, and they become available to a much broader audience, who are then invited to use any number of podcasting's interactive affordances to respond to what they've heard. And because podcast publishing is quick, and serialized, conversations can build not only within but also across episodes.

While the immediacy of digital publishing seems to push the podcast out into the brutal chaos of digital media flows, in fact, its production and consumption are slow, measured and respectful. Carl Leggo comments on how a digital medium like podcasting offers a link between the slow, reflexive production of scholarship and the immediacy offered by digital publishing:

> We're used to doing things in very slow kinds of ways. But that's not serving the role of scholarship in community contacts, in public dissemination. The real value, I think, of the new technologies, the new media, is immediacy . . . that we can speak to issues relatively quickly and not that we are producing the work quickly. The work is coming out of a lifetime of

commitment and reading and writing and so on. But that we can actually get work out there because we have something to say that people need to hear. So in other words, I would like to see, I guess, more of a connection between journalistic practices and academic practices. I think academic practices have accumulated a vast baggage that slows us down. (Leggo, Paré and Riecken 2014, 722)

Leggo focuses here on the *speed* of podcasting, but it isn't just the speed that appeals to us, it's also the rhythm. Rhythm in this sense is multiscalar and these scales interact. There is the rhythm produced by the seriality of podcasting: a podcast might come out every week or every two weeks or even every day, and that rhythm creates anticipation among listeners. There's often also an internal rhythm to each episode: maybe an introduction followed by some friendly banter, followed by an interview, followed by whatever it may be. And this internal rhythmic structure, combined with repeated motifs and even repeated phrases that a podcaster might use,[17] ties together episodes across a series. Then there is also the rhythm of the voice: the cadences, intonations and modulations the speaker uses to express emotional information and affective qualities. All of these rhythms can be transgressive of academic norms. As Ian explained during one of our Zoom meetings while feeling under the weather and possibly a little grumpy (note, if you have small children and they are reading this book, you may want to stop them now):

Ian: So we have a rhythm within the voice, we have a rhythm within the podcast's repeated elements, and we have this rhythm of seriality at the same time. And they're all really interesting and interactive rhythms at different scales. Maybe why they're transgressive is because they are rhythms which cannot be controlled [by the academy] – or at least not yet. They are not yet to be controlled by the rhythm of the fucking horrible machine that is academic production norms, the fucking waiting two years for someone to give you a

---

[17]Some popular podcasts even have bingo cards or drinking games related to certain phrases that the podcaster(s) are known for using regularly. See, for example, the *Jordan Jesse Go* drinking game (Thorn 2020).

fucking shitty half-paragraph review from a journal. The annual conferences and all of their fucking you know, blah blah blah, in some horrible fucking hotel somewhere, you know, all of the sort of. . .

Hannah: [laughing] 'All of their fucking blah blah blah!'

Ian: [with increasing intensity and speed] All of their, all of their super regimented 'You have 15 minutes to talk about your research. Now you're finished! You're finished! Stop speaking! Stop speaking!! STOP SPEAKING!!!'

Lori: [laughing]

Hannah: 'Now everybody go to the next session! Don't talk about this anymore!'

Ian: Exactly, exactly. 'Silence! Conversation over!' Those rhythms are like the school bell, they are sterile rhythms.

Hannah: Yes!

Ian: And the uncontrollable rhythms of podcasting are super fucking exciting in everything from the voice to the familiarity created to the anticipation created. And no wonder so many people don't like it because they disrupt this carefully constructed world that has been created over all these years. Even the rhythm of an academic article. Every discipline has its norms, but some journals are so super strict: 'These are your Findings! This is now your Literature Review! This is now your . . . whatever!' [makes barfing noise, sending Lori & Hannah into hysterics] It's all so controlled, you know? And this is what's amazing, I think: the rhythmic transgressions of podcasting on all these different scales, and the ungraspability of it all. Yeah, yeah . . . am I making sense? I really, like, I feel like . . . . [laughs]

Lori: [laughing and applauding]

Hannah: I love when you get a bee in your bonnet! It's so fun!

Lori: I feel like Ian might just drop dead now, though. That was a lot of energy!

Ian: [laughing] Should I drink a tea? Or should I drink a beer? I need something to keep me going.[18]

---

[18]We'll end the transcript here and spare you the devolution of the conversation into juvenile humour about 'academic rhythm method' and 'pulling out of scholarship'. We juveniles laughed pretty hard, though.

Digital Publishing + Voice = Expansive Micropublics

Scholarly podcasting (as a public and participatory sonic action) generates micropublics that understand themselves to be part of an expanded notion of knowledge creation.

As Dr Gigi knew when she started her podcast on historical representations of butterflies, no topic is too niche for a podcast. As a medium that evolved with a DIY ethos, little gatekeeping and fairly low-cost access to production and publishing, podcasting's soundscape has embraced a wider range of voices speaking about a wider range of subjects than would normally be heard on more traditional, mainstream media. While we don't want to overstate claims about podcasting being low barrier-to-access,[19] it nonetheless lacks the institutional barriers of traditional media such as radio. Whereas being permitted to present on radio airwaves requires everything from a coveted broadcasting licence to a rigorous screening and training process, theoretically anyone can start a podcast. Furthermore, any podcast has the inherent possibility of global reach. This wide reach along with the chance to be as niche as you like means the medium is ideal for public dissemination of research inquiry – often itself hyper-niche and of interest to a small number of people. As Sean Guillory, host and producer of the *SRB Podcast* told Ian:

> Those of us who are intellectuals or academics, who spend a lot of time studying very esoteric topics, need to think about different ways to produce intellectual content beyond the very conservative avenues of academic publishing or paywalled academic journals or conferences or lectures. I think podcasting, because it's democratised so much of the apparatuses of producing audio, allows for a different type of intellectual expression than writing texts, and writing texts that are often inaccessible to

---

[19]See, for example, Reginold A. Royston's 'Podcasts and new orality in the African mediascape' (2021), which explains why, 'For many African Internet users, such audio downloading could remain financially out of reach' (n.pag.).

wider audiences. Audio, I think, provides a potential remedy to all that.

While it has become rather in vogue to bemoan how many people have podcasts, the reality is that the origin of the medium in blogging assumes an ever-expanding web of creators with their own micropublics. We use the concept of the micropublic here in relation to publishing as an activity that calls a public into being, drawing on Michael Warner's (2002) definition of 'the kind of public that comes into being only in relation to texts and their circulation' (50). Where counterpublics are publics that 'differ markedly in one way or another from the premises that allow the dominant culture to understand itself as a public' (2002, 81) (e.g., queer counterpublics), *micro*publics understand themselves as niche, not necessarily in a way that counters dominant culture (though micropublics can also be counterpublics) but in a way that fractures off from dominant culture; micropublics are often characterized by an intensity of attachment to a non-dominant publication, like readers of zines or other underground publications. Xine Yao, co-host of *PhDivas*, had an unexpected fan interaction that reveals the way connections are made within micropublics. She had started a new job at University College London and had been invited out for dinner, then, as they told Ian,

> [I and one of the other dinner attendees were] walking home together and then sort of got chased by a man in a way that was very scary. And she was the one who actually helped me, because I froze and she grabbed me and dragged me across the street and brought me to her place. And then on the way, when once we stopped, she's like, 'oh, I just recognized your voice. You're one of the PhDivas.' And so, yes. So it's not just connected, but like she literally helped where this guy was being very menacing late at night, and then transitioned to podcast listener.

While the publics for academic podcasts might not be large, they can be, as the previous anecdote demonstrates, extremely powerful.

Digital publishing has fostered the growth of countless micropublics because digital publishing is so often *micro*publishing. In publishing, we refer to this as the 'long tail' effect. Physical media takes up a predetermined amount of space (you can't, for better or for worse, compress a print book or create an infinitely long newspaper), which means that publishers, media creators, booksellers, and other people and organizations responsible for deciding what media will be readily available are always in the process of curating for an anticipated public. That 'curatorial paradigm,' to borrow Michael Bhaskar's (2019) phrase, will be underpinned by a variety of explicit and tacit understandings of what makes some media more important than others: what is front page news, what are the important new books this season, what blockbuster movies are going to bring people to the theatre and so forth. Online, however, the storage space required to make media available, while not technically infinite, certainly approaches infinity: Amazon can make every in-print book available, Twitter can give every interested person access to a microblog and Apple Podcasts has yet to reach a limit on how many RSS feeds they can include. In a long tail media environment – one with a huge, almost infinite variety of titles available – there will be a small number of media properties with a significant or mass following, and a vast number of properties with extremely small followings.

Podcasting is an exaggeratedly long tail phenomenon. In practice, that means that while there is a relatively small number of smash hit podcasts with huge audiences, there are hundreds of thousands of podcasts that sustain themselves with comparatively small audiences. This in turn means that there is room for deep-niche rather than populist or mainstream content in the world of podcasting. And what *that* means is the expansion of whose voices are heard and what perspectives can be included. Keep in mind the next time someone eye-rollingly tells you that 'everyone and their dog has a podcast' that the democratization of media production is directly linked to the expansion of whose voices we're exposed to, and that calling a medium oversaturated is often a coded way of complaining about an absence of gatekeeping.

For scholars, the long tail of podcast distribution signals an opportunity. While podcasting audiences might be tiny in comparison to other mainstream media, they're still much larger than the audiences for the vast majority of academic publications. Hannah's podcast, *Witch, Please*, was once included in a WNYC piece on 'The Delightful World of Super-Niche Podcasts' (Basu 2017), but on the scale of academic publications this feminist rereading of the Harry Potter books is decidedly *popular*. Our point here is not a simplistic equation of scholarly significance with number of listeners or readers or citations; if you've read Chapter 1 you'll know we're not huge fans of the metrification of academia. We are fans, however, of expanding the reach of scholarly communication, engaging new audiences and upturning institutional and disciplinary hierarchies of what knowledge and whose knowledge counts. And the micropublics of podcasting, we believe, offer one space in which this kind of work can happen. Bonni Stachowiak, from the *Teaching in Higher Ed* podcast reflected on this phenomenon when speaking with Ian:

> At first I just really had this sense of 'who would ever want to talk to me?' . . . [So] I tried to turn that around as a teacher, as a speaker. So, 'who could I serve?' And as soon as we ask the question, 'who could we serve?' it gets us over ourselves because it's not about us. . . .
>
> I get interested in the numbers [of listeners] simply because I think they're a way of seeing the reach, but I also try not to ever have it be about that [the numbers].[20] So it comes back to, again, service. Who are you serving? And there's really a core community of people, they call themselves the Completists. They have listened to every single episode. And some people have listened from almost the very beginning. But then some, they only started a year ago, but just started from the beginning. And they have long commutes! There's one woman, I think she's in Australia, she would take the train and she'd be tweeting to me about every episode. I thought I was going back in time five years!

Voice + Conversation + Digital Publishing = Podcasting

So what does this all mean, in practice, for scholarly podcasting and its relationship to peer review? For one thing, it reminds us

---

[20]Though she gets 10 to 15,000 listens on her most popular episodes, which is remarkably high for a scholarly podcast.

of the profoundly rich opportunity presented by the intersection of scholarship and podcasting. As a public and participatory sonic action, scholarly podcasting engenders trust and intimacy through the human voice, underlines the discursiveness and contextuality of knowledge creation and opens up possibilities of responsiveness and interactivity through the rhythms of serialized digital publishing. Where these pillars overlap, we catch sight of affordances, exploring the kinds of vocal performances made possible within the medium, noting how we expand our understanding of the 'peer' in peer review and celebrating the micropublics so many podcasts engender.

Of course, we wouldn't be academics if we didn't note the limitations alongside the affordances. Podcasting shifts the locus of academic authority, but we must ask who is in the position to give up their authority and who is more likely to carry it with them into whatever new medium they dabble in. The conversational dimension of so many academic podcasts increases the potential audience and makes the process of knowledge-creation more transparent, but it also leads to a loss of precision and specificity, which are often vital to discipline-specific ideas. Plus, any celebration of open digital scholarship that gathers new audiences risks falling into a more=better approach that simply reimposes the metrification of academia. Podcasting is a democratic medium with low barriers to access, but listeners can get overwhelmed by the sheer quantity of available podcasts, making discoverability an ongoing challenge.

What we need are more sophisticated ways to think about scholarly communication, about its goals, its audiences and its impacts. Conventional approaches to peer review are entangled with traditional notions of what scholarship should do and whom it is for, and are increasingly in service to the neoliberal university with its fixation on metrics. It would be naive to imagine that a similar set of conventions couldn't be applied to podcasting, such that the most privileged academics monologuing with great authority and gathering significant audiences along the way become the faces of scholarly podcasting. How do we maintain the values of scholarly communication – rigorous grounding in research, citational practices, expert knowledge – while also embracing the exciting affordances of podcasting? One way forward, we believe, is to let podcasting help us reimagine peer review.

Interlude

Should I Make a Podcast?

At this point you may be asking, *what's next?* Our answer: start a podcast. *Wait, everyone?* Okay, no, not everyone. Luckily for you, we've made this handy flow chart to help you answer the question: should I start a podcast?

*Check out Stacey Copeland and Hannah's *A Guide to Academic Podcasting* (2021) or Ian's book *Scholarly Podcasting: Why, What, How?* (2023) for help getting started.

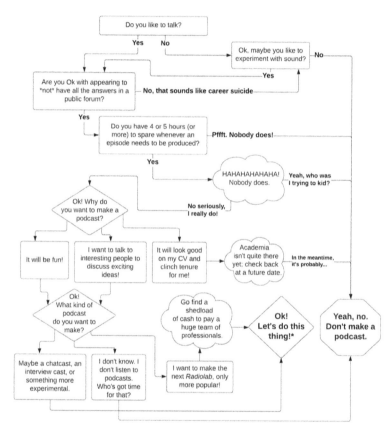

FIGURE 5 *Should you start a podcast?*

3

From Awareness to Appreciation (What Podcasting Can Bring to Peer Review)

As with written outputs, not all scholarly podcasting is the same. And, as with written outputs, not all review processes are appropriate for all forms of scholarly audio. Blog posts and book reviews are not treated the same way as monographs and journal articles, nor should they be. It follows that there are some forms of podcasting that, while engaged with the world of scholarship, may not be suitable to be peer-reviewed. There are also scholarly podcasts that *could* be reviewed but whose creators would (in fact, *do*) vehemently resist the idea of having them reviewed.

Our definition of scholarly podcasts focuses on reviewability, though not necessarily the fact of review. As discussed in Chapter 1, scholarly podcasts are podcasts that create new knowledge; whose content is accountable to a community of peers; that can be interrogated, cited and, in some disciplines, reproduced; and that can respond to comments, critiques or suggestions. Thus when *we* talk about scholarly podcasts, we are, perforce, excluding some work that may seem scholarly but that is not reviewable. Increasingly, for example, colleges and universities have podcasts that are intended to engage alumni, promote the work of faculty or communicate information to students. While these contribute important work to the university, peer review would be inappropriate as they are not generating new knowledge to be discussed. Similarly, podcasts that are simply recordings of classroom lectures, often uploaded to the internet unedited, do not warrant a review process. Some people may argue that these are not podcasts at all, lacking as they do some of those pillars we discussed in Chapter 2, such as seriality and audience engagement.

While other forms of scholarly podcasting may be reviewable, the podcasters may resist or outright refuse the process. Indeed, whatever the podcast form, there are many podcasters who resist being reviewed. Scholars enjoy using podcasts as ways to work out ideas that are not yet fully formed. The discussions or monologues they might have during a podcast function as a sort of sense-making in the moment. Peer review adds pressure to a process, threatening to stifle podcasting's informality, openness and even its *fun*. As *Archive Fever* co-host Yves Rees explained to Ian, 'peer review is kind of the last thing I would want to do, because I feel like that would put a layer of formality or pressure on, a sort of external framework for performance and productivity. Whereas actually, what I really love about this is that it feels so incredibly organic.'

Indeed, one of the most common concerns voiced by scholars who podcast is that peer review might kill the freedom that podcasting brings. They enjoy the fact that it is not noticed too much by their managers or tenure and promotion committees and hence, there aren't the same levels of oversight as there might be in other areas of scholarly production. Of course, these concerns presume the imposition on the podcast of a strict set of peer-review processes comparable to those of large journals, processes that restrict the ways in which scholarship can be presented and may therefore ruin the freedom and enjoyment of podcasting. But many scholars who podcast are becoming more forthright in their desire for recognition of this activity as meaningful scholarship in its own right. In other words, to create academic value via podcasting should not necessarily change the way podcasting is done to conform to peer-review principles created for another medium; any approach to peer-reviewing podcasts should be developed to support rather than undermine the medium's exciting and transformative qualities.

There is also a growing feeling among some scholarly podcasters that *some* kind of review process could help to bring the values of scholarly knowledge creation into the world of podcasting.

But what are these values, and how might we incorporate them meaningfully? If we aren't going to recreate a hierarchical definition of legitimate versus illegitimate knowledge – in which affiliation with an academic institution is synonymous with expertise – then the simple fact of the podcast host being a professor is not sufficient for a podcast to be scholarly. This might seem like a bold claim. After all, scholars are regularly invited as experts and authorities onto non-scholarly podcasts. Shouldn't the scholarly podcaster's qualifications and training give some sort of reassurance to the listener that what they are saying can be taken seriously? Sadie Witkowski from the podcast *PhDrinking* argues, 'I think academics do a good job of knowing where to hedge and where to have a stronger statement. But there are lots of research-based podcasts that are not by academics, and they can overstep or undersell ideas.' What her quote points to is that if scholarly work is based on a healthy sense of scepticism, it's not due to some inherent quality in the people who pursue an academic career, but, rather, in the ways we are trained to produce scholarly knowledge as reviewable. Stephanie Caligiuri, from *The People's Scientist* podcast, suggests as much in her articulation of how she sticks to her actual areas of expertise in her podcasting:

> I initially thought, well, maybe I'll bring on expert scientists to speak as well, or I could just speak to my own expertise. And I decided to speak to my own expertise. And that's why I'll stick to topics of nutrition, physiology, and neuroscience, because those are what I have my degrees in. I think for a scientific communicator it is always best to stick to your area of expertise, if you can, because sometimes there are small details that we don't realise because we're not an expert in that area that actually make it really important when we interpret the data.

While the integrity of the individual scholar-podcaster may help raise their credibility among their peers, who are positioned to recognize and appreciate critical humility, it is not always legible to a larger public of listeners, nor can it be taken for granted in the era of the academic turned pundit. Peer review, while not a replacement for fact-checking, allows for other positive outcomes; it can elevate and expand scholarship while also, vitally, credentialing emergent practices like scholarly podcasting. Whether peer-reviewing podcasts or using podcasts to conduct peer review, there are many ways in which podcasting can model and enact scholarly knowledge's reviewability. The question is *how*.

In this chapter we want to consider the intersections of podcasting and peer review more concretely, through examples, critique and the suggestion of potential models. Building on our definition of scholarly podcasting as a public and participatory sonic action that has the potential to be peer-reviewed, we consider what being able to hear the voice of a scholar does to traditional notions of review, along with the challenges posed when reviewing ongoing podcast series that defy the presumed singularity of scholarly production (the completed journal article or book manuscript). From challenges we turn to the opportunities and explore some of the new approaches invited by peer-review podcasting – that is, scholarly podcasts that are reviewable or reviewed, as well as podcasts that are enacting review – focusing on three characteristics: *creative*, *communal* and *care-based*, the three Cs of appreciative peer review. In this thinking about transformations to the peer-review process that focus on creativity, community and care, we're inspired by the vital work of HuMetricsHSS, the Humane Metrics Initiative, which since 2016 has been working to articulate alternate ways to frame the value of research, particularly in the humanities and social sciences, beyond metrics and rubrics. The framework they offer is based on the values of equity, openness, collegiality, soundness and community ('HuMetricsHSS: Our Values Framework' n.d.). While we identify with many of the same values, our argument is based around the specific affordances of podcasting.

We believe that scholarly podcasting as a public and participatory sonic action creates an *awareness* in listeners (including but not limited to potential reviewers) of who a scholar is and what they sound like. To be aware is to know, feel and perceive; reviewing scholarship necessitates 'having awareness' of not only the scholarship, but also how voices, which embody the scholar's interiority, and other sounds affect one's critical faculties. To have awareness is thus also to be conscious and cognizant of what sound and seriality, as vital forms of context, are doing to both scholarship and a reviewer's process of reviewing. In offering suggestions on different potential forms for peer-reviewed podcasting, we explore how awareness can, if done well, morph into *appreciation*. To be appreciative of podcast scholarship is to both seek to understand the scholarship and the scholar, and also to be grateful for the way its production suggests radical new ways of doing scholarship. After all, the comparative newness of sound-based scholarship means there is still space for experimentation in how we approach it. Appreciative review is humane, generative and ethically oriented – and, as much as some scholars have come to see peer review as a fundamentally grim process, it might even be fun.

With Open Ears: Known Scholars and Open-Ended Scholarship

The first, loudest and most oft-repeated challenge to peer review podcasts is anonymity. Advocates of anonymized review claim that anonymity reduces bias, nepotism, gatekeeping and academic revenge against negative reviews. We certainly sympathize with the sentiment behind this argument. Academia has its fair share of biased, nepotistic, revenge-seeking gatekeepers. However, anonymity is much less beneficial – and much harder to achieve – than it may seem, a fact that many university presses have long recognized; the standard for reviewing monographs is single anonymity, in which the identity of the author is known to the reviewer, though not vice versa. Even with journals, in which the standard continues to be double-anonymous review, it is easy enough for a reviewer to find out whose paper they are reading through a quick online search, or at least to make an informed guess and then allow that bias to frame their response. A title or niche topic might show up in conference programmes, workshops or other online forums. Even if a reviewer were not deliberately seeking to find out who an author is, they may do so inadvertently when looking up a reference or trying to verify a claim. There's no solid evidence that anonymity stops biased gatekeeping reviewers or disgruntled authors from behaving badly. Arguably, anonymity does more to reduce accountability and excuse this bad behaviour than it does to protect authors or reviewers (Ross-Hellauer 2017).

And yet, as anyone who has experimented in open-review processes already knows, adding the voice of the author into this mix is not without its problems. When we hear voices, as we've explored in Chapter 2, we hear them with multiple culturally constructed ideas about the person behind the voice. Because academia is still dominated at its highest levels by white, upper class (or at least upper middle-class) men (Lynch and Ivancheva 2015),[1] the 'neutral' academic voice is still characterized by these identifiers. We have little reason to suspect that the social injustices structuring relations of class and gender within institutions (Reay 2004) would not arise in scholarly podcasting as they are refracted through voice (and the structures within which voices are legitimized). After all, those dynamics are certainly playing out in the world of non-scholarly podcasting, where questions of the politics of voice remain a frequent topic of debate within the industry.

While ideologies of voice certainly pose a challenge to the peer review of podcasting, writing has similar issues. Writing also has a 'voice', with scholarly journal writing conventions in the humanities and social sciences creating demands that are easier for authors from certain backgrounds to fulfil than others. English language journals have cemented themselves at the top of the ranking hierarchies, compelling non-native speakers, including those from national university cultures that have little to do with English, to adopt the stylistic norms of these journals if they want to be part of 'international academia'. Feminist and queer scholars, Black and Indigenous scholars, as well as others hailing from under-represented communities, have pointed out that the need to anonymize their scholarship strips out the embodiment and relational dimensions of their work, forcing them to present themselves as isolated individuals rather than nodes in complex networks (McKittrick 2020; Cariou 2020). Cariou, for example, advocates for an open peer-review process that could 'acknowledge the relationality of the evaluation process' and 'engage with . . . the positionality of the reviewer' (2020, 11). Relationality and positionality are brought up in a lot of interventions into how 'expert' knowledge is circulated,

---

[1]While the increasing representation of women in some fields may suggest something like gender-based equity in universities as a whole, this impression is not supported by actual data. The American Association of University Women, for example, points out that 'women make up the majority of non-tenure-track lecturers and instructors across institutions, but only 44% of tenure-track faculty and 36% of full professors' and 'are still paid less than men at every faculty rank and in most positions within institutional leadership' (AAUW 2020). These gaps are, of course, significantly exacerbated by ethnicity, class, disability and other intersections of identity.

stemming from feminist understandings of situated knowledge, for example, or decolonial resistance to the idea of 'objective' facts that can be divorced from their contexts. At its heart, the intervention is this: we want to put ourselves, and our communities, back into our work.

Where scholars refuse to or cannot do this context-stripping, they may be punished for it, as Dada Docot describes in 'Dispirited Away: The Peer Review Process' (2022):

> Critiques of single-blind review note its exposure of the author's identity to reviewers, which might lead reviewers to make assumptions based, for example, on the author's non-Western name or gender. Furthermore, some authors who write self-reflexively or who research within their own community and family using autoethnographic methods may be easily identifiable. Thus, the review process becomes automatically single-blind for them. Reading the work of a scholar of color reflecting on her struggle with multiple forms of locatedness, exclusion, and colonial histories, Reviewer 2 saw only gibberish. (127)

Language and expression hierarchies already exist within conventional textual outputs, but they are often tacit rather than explicit. It is not our claim that scholarly podcasting is free from similar problems, but, rather, that peer-review podcasting can and should contain an awareness of voice and the structures within which it operates, and that expanding the range of modes of scholarly communication is likely to *reduce* barriers over all.

What we gain in context from podcasting, we may lose in academic authority – but that may be a good thing. As we explored in Chapter 2, one of the affordances of scholarly podcasting is shifting the locus of trust from the authority of the scholarly community (in which the traditional gatekeepers of trust are reviewers and editors) to the relationship between listener and podcaster. There is nothing fundamentally 'better' or 'worse' about this way of working out trust. Rather, the same way in which many academics critically assess the utility of peer-review processes for being slow, expensive, inconsistent, biased, and open to abuse (Smith 2006), we should critically assess the ways in which trust is engendered through podcasting.

A skilled writer creates authority by making the reader believe they understand a topic well, or have been deeply engaged in research or a fieldsite; a skilled podcaster can do the same if they know the craft. However, many academic podcasts do not appear as if they have been carefully crafted with the affordances of the audio medium in mind. Indeed, most are fairly unscripted (they usually have a structure, but conversations within them ebb and flow as conversations usually do). Leaving aside carefully designed series (e.g., *Somatic Podcast* or *Phantom Power*) or tightly scripted series (e.g., *How to Build a Stock Exchange*), most scholarly podcasts work through questions of trust and authority as they go, a sort of on-air trust-building exercise. This process injects a lot of vulnerability into scholarly knowledge production, which is antithetical to much of how we perform – or are expected to perform – our expertise in academia (Cook 2022). Departmental, national and disciplinary cultures vary greatly, but probably all academics have seen and heard others' (or their own!) work being criticized in unconstructive ways or seen classroom cultures develop in which displaying prior knowledge takes precedence over learning. For many of us, however, ideas are developed and worked out in different forums; not everything we say and do has to be perfect in its first attempt. Scholarly podcasting's vulnerability can therefore be part of its creative boon: it helps with the processing, developing, refining and restating of ideas in new and unpredictable ways.

Vulnerability thus becomes the strength of many scholarly podcasts. Expert knowledge is often attacked by those who seek to undermine its modes of inquiry or the wider system within which it is legitimized (see Chapter 1 for more on neoliberalism's suspicion of experts). Opening up the processes through which we create knowledge, either by talking about how we got there or working things out as we go, is not 'defending' work which is being 'attacked' or 'opposed', but, rather, engaging in a collaborative process of revelation. This approach requires a certain degree of trust – trust in oneself, as well as the trust that is generated with listeners over time. Building up trust with listeners is tied to the intimacy afforded by the podcast medium and allows for hosts to experiment as the show develops. Trust, as a mutual contract between podcaster and listener, allows for increased vulnerability.

Sociologist and host of the *Annex Sociology Podcast* Joseph Cohen explained to Lori how moving away from the 'monologue' of the finished paper and into the more conversational mode of an interview podcast can create discursive space for this openness and vulnerability in a way that can actively improve scholarship. Distinguishing between the monologic mode of the conference presentation and the more dialogic mode of many podcasts, Cohen explains:

> There is a pretence in monologues, there is a defensiveness, there's an incentive to puff up our findings or the integrity of our methods, there is an incentive for us to overplay the importance of what we have found, or theoretical insight. . . . I find when I engage in dialogue with people, and I start off by asking them to detail the lived experience of performing the research project, the tone, the language shifts towards one where people are more open about the warts of their study, or the uncertainty, or the fact that they're just making an interpretation based on what they see. And then when we get to the interpretations, I can really understand where they're coming from . . . We're just open about what it is we do, because it's still valuable, it's still good.

Cohen's perspective is echoed by Kinkaid, Emard and Senanayake (2020) who argue that monologic presentations tend to force consensus and make invisible any disagreements among researchers, while 'the dialogic potential of the podcast' allows for 'difference, dissent, and multiple perspectives in collaborative knowledge production' (85). Dialogue has the potential to reveal the processes through which scholarly knowledge is made.

Such an openness and vulnerability, however, might not appeal to all because of their position within academic structures and wider society. It may be the case that those who feel secure in being vulnerable are, in fact, already in a more secure position. The freedom to be vulnerable accorded to a tenured, and therefore virtually unfireable, professor, for example, is not the same as that accorded to a student or precariously employed academic. The level of freedom plays out in part via the content of the podcast – those with less job security or academic prestige often worry more about expressing something that is not backed up with iron-clad references – but also in terms of what kind of scholarly production is demanded of academics.[2] The expected modality of scholarship is to keep your thoughts, your data and your questions to yourself until you have created a polished diamond to present to the world. Thinking out loud in public is almost unseemly in this context.

Vulnerability and uncertainty are not the only risks early career or precariously employed academics may face when choosing to podcast; they are also likely to come up against academia's often-unspoken hierarchies of who is worthy of having a public platform such as a podcast. An academic star within their field might expect to be able to speak to a few hundred people as a keynote at their discipline's annual regional conference, but an 'upstart' PhD student might be speaking to as many people if not more on a weekly basis through their podcast, which can certainly cause disquiet among those who believe and have invested in hierarchical systems of academic recognition and rewards. These systems have, often for very good reasons, traditionally been based on the slow accruing of expertise and recognition. The young podcasting scholar can potentially operationalize their academic and digital scholarship capital as a means of gaining acknowledgement both inside and outside the academy in a way that leapfrogs established norms. However, as more and more scholars model the production of knowledge via public-facing mediums like blogging and podcasting, transforming the academic culture of authority-via-invulnerability and its accompanying hierarchies seems possible. Maybe we can carve out a space in academia for probing and uncertainty, not just as the starting points for inquiry, but as the starting points for public dissemination of scholarship. We have hope in this possibility, in part, because of the ways in which digital publishing continues to disrupt scholarly publishing norms.

After anonymity, the second major 'obstacle' faced when peer-reviewing some podcasts is their unfinished, serial character. While some podcasts are created as a finished whole, many scholarly podcasts explore topics and themes over a series or in an ongoing

---

[2]While this section focuses on the voice of the podcaster and the implications of the loss of anonymity, it is equally true that scholars from marginalized backgrounds may hesitate to participate as reviewer in an open review process, aware of how their identities may curb the kinds of critique they can offer.

fashion without an obvious end. How can a reviewer review something that is not yet finished? How can a reviewer review something that is both published but not *fully* published because it's the middle of a series? Some of the concern, quite understandably, is that scholarship might be published over-hastily, without the time and care represented by the peer-review process. If a podcaster puts out ideas into the world that are not yet fully formed and that contain factual errors or unsubstantiated claims, only to retract them in a later episode, isn't there a risk of spreading disinformation or undermining the already embattled expert voice? These are legitimate concerns. But as we established in Chapter 1, peer-reviewing has not, by and large, been about spotting and correcting factual errors. Ideally, peer review should be about improving and developing scholarship.

At their worst, the current dominant peer-review models practised by many corporately owned journals and academic publishers produce gatekeeping and box-ticking exercises, making sure that new scholarship pays proper homage to a conservative notion of canonicity and disciplinary norms. Serialized scholarship, however, demands that reviewers think not about gatekeeping but, rather, about improving future iterations by engaging in an ongoing conversation. While this ongoingness is comparable to the unfinished quality of many digital humanities projects,[3] ongoingness and unfinishedness are not quite the same thing, as we're conceiving of them. A review of a digital humanities project might, for example, capture a 'snapshot' of the project before further changes are made. A podcast, on the other hand, must be engaged with at the level of the episode. A podcast is not a single text that a creator might return to, adding to or modifying what's there, fixing bugs and creating new features; rather, individual complete episodes exist within an ongoing podcast series that demands listeners (and creators) think about the relationship of the individual episode to a series with a perhaps undetermined conclusion.

While ongoingness is not a characteristic of all podcasts or all sound-based scholarship (in the case studies that follow, we will look at some examples of peer-reviewed sound-based scholarship

---

[3]For more on the conundrum of unfinished digital humanities projects, see Brown et al. (2009).

that is not serialized), it is certainly one of the central and structural challenges of peer-reviewing podcasts. It is not merely a challenge, however, but also an opportunity to imagine different possible relationships between reviewer and scholar. For example, when the reviewer becomes a listener to an ongoing podcast series, their experience of the scholarship is shaped, in part, by how seriality impacts the listening experience (see Chapter 2 for more thoughts on seriality and its inviting rhythms).

Of course, when it comes to reviewing, especially if a reviewer has been specifically asked to review a podcast and listens to a lot of podcast episodes in a short period of time, the serial rhythms of the podcast, and of the reviewer/listener's engagement with it, are interrupted or compressed. However, within podcast episodes there are still recurring elements or segments or even turns of phrase that create relations of expectation to differing degrees. This expectation has the potential to create an effect that is not simply *non*-anonymous, but is, in fact, the opposite of anonymity: it is an awareness of voice and of what seriality does to reviewer–scholar relationships. And this awareness, we contend, is an important step in establishing the grounds for appreciative reviewing.

Appreciating Scholarship: Case Studies

Considering the proliferation of new digital platforms for publishing multimedia research, well-documented critiques of current models of peer review and the affective displeasure so many of us experience in the traditional processes of peer review, it isn't at all surprising that scholars and editors alike are clamouring to do things otherwise. We are seeing academic publishers, for example, evolve from text-only repositories to platforms that can accommodate a variety of digital assets that are produced in the course of scholarly research; data sets, visualizations, recordings, digital artworks and the like are increasingly being considered an integral part of the research story rather than something that must be removed and replaced by literal – and often inadequate – description. The development of new digital publishing platforms has similarly opened up new possibilities for the form of scholarly communication as well as the development of appropriate peer-review processes for multimodal scholarship, including, of course, sound-based scholarship.

Scholarly podcasting and sound-based scholarship in general are only part of this landscape, but they are an exciting part. The case studies that follow are far from exhaustive, and it's worth noting that they get a touch autoethnographic, because the experiments we are most familiar with are the ones we've been working on ourselves. As you may already be able to guess, we've had generally good experiences peer-reviewing our podcasts and/or podcasting our peer reviews, and are eager to elucidate these processes in the interests of encouraging their uptake by the many, many scholars already engaged in podcasting – and the many more who are curious but concerned about making this work count. At the same time, because the relationship between peer review and podcasting is actively being developed, the approaches are wide-ranging and diverse, which can be both exciting and a bit confusing. We need to consider the nature of the work being reviewed: is it an ongoing podcast series, a limited series or a one-off work of audio scholarship? Or is it written scholarship that is being peer-reviewed *via* podcasting? We also need to look at the form of the peer review itself: is it written or sound-based? Open or anonymized? Is the author involved in the conversation of the peer review, and if so, how? Did the peer review happen prior to or following the publication of the work, and if the latter, how was the review integrated? We also want to consider the peers in question. How is 'peer' being defined? Who is included in (and excluded from) the peer-review process?

Rather than spelling out guidelines for peer review, we turn to the case studies that follow to gather a list of approaches to peer-review processes for sound-based scholarship. These approaches are not mutually exclusive – indeed, they frequently overlap and complement each other. For that reason, we've developed a vocabulary of approaches that we'll use to **tag** our case studies as we develop a framework for appreciative reviewing. The six (potential) approaches to appreciative peer review we've identified[4] are as follows:

---

[4]Some of our approaches overlap with various dimensions of open review as defined by Tony Ross-Hellauer (2017). What we call public review, for example, he calls open reports review; our conversational review is similar to his open interaction

- **Public** reviews are shared publicly, such that reviewer comments can be heard or seen by anyone interested; when review is done publicly, reviewers are likely to be more respectful, attentive and explanatory in their feedback.

- **Conversational** reviews take place via conversation between reviewers, or between reviewer and reviewee, making space for the back-and-forth of talking ideas through together.

- **Media adaptive** reviews recognize that many of the norms of peer review were designed with written scholarship in mind, and that review processes for multimedia scholarship must take into account the particular affordances and concerns of the medium in which the scholarship has been created. This recognition may take the form of a peer review that develops new questions with the medium of the work in mind, or may involve bolder structural experiments, such as conducting the review in the same medium as the scholarship.[5]

- **'Summiterative'** reviews – a portmanteau combining the ideas of both completed (summative) and ongoing (iterative) – allow for work to be published first, and then reviewed and improved in public, thus mitigating the long delays typical of scholarly publishing.

- **Community accountable** reviews expand the understanding of who constitutes the 'peer' in 'peer review' by putting scholarship in conversation with those whom it is for and/ or about.

- **Recirculating** reviews put published scholarship through new cycles of review, reflection and conversation, to keep the knowledge creation process going. Recirculating review contrasts the current norm of treating published scholarship

---

review; and our community accountable review is similar to his open participation review. The terminology we have chosen here is not meant to replace the valuable work being done on open review, but, rather, to emphasize approaches to the review of scholarly podcasts in particular.

[5]With thanks to peer reviewer Megan Lyons for encouraging us to flesh out our draft definition of this.

as a finished object that can be engaged with only as a citation. You might read this and think 'how is this a review if it's not open to change?' to which we would say, 'knowledge is not synonymous with outputs; rather, it is ongoing, fluid and open-ended.'[6]

Each of the case studies that follow highlights one or more of these review approaches, and thus models a possible form of appreciative review. Our goal here is not to create an exhaustive list of platforms that practise appreciative review, nor is it to draw narrow boundaries around the right and wrong ways to *do* appreciative review. Rather, we use the format of the case study to demonstrate the complexity of review in practice, as well as how many existing projects are already working through the radical possibilities we're describing here.

Open Peer-Review Podcast *and* The Podcast Studies Podcast

Our first example is one close to our hearts: the *Open Peer-Review Podcast*, an experiment in podcast peer review initiated by Lori Beckstead. Starting with either a draft of a paper or simply a work-in-progress, the scholar who wishes to present their work invites a peer to join them for a **conversation** on the podcast. In a proof-of-concept episode of the *Open Peer-Review Podcast*, Lori presented her work-in-progress on what she calls the 'genetic code' of podcasts to scholar and podcaster Dario Llinares. Taylor MacLean from Toronto Metropolitan University's Centre for Communicating Knowledge acted as host and moderator for the ensuing questions and discussion. Both Taylor and Dario were provided with a summary of the research-in-progress in advance, while Taylor was also provided with a list of suggested questions and prompts to keep

---

[6]All published scholarship should be part of an ongoing dialogue with other work, pushing ideas forward. It should circulate. We're referring to something more specific here: scholarship that remains open and ongoing without the strict need to 'defend' something that was published, but, rather, being open to amend positions/arguments and further scholarship in an ongoing, dialogical and more immediate fashion.

the conversation moving as needed. The purpose of this strategy was to allow the scholar an opportunity to 1) organize and summarize their work in order to communicate it well to the peer reviewer and podcast host; 2) get dialogic, engaged feedback from a peer; and 3) invite comments and feedback on a **public** platform not only from other scholars but also from the wider public. Peer review is intrinsic to the process and therefore the resulting podcast episode can be seen as not only part of the peer-review process but also as a work of scholarship in and of itself. However, the process can also be employed as a step along the traditional publication pipeline.

An episode of *The Podcast Studies Podcast*[7] released in 2021 demonstrates the latter approach: Lori invited both Hannah and Ian to read a chapter she had drafted for an edited volume and then record a podcast episode to discuss it. In this discussion Hannah and Ian were able to give valuable insights and feedback on the draft, which Lori eventually incorporated into the final version of her chapter.[8] In a follow-up episode in which we all reflected on the experience, we discussed some of the affordances and limitations of this method, beginning with the sacrifice of thoroughness in favour of energetic **conversation**: we arrived at more interesting interventions than any of us would have independently, while not necessarily capturing the syntactic specificities that a traditional peer review might.

We also discussed the lack of anonymity: not only knowing who the author is, but having the author present for the review and included in the review-as-conversation. The author wasn't the only additional voice added into the peer-review process via this experiment, though. A conversation between authors and peer reviewers that happens behind metaphorically closed doors will have a very different dynamic than one that happens openly and publicly, particularly when you add in an awareness that the audience may not have certain forms of area expertise. The presence of that imagined listenership of non-experts, as Hannah argued in our discussion, encouraged us to be more transparent and even pedagogical in our recommendations. And that pedagogical

---

[7] Founded and co-hosted by podcast scholar Dario Llinares.
[8] See Beckstead, 'Context is King: Podcast Paratexts' (forthcoming).

approach to peer review has further benefits. To quote directly from our conversation on the *The Podcast Studies Podcast*:

> **Ian:** This is potentially – also, hopefully, maybe – serving as a model to younger people than ourselves. Like, this is actually how you give feedback in a constructive way. Which isn't always displayed, because we never get taught how to do peer review, right?
>
> **Hannah:** In that sense, it is another example of the way that well-done scholarly podcasting always has a little bit of the pedagogical to it. And that when we think about peer review as another form of pedagogical discourse, rather than [as a form of] gatekeeping or policing boundaries, we produce better peer review.

That pedagogical dimension of doing peer review in public hinges on the idea of social modelling via example, of showing how peer review might be done in a **community accountable** way that remains open to people not only appreciating your approach, but also having issues with it. That possibility – that in the process of modelling you open yourself up to new forms of critique – is also central to appreciative review. As Ian explained in the same conversation, many early career scholars when approached to be on podcasts are hesitant to talk about their work in such public and informal ways:

> **Ian:** . . . maybe this [scholarly podcasting] can be a way [that] we start to get more used to the idea that we can have a conversation, record it and put it out there, and we don't have to be perfect . . . . So I guess, normalizing owning small mistakes and moving forward is also a very healthy thing to promote inside scholarly work.

In fact, we agreed so entirely with Ian's point about normalizing making mistakes and embracing vulnerability as an approach to peer review that we ended up incorporating it into our understanding of appreciative peer review – but more on that later. For the moment, we want to note here that doing peer review out loud, *on* a podcast, enacts open and transparent review, while releasing that podcast prior to the publication of the scholarship invites a wider range of listeners into the process, thus expanding who constitutes a peer. That temporal difference is also an interesting variation on a theme of when peer review happens, and when (if ever) it is shared with a wider audience.

'Mapping the Fit Between Research and Multimedia: A Podcast Exploration of the Place of Multimedia Within/as Scholarship'

Ted Riecken's 'Mapping the Fit Between Research and Multimedia: A Podcast Exploration of the Place of Multimedia Within/as Scholarship' (Riecken 2014) and the follow-up peer review round table (Leggo, Paré and Riecken 2014) provide another key example of using podcasting for peer review – in this case for the peer review of a scholarly podcast. Riecken's podcast uses interstitial music, natural outdoor sounds and Riecken's voice to create both a narrative and an atmosphere through sound – features that create an experience that is strikingly different from reading a paper. While Riecken's podcast episode was more of a proof of concept than an example of an ongoing endeavour (it was a one-off recording, as was the subsequent peer review), its publication inspired hope that there was room for innovation in the use of multimedia scholarship in our classrooms and our wider research agendas. The peer review conversation, conducted by Carl Leggo, Anthony Paré and Ted Riecken, is particularly interesting for our purposes, offering an early model – perhaps the first – of peer-reviewing a scholarly podcast via another podcast, thus modelling how podcasting your peer review can be at once **media adaptive, public** and **conversational**. In this review, Leggo, Paré and Riecken articulate many of the concerns and challenges we address in this book, including the difficulty (if not outright impossibility) of anonymizing the human voice (Leggo, Paré and Riecken 2014, 718), the delayed timelines of scholarly publishing (723–4) and the need to recalibrate our understanding of metrics around the realities of digital publishing (724–5). They conclude that multimedia publishing provides an opportunity to diversify our approaches to knowledge-making beyond the model of the scientific journal that, as Paré articulates, is based in a centuries-long tradition that, 'in a world that's gone multimodal and multi-literate', is no longer the only or best way for scholars to communicate (719).

As a proof-of-concept about the potential of multimodal scholarship, this podcast exploration continues to be an important milestone in the development of scholarly podcasting, one that paved the way for more extended and resource-intensive experiments in sonic scholarship that are even more experimental in their use of sound.

A History of Central Florida: *The Podcast Project*

Another landmark experiment in scholarly podcasting, and the challenges of reviewing it, is *A History of Central Florida*. The fifty-episode podcast series was created by University of Central Florida history professor Robert Cassanello between 2013 and 2015 as an ongoing collaborative project with his students, inspired by the BBC podcast series *A History of the World in 100 Objects* (which ran in 2010 and marked one of the BBC's first significant successes in the world of podcasting). *A History of Central Florida* features short podcasts that introduce the audience to significant objects and artefacts through which we can learn more about Central Florida.

In 2019, the journal *The Public Historian* published a **public** (albeit paywalled[9]) review of *A History of Central Florida* by Erin L. Conlin. In addition to publishing scholarship in the area of public history, *The Public Historian* also publishes reviews of 'exhibits, historical films, media productions, videos, and digital projects' ('The Public Historian') as a means of engaging with the many forms that public history can take. Conlin described *A History of Central Florida* as 'an exemplary digital public history project' and 'an inspirational example of how to engage students in direct historical inquiry, digital media, and community partnerships' (156).

Interestingly, it took Cassanello four years to get the series reviewed. He sent multiple emails to review editors about the series, but with no luck. It was only after he, as he told Ian, 'blew up' at

---

[9]While a review published in a paywalled journal may not be *open*, it is still public, as opposed to most reviews which are never made available to anyone beyond the author(s) and editor(s).

the Organization of American Historians in response to hearing the review editor of *Journal of American History* complain that people weren't sending digital projects for review that things started moving. After pointing out he'd been trying to get a review for years, he was told the problem was finding people to review the podcast series, with potential reviewers claiming they did not have the expertise. Cassanello managed to get the collaborative series reviewed because of his persistence, and as he told Ian, he was motivated, in part, by a desire to get the work taken seriously as scholarship. While some of his peers did begin to understand what he was doing, others refused to acknowledge it as proper scholarship. As Cassanello recalls an interaction with one of the doubters:

> I said, well, '. . . come by my office, we'll take some coffee and let's talk about this. And give me the opportunity to convince you.' [. . .] He said, 'no, I don't want to.' So I had to essentially tell him, 'you know that what you represent is kind of an anti-intellectual strain because you won't even hear the argument. You're going to cower instead and close your ears and say, "I don't want to hear this".' I said, 'I don't know how that puts you in an esteemable position. You're running away from me. I'm giving you the chance to shoot this down and we can have a dialogue. And you're saying, "no, I don't want the dialogue".' And I said 'that is contrary to your role as a scholar, you should be engaging with arguments, not running away from them.'

The refusal to engage that Cassanello describes here is symptomatic of a general suspicion towards work that blurs the lines between teaching and research. As one reviewer of this chapter noted, large-scale collaborative and public-facing projects like this demand 'an additional skill set around project management, community relationship building, public interfacing, and often, for teaching public historians, incorporating and managing students in the process.' Had it been possible for Cassanello to find reviewers in less than four years – had he encountered less resistance to the very idea of *engaging* with the podcast – then incorporating **summiterative** review into the ongoing project may have been more feasible. As with so many of the approaches we describe in this chapter, this experimental scholarship could not be created in isolation but relied on a scholarly community willing to engage in the same experimental process.

Reviews in Digital Humanities

Luckily for all of us, the landscape for reviewing digital humanities scholarship has shifted in recent years. One such shift is the creation, by Jennifer Guiliano and Roopika Risam, of the journal *Reviews in Digital Humanities*, a pilot project that offers peer review for digital humanities projects including 'digital archives, multimedia or multimodal scholarship, digital exhibits, visualisations, digital games, digital tools, and digital projects' ('About Reviews in Digital Humanities' n.d.). This model of review responds to the ongoingness of many digital projects, as well as the multiple publishing approaches that are often chosen for community-engaged and/or non-traditional research. Project creators can submit their projects to the journal, which will solicit an open and **public** review from an area expert. Reviews are published, along with a 500-word project overview written by the project creators, on the journal site, which serves as a kind of directory of peer-reviewed digital humanities projects. The journal has a policy of not publishing reviews that are 'categorically negative', instead forwarding those reviews privately to the project creators. In this way they maintain the need for negative critique while also recognizing the impact of **public** reviews on scholars' careers, especially junior or precariously employed scholars.

While *Reviews in Digital Humanities* is not explicitly focused on sound-based scholarship, they have peer-reviewed multiple podcasts, demonstrating that the use of **summiterative** review for ongoing digital projects can be appropriate to podcasts as well. For example, in a February 2023 review of the podcast *Dig: A History Podcast* – a public history podcast that is still in production – reviewer Elizabeth Keohane-Burbridge offers both feedback for the ongoing improvement of the series and framing that helps to explain its legitimacy and relevance as a work of public scholarship. They suggest 'that the co-presenters who have not written the script or prepared the research for the episode review the script in more detail before recording' but conclude the review with a full-throated defence of public history as a valuable form of scholarly work:

The team at *Dig* demonstrates how public history by academic historians can be enjoyable and educational – a fact that is often dismissed, like many of the topics that this podcast examines, because they focus not on political or military history but on social history. (Keohane-Burbridge 2023)

It's no coincidence that the non-traditional approaches to peer review modelled in these case studies are more amenable to non-traditional forms of scholarship, including public history and digital humanities. The example of *Reviews in Digital Humanities*, like the case study to follow, is a response to structural critiques of peer review's limitations, and an attempt to model that other approaches are possible.

Kairos: A Journal of Rhetoric, Technology, and Pedagogy

The open access journal *Kairos: A Journal of Rhetoric, Technology, and Pedagogy* publishes what they call 'web texts' (Ball and Eyman 2015) or 'projects developed with specific attention to the World Wide Web as a publishing medium' ('Submissions' n.d., para. 1). Their inclusive and anti-racist peer-review practice values transparency, accountability and inclusivity among reviewers, via three tiers, or stages, of review. In Tier 1, the editors review each submission to determine its appropriateness for *Kairos*, before forwarding it to the editorial board. In Tier 2, the full editorial board discusses the submission and collaboratively assesses it based on a posted rubric that includes intellectual contributions, rhetoric and design and inclusive citations. If authors are asked to revise and resubmit, they have the option of proceeding to Tier 3, in which they are mentored directly by a *Kairos* staff member for up to three months as they respond to the editorial board's evaluation ('Editorial Board and Review Process' n.d.). This approach is collaborative and process-based, modelling an investment in working with authors on their pieces that has the potential to address inequities such as access to institutional resources.

In their explanation of the development of this approach, *Kairos* editors Cheryl E. Ball and Douglas Eyman (2015) explain that web texts simply cannot be reviewed in the same way as conventional manuscripts. Multimedia scholarship so frequently includes video and/or audio recordings of the author(s) that scrubbing their identity would be impractical if not completely impossible. As a result, *Kairos* embraces collaborative review in which multiple editors work together to produce the review. The editors say this helps to overcome the potential bias of knowing who an author is and is 'more rigorous and more informative than traditional gatekeeping peer reviews' (Ball and Eyman 2015, para.18). Furthermore, the exact form the peer review takes can shift to suit the nature of the web text submitted.

In a personal example, Hannah and feminist media scholar Stacey Copeland have published a three-part podcast miniseries with *Kairos* (Copeland and McGregor 2023) that, as *Kairos* Managing Editor Erin Kathleen Bahl explains in the miniseries' Appendix, 'encouraged and challenged the editorial team to think about and structure the review process in a different way that resonates with both the design and spirit' of the submission, as well as 'to expand on our commitment to even greater transparency in the review process'. The editorial board made the decision to conduct their **media adaptive** and **conversational** peer review as a podcast: they recorded their conversation in lieu of a more traditional peer review response. While *Kairos* often experiments with their approaches to peer review, this collective review was a first for them:

At *Kairos*, Tier 2 peer review takes place by our editorial board members through an open conversation via email, and reviewers' comments and names are shared with the authors along with a letter synthesizing editorial feedback and decisions. In the past, individual *Kairos* reviewers have provided experimental feedback via annotated images or even zines. However, this is the first time that *Kairos* editorial board members have come together collectively for a more holistic multimodal review process. (Bahl in Copeland and McGregor 2022)

The result was a review that Bahl describes as 'robust, collegial, supportive, critical, and generally enthusiastic. It is still clearly structured, but a little more informal and conversational, echoing some of the intimacy of the personal voice that the authors describe.' Indeed, Copeland and McGregor were so struck by the effectiveness of this approach that they decided to make the peer review podcast **public** by including it, alongside a transcript and a framing introduction by Bahl, as an Appendix to the submission. In this sense the reviewers became not only publicly identified participants in the review process, but also meaningful co-authors of the final web text via a fourth episode of the miniseries that is in dialogue with the original work, rather than invisibly reshaping it.

Society for Music Theory Podcast (SMT-Pod)

Other online journals have similarly taken advantage of their platforms to embrace multimedia scholarship. Unsurprisingly, many of the most exciting experiments in peer review of sound-based scholarship are emerging from scholars of sound and/or music. The *Society for Music Theory Podcast*, for example,

> is an Open Collaborative Peer-Reviewed and creative venue for timely conversations about music theory. Audio-only podcasts offer a unique – though non-traditional – way of engaging with music, analysis, and contemporary issues in the field. As opposed to the heavy, jargon-laden publications we are used to working through at our desks, SMT-Pod publications are easy to listen to and think about in the car, on your run, or while grading. ('SMT-Pod' 2021)

Their first season, released weekly between January and April 2022, consisted of sixteen episodes produced by a range of scholars working in the field of music theory. *SMT-Pod* uses a **public** and **conversational** peer-review process created through a collaboration among the scholar who proposed the episode, a peer reviewer and an SMT board member. Thus the peer review process 'happens not only at one point, but organically and continually throughout production' ('SMT-Pod' 2021), and is intended to help produce scholarship with public appeal in a more timely fashion than conventional peer review. Peer reviewers are named and thanked in episode show notes, further emphasizing the public nature of this review process. *SMT-Pod* also offers production assistance for scholars who don't already have audio production experience. The collaborative ethos of their editorial board focuses on accessibility and transparency, an approach that encourages scholars new to podcasting to try their hands at the medium.

The explicit guidelines that *SMT-Pod* spells out via their peer review timelines demonstrates how **media adaptive** review, that engages with a new medium by conducting review *in* that new medium, often requires a return to basics in which we ask ourselves what peer review is actually meant to accomplish. A key value of *SMT-Pod*'s approach is to engage work on the author's terms, understanding what the author is seeking to do rather than imposing the reviewer's own, often unstated, values. As the next case study also demonstrates, public review can be a key strategy for demonstrating the particular affordances of sound-based scholarship.

Seismograf

As Sanne Krogh Groth and Kristine Samson write in 'Audio Papers – a manifesto' (2016a), sound-based works emphasize 'sensory and affective modes of knowledge', demanding a peer-review process that asks different kinds of questions. Notably, they end their manifesto – which also serves as the introduction to a special issue of *Seismograf* comprised of Audio Papers – with **public** and non-anonymized excerpts from various peer reviews, a testament both to the rigour of this scholarship and the need to consider different qualities when conducting **media adaptive** review for sound-based scholarship, such as affect, 'corporeal listening experiences', and 'the techniques and tools needed to create a convincing audio dramaturgy' (2016a).

Seismograf is a Danish sound art magazine and a platform for peer-reviewed scholarship on 'practical and theoretical issues in relation to contemporary music and sound art' ('Seismograf Peer' n.d.). Since 2016, *Seismograf* has published both written scholarship and audio papers, which aim to consider not only how scholars might write *about* sound, but also how they might articulate arguments *in* sound:

> The audio paper is an extension of expressive means: Not only words and syntax are means of expression – so are tempo, time, voice, sound and music. Our goal is to bring analytical and performative awareness to academic means of expression, and the audio paper provides us with a new and experimental platform to do so. (Groth and Samson 2016b)

Since that 'Fluid Sounds' special issue in which *Seismograf* first experimented with peer-reviewing audio papers, they've incorporated audio papers into their regular submission guidelines. While *Seismograf* practises anonymized peer review, they specify that their goal is 'to make the peer review process transparent, aiming for a dialogue instead of a one-way communication. In practice this means additional publications in direct relation to the final article that display, reflect and communicate the processes of knowledge production (e.g., the reviews)' ('Seismograf Peer' n.d.).

i used to love to dream *by A. D. Carson (and other soundworks at University of Michigan Press)*

While we've largely focused thus far on journals, one of the most exciting venues for experimental, sound-based scholarship in recent years has been University of Michigan Press, specifically their eBook collection, hosted on the open-source Fulcrum platform. In 2020 they published A. D. Carson's *i used to love to dream*, the first ever peer-reviewed rap album. Carson refers to this project as 'a mixtap/e/essay – a combination of storytelling and academic scholarship that uses sampled and live instrumentation, repurposed music, film, and news clips, and original rap lyrics to perform an engaging meditation on authenticity, belonging, and home' (Buckler 2020).

The unique nature of this scholarship demanded a similarly unique and **media adaptive** approach to the peer review, which was facilitated by senior acquisitions editor Sara Jo Cohen and series editor Loren Kajikawa. In an *Inside Higher Ed* article on the piece, Cohen describes how they revised their standard review questions to accommodate and consider the sonic essence of the work as well as its deeply personal nature and to ensure it was useful to Carson on the terms of his own project (Flaherty 2020). It was equally important for Cohen, however, to consider this project as part of a larger intervention:

> In Carson's project in particular, she said, 'I saw an opportunity to challenge what counts as scholarly publishing in terms of both form and content.' *i used to love to dream* was an 'opportunity to support cutting-edge scholarship that we were uniquely able to take on because of the digital affordances of Fulcrum.' Not only was

the press able to publish tracks, she said, it could publish a short documentary and lyrics and notes in a book-like format accessible to scholars and tenure and promotion committees. (Flaherty 2020)

This creative experiment became an opportunity to demonstrate both that peer review practices must be adjusted to fit sound-based scholarship and that such adjustments do not reduce the rigour, seriousness or value of this work.

University of Michigan Press's commitment to encouraging experimental sound-based scholarship is also evident in the work of Jacob Smith, including *ESC: Sonic Adventure in the Anthropocene* (2019) and *Lightning Birds* (2021), the latter being 'a multi-media project that consists of a five-episode, podcast-style audiobook, a curatorial essay, and a bibliography'. *Lightning Birds* is a richly sound-designed project, incorporating archival radio with soundscapes to articulate an ecological understanding of the airspace that birds and radio share. In order to embed the work in relevant scholarship, *Lightning Birds* is accompanied by a 'curatorial essay' that functions as 'liner notes' for the project's five episodes, as well as a lengthy bibliography; combined, these two textual supplements both establish the rigour of the project and free the audiobook itself to focus on its sonic affordances. As a scholar of sound, Smith demonstrates through his work how sound itself is capable of making arguments that exceed the written word while also satisfying the needs of scholarly communication via the scholarly apparatus of his works. In general, the experiments of University of Michigan Press in publishing sound-based scholarship within the structures of a university press demonstrate that the conventional structures of peer review can continue to be useful as long as they are updated to be appropriate to the scholarship in question, that is, that they are media adaptive.

Marrying Out

Carson's *i used to love to dream* is a strong example of what are referred to in Australian universities as Non-Traditional Research Outputs, or NTROs. This concept emerged in response to the rise of an academic 'audit culture' in the early 1990s that sought to quantify the amount and impact of research outputs (Welch 2016);

NTROs were a way to account for knowledge creation that does not strictly adhere to the usual logics of academic publishing. NTROs must meet the Australian Research Council's definition of academic research, namely 'the creation of new knowledge and/or the use of existing knowledge in a new and creative way to generate new concepts, methodologies, inventions and understandings. This could include the synthesis and analysis of previous research to the extent that it is new and creative' (Australian Research Council 2015). While some grumpy-pants pundits might think that anything non-traditional is somehow less significant or rigorous, NTROs, in fact, are subjected in most cases to more scrutiny than traditional published scholarship, passing through three layers of peer review (Woodrow 2016).

In contextualizing 'crafted audio storytelling' as an NTRO, journalism scholar and podcast producer Siobhan McHugh (2019) argues that getting her audio documentaries accepted for broadcast constitutes a form of **community accountable** peer review, as does receiving critical recognition or industry awards. But beyond justifying audio storytelling as research, McHugh's work exemplifies what sound-based scholarship can add to the quality and experience of the 'research'. Here she speaks about her audio documentary *Marrying Out* for which she interviewed couples who had married across religious divides:

> What was new in my synthesis [of the research] was the visceral experience for listeners of sharing the pain of family feuds and societal bigotry: it was carried affectively in the interviewees' voices and in their non-verbal sighs and tears. It was amplified by specially composed music and historical references powerfully evoked by the archival recordings and actuality I selected . . . This effect on listeners was maximized by the relational way I mixed these sounds in order to heighten their affective power: e.g. having the taunts float over an ethereal boy soprano singing a Catholic hymn, in an emotive evocation of the conflict between prejudice and spirituality. (2019, para. 12)

Similarly to how Sara Jo Cohen described the need for peer review to consider the sonic components of Carson's *i used to love to dream*, McHugh advocates for **media adaptive** peer review in the form of critical appraisals of her work by industry experts qualified to appraise the use of sound and sophisticated production techniques. If rigorous peer review of sound-based scholarship is going to be possible, our methods will need to take into account how podcasts make use of sound – although, as projects like H-Podcast point out, focusing too much on polished production can contribute to widening gaps between scholars based on institutional resources.

H-Podcast

H-Podcast is an extension of H-Net, an online community for scholars of the humanities and social sciences that has been in operation since 1993. The primary goal of H-Net is to encourage 'electronic networks, using a variety of media, and with a common objective of advancing humanities and social science teaching and research' ('H-Podcast'). H-Podcast has become a robust community for scholars interested in podcasting; it hosts several scholarly podcasts as well as a user-generated 'Academic Podcast Round-Up'. Under the guidance of Robert Cassanello (creator of *A History of Central Florida,* discussed earlier), H-Podcast has also begun not only to facilitate conversations about podcast studies as a field, but also to encourage the **summiterative** review of podcasts themselves. Building on the model Cassanello used for his own podcast series, these reviews are meant to be summative appraisals of a podcast series that speak to its significance as scholarship while also offering the kind of formative feedback that is central to peer review:

> For born-digital scholarship, like podcasts, an academic review might be the only or one of the few opportunities a scholar or team of scholars might have to receive critical praise, scrutiny, or evaluation of their creative and research production. Peer review is the backbone of tenure and promotion, so the reviewer should be sure to include in the review the significance (if any) and greater contribution a podcast series might offer. ('Guidelines' n.d.)

Recognizing that the review of podcasts is still an emergent practice, H-Podcasts' 'Guidelines for Reviewing Podcasts and Podcast Series' offers various suggestions for how to approach writing a **public** podcast review. Reviews, they suggest, should attend not only to the possible scholarly contributions of the podcast, but also, true to the values of **media adaptive** review, should note its sound design, accessibility, publishing choices (including home page and/or hosting platform) and scholarly apparatus (e.g., citations and footnotes). The guidelines also highlight the importance of considering funding availability when evaluating podcasts, noting that, while production quality might be a significant feature of a podcast, 'reviewers should likewise be cognizant of the different forms of institutional funding and support that different podcasts receive, and be sure to consider whether a podcast is produced independently, with minimal institutional support, or with the support of a commercial network' (Guidelines' n.d.).

The guidelines also explicitly recommend that reviewers look at Siobhan McMenemy's experiments in peer-reviewing podcasts, so why don't we do that as well?

Secret Feminist Agenda

Secret Feminist Agenda was Hannah's pilot podcast for her ongoing collaborative work with Siobhan McMenemy, Senior Editor at Wilfrid Laurier University Press.[10] The podcast underwent a post-publication **summiterative** review, season by season, mirroring and extending Cassanello's experiments. The review was open and **public**, in part because the intimate nature of the podcast made it fundamentally non-anonymizable, but also because anonymity would be at odds with the ethos of the podcast, engaged as it was with the specificity of situated and embodied understandings of feminism and with the feminist value of **community accountability**. The peer-review questions asked reviewers to engage both with the podcast as scholarship and with the peer-review process itself. As McMenemy explains, 'We encouraged the reviewers to reflect on whether they considered the peer review questions themselves to be relevant and helpful to their task as peer reviewers and to

---

[10]The creation of *Secret Feminist Agenda* was funded by the Social Sciences and Humanities Research Council of Canada as an experiment in using podcasting as a form of scholarly communication, including developing methods for peer-reviewing podcasts.

our responsibilities as editors, producers, and publishers of the podcasts' (2018).

In addition to being open, this review also built in the possibility of responsiveness: Hannah was invited to write a formal response to each season's review, which was published alongside the reviews. These responses exemplify much of what we have been saying about the vulnerability of sound-based scholarship. Responding to the first season's review, Hannah wrote:

> I was deeply nervous about this peer review process, in a way that I have not experienced since getting the reviews for my very first journal article nine years ago (wow hi I am old). The work I've been doing in *Secret Feminist Agenda* feels deeply personal in a way none of my other scholarship has felt. By speaking in my own voice, about my body and my mental health and my sexuality and my intimate relationships, I'm working to model a form of feminist scholarship that makes space for vulnerability – and that includes the vulnerability of an open peer review model, in which everyone gets to read what people think about my work! (McGregor 2018)

Notably, while McMenemy was concerned that the openness of the review process might discourage some reviewers from participating, the reviewers themselves, in fact, pushed for greater collaboration and openness. As a result, the review of Season 3 was conducted as a **conversation** between Season 1 reviewer Cheryl E. Ball (of *Kairos*, discussed earlier) and Season 2 reviewer Carla Rice, with McMenemy and Hannah recording a conversation in response to the review. These conversations were posted publicly to the Wilfrid Laurier University Press website and released as episodes of *Secret Feminist Agenda*, where they were downloaded thousands of times, demonstrating the listenership's interest in engaging with the review process of a podcast that mattered to them.

As with *Reviews in Digital Humanities*, the review for *Secret Feminist Agenda* and that practised by H-Podcast is **summiterative**, a post-publication response to an ongoing series that attempts to capture something of its ongoingness. Another function of this kind of post-publication review is that it extends the lifespan of conversation around scholarship, making it a form of **recirculating** review as well. Rather than reviewing necessarily happening between author(s) and reviewer(s) prior to publication, it can also unfold as a conversation post-publication, one that invites a wider audience into the conversation while also making more transparent and inclusive the meaning-making processes of scholarly disciplines. The next examples we'll look at model the use of peer-review-style conversations that happen after the publication of scholarship as a way of extending that scholarship temporally and communally.

ResonanceCast

ResonanceCast is a new idea from Allegra Lab, an anthropology publishing platform where Ian is part of the editorial collective. When the editors find articles that speak to one another, no matter when they have been published, the authors of these papers are invited to read each other's contributions, start commenting on each other's work via a common google doc, and then create a podcast together with one of Allegra Lab's editors. This all takes place after the papers have been published, and thus already been through Allegra Lab's care-based review process (about which more in what follows); it allows for the **recirculation** and continued reassessment of work, for work to be revisited in light of developments in the field (as well as reminding the author and editor about what excited them about it), and for authors themselves to critically assess their work through **conversation** with a peer in the same situation. This is a mutual, vulnerability-embracing, post-publication **public** review process in which the reviewer and author are both reviewers and authors of one another's work at once.

Jastinder Kaur took part in the second *ResonanceCast*, bringing her article 'Towards an Anthropology of Coups' (Kaur 2021) into conversation with Daniel White's 'Incitement! Incremental Theory for an Imminent Fascism' (White 2021). Ian, who hosted *ResonanceCast*, asked her to reflect on her experiences, and she wrote back describing her negative experiences in the past with 'review as gatekeeping' and her decision to participate in this experimental approach because of how Ian and his co-editor Felix Girke have 'cultivated trust' with their authors through a review process that is 'open, transparent, [and handled] with care, encouragement, and some new directions to ponder.' Despite that trust, Kaur still approached the podcast recording with some trepidation, rooted in her position of academic precarity:

> A precarious postdoc anthropologist and academic, it seemed like an unworthy spotlight to be shining on my research. Especially compared with Daniel's [who is a Senior Researcher in Social Anthropology at the University of Cambridge]. But I found a spirit of freedom and excitement emerge as we read and commented on each other's articles. We were making connections, thinking comparatively, able to engage with the kind of respect and care that academics don't often feel encouraged to show each other.
>
> And to be able to do this by just having a conversation – guided carefully and thoughtfully by you [Ian] – was another freeing aspect of the experience. Because we get so caught up in the performance of writing for each other, following set formulas and ways of expressing and writing, performing authority through the deployment of jargon that marks us out as being authentic academics. The podcast format helped strip away these tired old modes of critical engagement. And in a way, without the constant self-editing, and the search for the most up to date terminology, it was possible for my and Daniel's ideas to surface more clearly. And through this to make better connections between our ideas, and then of course to riff off each other, let our research and theories travel in new directions. Together.
>
> Academics are always trying to impress each other, if you think about it; we are our main and sometimes only audience. The traditional linear review process confirms our worth or lack thereof. But with the podcast, our value is taken for granted, so we are freed up to explore our own and each other's ideas, to engage intellectually without inhibition. And that is its own reward, because it reveals that good review is one which is an ongoing and emergent process, composed of difference and disagreement, but undertaken with care. And in the hands of a guide who is themselves good at nurturing conversation, critical engagement, and respectful relationships.

The values that Kaur centres here – trust, care and respect, alongside critical engagement and rigour – are not unique to the kinds of non-traditional approaches we're outlining in our case studies, but they can be deliberately fostered in a variety of ways, including by thinking seriously about the affordances of a medium like podcasting, which has conversation as one of its foundational pillars.

Mundaréu

The Brazil-based podcast *Mundaréu* invites anthropologists to bring their work into **conversation** with one of the interlocutors they've worked with. As such, it's an example of how scholarship, once published in text form, can be subjected to a **community accountable** review, in **public**, by those who are the subjects of research. *Mundaréu* thus brings those whom social scientists often talk *to* in private and *about* in public, to speak *with* them and *about* them in a public setting. The podcast allows for a critical reflection on and a challenge to the conclusions drawn by the expert anthropologists by someone from the community. This pushes the expert to become vulnerable in the face of interrogation by someone who is an expert by virtue of where they come from and who they are and can lead to new rounds of reflection and, thus, knowledge production. As Soraya Fleischer, co-host of *Mundaréu* explained to Ian:

> We invite an anthropologist and then we say, 'please now invite your interlocutor. Invite somebody that works with you in your research.' We always have this pair together, and that's what we wanted to bring to the programme. We didn't want what we had seen already, that you call an anthropologist and you interview her for a long time and she talks about the people she works with. She talks about the community. She talks about her results. The way that we designed it, they're talking together. It's really interesting because sometimes the researcher says something and then the person says, 'I didn't know you were doing that' or 'I disagree. I wouldn't put it in those words.' It's very interesting. And the idea is not to put them in conflict . . . they have this bond beforehand, they have been working on the research for years. So they have a lot of trust in one another, and they recognize how both are specialists in their own way, you know? So we're bringing this relationship into the studio.

This **conversational** and **accountable** review also has the added bonus of **recirculating** published scholarship, breathing new life into it and introducing it to potential new listening publics.

Witch, Please

Our final case study is probably the one that will raise the most eyebrows in a book on peer review, because it is also the one that most overtly challenges the definition of 'peer'. *Witch, Please* (2015–23)[11] was a fortnightly podcast co-hosted by Hannah and her collaborator Marcelle Kosman that introduced listeners to various forms of critical theory through a close and ongoing engagement with the Harry Potter series. While the podcast was never peer-reviewed conventionally, many of its listeners were also academics who were encouraged to pitch episode topics from the perspective of their own areas of expertise. In addition to formally pitching, listeners provided a regular stream of feedback through emails, Apple Podcasts reviews, tweets, Instagram DMs and Discord conversations. This process of ongoing response speaks to both scholarly podcasting's expansion of whom we think of as our peers, and to the communal accountability made possible by podcasting as a form of public scholarship. When your peers become expansive and diffuse, you also need to make more deliberate decisions about whom you're accountable to; rather than two or three formal reviewers whose response to your work determines its publishability, **community accountable** review might involve hundreds or even thousands of listeners that you, as the podcaster, must choose whether to respond to.

In the case of *Witch, Please*, the question of accountability was a constant negotiation, a conversation between the production team and the wider listening community. It is impossible to respond to all feedback, nor is all feedback offered in good faith. Not all formal peer review is offered in good faith either, but with

---

[11]In 2023 the team behind *Witch, Please* made the decision to pivot the direction of the podcast both because we completed our read-through of the Harry Potter series and because we were tired of talking about how terrible J. K. Rowling is. The new podcast, *Material Girls*, focuses on materialist readings of pop culture and will continue to emphasize introducing listeners to critical theory.

communal review academics gain the ability to define our peers for ourselves and to decide which communities we are speaking to and can be held to account by. *Witch, Please*, as a queer, feminist and anti-racist podcast, was particularly responsive to the feedback of Black, Indigenous and racialized listeners, trans and gender-non-conforming listeners and disabled listeners. The rhythms and ongoingness of podcasting, as a serialized medium, also lend themselves to these forms of communal accountability; there is always the possibility of response in the next episode, a reality that invites feedback as well as humility.[12] The idea is not to create a perfected piece of scholarship, sealed forever in amber, but, rather, to generate an ongoing conversation that will, by definition, change as the makeup of the listenership changes. This ongoingness lends itself to **summiterative** review and to review that happens in **public** as we strive for transparency in our responses to listener feedback.

Framing these listener responses to *Witch, Please* as peer review requires us to set aside a whole number of assumptions about the practice: that it's enacted anonymously and behind closed doors, by institutionally affiliated experts, prior to the publication of scholarship. It also undermines any tidy distinction between podcast listeners, as a kind of passive audience, and peer reviewers, if we understand that every reviewer is a listener and every listener a potential reviewer. If we understood peer review to be characterized not by its compliance to a set of practices, however, but by its embracing of a process through which dialogue within an intellectual community helps to improve, refine, extend or otherwise enhance scholarly work, then our sense of what peer review can look like really begins to change.

The Three Cs of Appreciative Reviewing: Creative, Communal, Caring

The bevy of examples we have offered previously demonstrates a number of things. First, that podcasts can be, and, indeed, *are being*,

---

[12]Hannah details an example of this accountability process in her book *A Sentimental Education* (2022b).

peer-reviewed. Second, that podcasting is also a great medium for experimenting with open peer review. Third, that review for sound-based scholarship must be responsive to the affordances of sound. Fourth, that good peer review can be flexible, open, collaborative and conversational. And fifth, that the conversations that happen on podcasts can help to extend the life of scholarship and expand its audiences. And within these examples, we can also see themes beginning to emerge: that sound-based scholarship is often non-traditional or creatively experimental, and benefits from review that embraces that spirit; and that we have the potential to make our scholarship more expansive, inclusive and humane. Using the six approaches to appreciative peer review we've identified in the foregoing case studies (public, conversational, media adaptive, summiterative, community accountable and recirculating), we want to highlight a set of recurring values that we believe underpin them, offering our own model for appreciative reviewing as *creative, communal and caring*.

This framework isn't a concrete model for how to peer-review podcasts but, rather, a set of values – an ethic, if you will – that characterize an appreciative mode of review, one that seeks to understand the scholarship and the scholar, and to be grateful for the work they are doing. These values highlight what we find exciting in the possibilities of peer-reviewing all kinds of scholarship, including podcasts, pointing to how transformative peer review as a process can actually be.

Peer review should be forward thinking, open and generative, contributing to the *creation* of something new – indeed, to the creation of knowledge itself. This value can be seen in the **recirculating** reviews that take published scholarship and bring the scholar into dialogue with an expanded pool of peers or experts, thus keeping the knowledge creation/revision process alive. It can be seen in how **summiterative** reviews do not attempt to pin down scholarship on the move, but, rather, respond dynamically and iteratively to knowledge creation. And it can also be seen in the way **media adaptive** reviews open up scholarly norms about how review should be conducted.

When we refer to creative peer-reviewing practices we are considering the modification of existing peer-review practices to fit creative practices, as seen in the example of Siobhan McHugh's use of industry evaluations as the review for her NTROs. But we are also thinking about creativity as an activity, one that aspires to be non-commodifiable, anti-celebrity and uncontainable: an ongoing and emergent creative practice that is alive with a multitude of values and produced communally. As the anthropologist Tim Ingold (2011) has argued in relation to creativity and artistic practice more generally,

> [M]aking is less a matter of projection than one of gathering, more analogous, perhaps, to sewing or weaving than to shooting arrows at a target. As they make things, practitioners bind their own pathways or lines of becoming into the texture of the world. It is a question not of imposing form on matter ... but of intervening in the fields of force and flows of material wherein the forms of things arise and are sustained. Thus, the creativity of making lies in the practice itself, in an improvisatory movement that *works things out as it goes along.* [our emphasis] (178)

This is what it means to search for creative review processes within the current academic climate: to delineate review processes that speak to the ongoing open-ended nature of some podcasts, as with the **summiterative** review of *Secret Feminist Agenda*; to fast evolving changes in reviewing practices more generally, as in the **media adaptive** review modelled at *Kairos*; and to an idea of review that seeks to generously support scholarship as it continues to find new audiences beyond its publication, as in the **recirculating** review of *ResonanceCast*.

To this understanding of peer review as a creative activity, we add the possibility of peer review also being *communal*. This value can be seen in the **community accountable** reviews where those whom the research is for or about can directly intervene in the reviewing of the scholarship. Communal forms of review often mean talking not only about the content of what's being reviewed, but also about the process of the review itself. We're put in mind of how Spinelli and Dann (2019) discuss the famous true crime podcast *Serial* as not only exploring a murder, but also – maybe even primarily – modelling the move *away* from established journalistic ethical codes that traditional media and their journalists have purported to follow, and *towards* transparency and self-reflection on air. Essentially, it is about opening up the closed box of professional norms that journalists have relied on to distinguish themselves from non-objective, non-professionals and finding a way to talk ethics through with an audience as part of an ongoing relationship rooted in trust. Something similar is at work in how scholarly podcasting can open up the processes of knowledge creation.

Focusing on peer review as an open and communal process lets us rethink the role of trust, not only between podcasters and listeners but also between universities and the wider public. There have been notable shifts in what universities – particularly public universities – mean to different groups and how they are positioned within society. These include the growth of entrepreneurialism and competitiveness, the reduction of state funding, a reconceptualization of education as a private rather than public good, a rebalancing of the labour force to include a higher ratio of administrative staff over permanently employed academic staff and a shift of governance power from academics to managers (Wright and Shore 2017). The more universities are reframed as businesses, the less they are invested in any sense of public good – and the less the publics that the university should be serving can actually *trust* that the university has any significant role in society beyond training.

Rather than universities built on inter-academic, inter-institution and inter-student competition, Cris Shore and Susan Wright (2017) argue for universities built on trust. In the context of the UK, a trust, as an organization or arrangement, has inalienable assets and thus cannot be privatized; in such organizations, trust as a feeling or belief is nurtured through shared governance mechanisms and purpose (which could include, for example, limits on differences in pay). More directly relevant for podcasting and peer review, a university as a trust would have a different relationship with the society in which it resides, a social contract that puts the public responsibilities of academics at the fore. Such institutions could (re)inspire a trust in universities as places that can create a better world in the future, not only for those who attend them, but also for society at large. Similarly, Katherine Fitzpatrick (2018) has argued that the modern university needs to be rebuilt on a foundation of generosity. By this, Fitzpatrick means not only 'adopt[ing] a position of greater openness to dialogue with our communities' through publicly engaged research, but also 'plac[ing] a greater emphasis on . . . collaboration in academic life' (37). At the core of her call to generosity is an understanding of universities as a public and communal good, 'worthy of the public trust' (228). Only through a reorientation of academia's mission towards generosity and community can the current crisis of neoliberal metrification, and accompanying systemic defunding, be overcome. We see such trust-building at work in the *Open Peer Review Podcast*, which invites listeners into the process via **community accountable** review, and in a project like H-Podcast, which encourages a practice of **summiterative** review that identifies and takes seriously scholarly podcasts that may not have previously benefited from critique.

Conceiving universities as places that create trust – through relationships with publics and as places that seek to create better societies – speaks directly to the potential of scholarly podcasting with a review process opened up for communal critique. A generous and trust-informed communal review process is one that could be accountable not only to the community within which a university resides, but also the communities scholars work among or come from, as *Witch, Please* models through its practices of accountability to communities of listeners. In this way, by opening itself up to communal review, a podcast can enact an ongoing and responsible form of review based on principles of answerability and respect. Such a mode of review reconceptualizes peer review away from being a box that needs to be ticked or a hurdle to be crossed on the way to final publication, and towards ongoingness and responsiveness. Similarly to how wikis have redefined trust in communally produced knowledge platforms, an open, trust-based communal form of peer review can change the relationships between scholarly knowledge, those who produce it and the publics who consume it.

But hand in hand with a culture of creativity and communal trust goes a heightened sense of vulnerability, and vulnerability, we believe, must be met with *care*. This value can be seen in how **public** reviews make an effort to explain and educate in a way that is free from meanness and pettiness and awash with generosity. It can also be seen in the **conversational** reviews in which the reviewer(s) speak with one another and/or the scholar in ways that seek to understand, challenge and expand collective understanding of the scholarship under review.

The anthropology platform *Allegra Lab* – the same one that created *ResonanceCast* – does not practise conventional peer review, rather opting for something they call 'care review'. Inspired by a feminist ethics of care, they propose a review model based on mutual support (versus the competition and the lonely, fearful life of an academic) that centres the person behind any piece of research, attempting 'a constructive, open, and productive process through which both reviewer and reviewee come to feel emboldened and respected' (Allegra Lab, February 2022). In practice this involves an initial assessment from an editor, who then either provides feedback themselves or asks another editor to do so. Once a piece is ready for peer review, an external peer reviewer is found, usually from among past authors. However, this reviewer and the author are not hidden from each other. The aim is to create genuine collaboration via a conversation in which the author, reviewer and editor allow a review to unfold and grow with the shared aim of making the piece better. This approach fosters collegiality and trust, but is also 'predicated on vulnerability (on openness, on willingness to be affected) on all sides' (Allegra Lab, February 2022). The editors hope that a care-based approach might change the attitude towards the review, not only by encouraging reviewers and reviewees to enact a shared commitment to making something as good as it can be, but also by transforming the feeling of doing a review from a chore to 'a (critically rigorous and serious) joyful and creative task' (Allegra Lab, February 2022).

Čarna Brković calls for a similar transformation to the peer-review process in '"Thinking With" When Peer Reviewing: Introduction to the *PoLAR Online* Emergent Conversation on Peer Review' (2022). 'Thinking with,' as described in the article, is 'an ethical practice premised upon certain forms of relationality' in which 'the reviewer attempts to step into the shoes of an author and to think together with them on how to develop their point and how to make it in a more convincing manner' (2022, 113). Like care-based review, 'thinking with' demands an ethical leap in which the reviewer takes the time to consider the author as a human being, imaginatively identifying with them and 'making an interpretive effort to understand what the author tried to do and to help them to get the paper there – just like we aim to do with our students' (114). Reorienting peer review around a model of mentorship and pedagogy reminds us that, within academia, we have many models for producing rigorous and rich scholarship that aren't fundamentally combative. As we noted in our discussion of collectively reviewing Lori's work on the *Open Peer Review Podcast*, care-based review can sometimes take the form of literally *thinking with* the author, which in turn models the possibilities of scholarly knowledge creation built on vulnerability and transparency.

Let's consider our hypothetical scholar of Pannonian Avars, Dr Marina Makandar. Dr Makandar struggled with confidence. Whenever she thought she had insights about the Pannonian Avars, she got excited. But when she tried to put them down on paper, she couldn't find the words. She knew there was something interesting and important she was trying to say, but needed to test it out in conversation before adding the needed nuance and sophistication to her initial ideas. So she started *Podonian Avatars*, a monthly show in which she talked through the latest research in the field with different guests. This project not only allowed her to test her ideas before committing them to paper, but also provided opportunities to make mistakes, ask questions and find out not only what she didn't know, but what she didn't *know* she didn't know. And rather than pushing herself to perform a level of authority and certainty she didn't feel, the podcast let her embrace her uncertainty. Sure, that meant certain scholars in her field might take her a little less seriously, but at this stage in her career, those weren't the people she was concerned with; it was much more exciting to her to find out that, for emerging scholars in her field, *Podonian Avatars* was empowering them to display their own uncertainty, to ask more questions and to put their vulnerabilities out into the world with the hope that they would be met not with mockery or rejection, but with care.

Such a notion of care is maybe even more suited to a podcast-review form than to text, because the speculative, exploratory and discursive nature of many podcast series injects a serious amount of vulnerability into the scholarship, as Hannah reflected on in her experience of having *Secret Feminist Agenda* reviewed via **conversational** and **public** review rooted in care. Vulnerability is antithetical to much of how we perform – or are expected to perform – in academia, but it is also one of the strengths of podcasts. In a very different context, it has been suggested that vulnerability does not necessarily create the need for defensiveness, but, rather, creates an awareness of a predicament and, further to this, it is by putting oneself or a thing in harm's way that vulnerability is operationalized (Butler 2012). Vulnerability wouldn't be vulnerability without risk, and we don't intend to pretend that you can open yourself up like this without the risk of negative consequences. As Soraya Fleischer from the *Mundaréu* podcast reflected when speaking to Ian about how podcasts open up methods to a wider public:

> If you're being attacked and you open the box and even show how it's done maybe it makes us even more vulnerable to attacks, but maybe also it can win some hearts on the way by showing how we work and how serious we are about people and how we take in consideration what people are saying and learning with them.

Care-based review also creates the possibility for deeply compassionate and generative scholarly conversations by 'adopting a mode of exchange that begins with *yes* rather than *no*', a response that 'creates the opportunity for genuine dialogue, not only among colleagues but with many more potential colleagues' (Fitzpatrick 2018, 34). When we open ourselves up to having a real conversation about our scholarship, we create cascading possibilities for making our work better, more accessible and, ultimately, more rigorous.

* * *

One critique of appreciative review, and one we have received from our peer reviewers when advancing our argument in this book, is that such a system fails to take into account assessment of 'quality'. As one reviewer wrote:

> [T]here is an honest question to be answered about how Appreciative Reviewing should happen when an article or manuscript is bad, just plain bad. Bad is a thing. . . . I wonder if there is a way to include the notion of discernment/judgement/ expertise into this somehow? Does 'quality' scholarship exist? Or are we throwing that notion out in its entirety with the patriarchy? I love the idea of 'ungrading', but I also really resent being asked to read awful student essays, which are a real/ objective thing? Can you help me resolve this?

While this response is understandable given the impossible workload of higher education staff, we need to distinguish between the role of the editor on the one hand and the reviewer on the other. If an editor asks a reviewer to review a piece, then, within our appreciative approach, this means that the journal is invested in the idea of publishing a particular bit of research and wants the expert reviewer to guide the process in a caring, communal and creative fashion. Likewise, a teacher's job is to teach, and if a student fails to display an understanding of what has been taught (to an examiner or the teacher), then a teacher's role is to guide the student, including giving feedback in regards to how a student might approach their learning or essay writing more successfully.

The discernment, judgement and expertise of editors is key in making sure that a submitted piece fits the aims and scope of a particular publishing venue. Unsurprisingly, academics often spend less time discussing the role of editors and their part in the academic knowledge production process than we do that of peer reviewers, since more of us participate in the latter. In our scholarly lives, we have had mixed experiences of editors, for instance, being asked to review research that we were surprised editors sent out for review (as it was almost identical to previously published research by the same authors, or lacked any discernible contribution). This is not to blame individual editors, but, rather, to critique the system that has resulted in a massive increase in research submitted for publication, and to journals in particular, and a wider academic culture in which individuals can wield power in a relatively unchecked manner.[13] As argued in Chapter 1, the breakdown of the system is linked to the demand for increased production as a means of assessment of a scholar's worth.

Within such a system of overproduction and overwork, calling for a type of review that needs more time may make many scholars scream. As one reviewer of the draft of this book pointed out:

> While there is a laudable focus on the author submitting work to be reviewed and the pressure and stress caused to them by the current peer review process, more can be included here on the demands being placed on the reviewer. . . . I can't help but feel that Appreciative Reviewing is going to add to my (unpaid)

---

[13]An extended discussion of the role of editors in promoting/withholding original research, the ability of high-status individuals to circumnavigate editorial systems of control, the rise of 'alternative journals' and how this fits into the wider academic culture is beyond the scope of this book. Let us know if you write that book!

workload. I need to be efficient and direct in many of my comments sometimes without walking on eggshells. The system is bad for us all.

Appreciative reviewing might well be something that takes more time than most reviews currently do, but reviewing is also something that can be – and even should be – an engaging and rewarding process for the reviewer as well (in Chapter 4 we'll talk about the freedom to publish slowly). The system of academic production is truly broken, but for us this means we need to suggest new ways of creating knowledge, not only critique the current state of play.

Another worry reviewers of audio might have is that they do not have the expertise to review audio content because they are not familiar with the medium. Again this is a concern we understand, as it's hard sometimes to imagine our scholarly expertise can be useful if it isn't a perfect match to the work under review. However, such situations already often arise with text-only scholarship: for instance, if we are asked to review journal articles about which we have theoretical expertise but not regional knowledge, or where we intimately know a topic, but are in a different discipline than the authors and journal. Here, a good editor and an honest reviewer can work together to overcome any potential issues, that is, saying what one can and cannot provide a review about and making sure expertise gaps are filled. Likewise, scholars with no podcasting experience might feel comfortable commenting on the content and argumentation, but not on the form this takes. However, podcast producer and scholar Siobhan McHugh believes that an understanding of the medium is vital from the side of the reviewer. As she wrote in relation to the earlier-discussed *Secret Feminist Agenda's* review process:

> The reviews provide a valuable assessment of many aspects of the podcast, but neglect to appraise the use of an audio format: a bit like having a review of a journal article fail to address the clarity, correctness and style of the writing – an integral aspect of its ability to communicate research. If podcasts are to be put forward as research outputs, they need to be evaluated by someone who is also audio-literate. (2019, n.p.)

We think this is an important critique – we spent Chapter 2 working through the particulars of audio scholarship – however, we think it needs to be understood within the current context of scholarly expertise and framed as an invitation to extend such expertise among reviewers. While it is true most scholars have little or no experience of reviewing audio, this doesn't mean they cannot be guided as to what to listen for and given suggestions as to how to extend their skill set, namely, that they are provided with clear guidelines from the editor. To be clear, this doesn't mean a scholar must be a podcast maker to be a reviewer of a podcast, but, rather, that they can be provided the resources to help them better understand the medium as they bring their expertise to the review process. Some types of podcast, for instance those with rich audio design, may call for heightened levels of audio-literacy, but when reviewing interview podcast series this becomes less important (though important, nonetheless). In our ideal world, peer reviewers would be open and engaged in the process in such a way that they are willing to expand and develop their abilities as a scholar so as to speak to scholarship across mediums. Peer review is currently unsound in part because reviewers see it as a chore; we want to change the process, paradigm and, when needed, the medium of review for the sake of the authors *and* the reviewers. Such a positive change is something that, we hope, can reinvigorate knowledge creation more broadly. At the heart of appreciative review is the belief that creativity, trust and vulnerability bring something powerful into our scholarship, and into peer review. The vulnerability of care-based reviews, alongside the responsiveness built into creative reviews and the expansion of notions of 'peer' inherent in communal reviews, allows us to re-envision how scholarship is made and whom it is for. While these interventions are not unique to podcasting, they are well suited to the medium, making experimental peer-review approaches to scholarly podcasts an ideal site for the experimental expansion of how we think about the creation of knowledge in the 21st century. And that, as we will argue in Chapter 4, is precisely what knowledge creation needs right now.

Scholarly podcasting is an emergent practice rich with potential and accompanied by often overblown claims of reinventing scholarly communication as a whole, even of saving academia (a project that frankly doesn't interest us all that much). What *does* interest us is how sound-based scholarship breaks open the systems of scholarly communication precisely because academia has not yet figured out how to track it. Sound-based scholarship isn't an exciting prospect because sound is somehow inherently anti-capitalist, or decolonial, or feminist or otherwise subversive; looking to the formalization of the podcasting industry demonstrates that sound can be as thoroughly incorporated into capitalist logics as any other medium (Sullivan 2019; Ketchum 2022). Sound is exciting, rather, because it offers a site of slippage, a liminal space that has not yet been fully incorporated into the institutional logics of how academics do their work; it is a space in which to play, and as these many examples demonstrate, play we shall. And within the playful embrace of peer-reviewing podcasts and podcasting peer review, some overarching themes have begun to emerge: these experiments tend to be *communal*, expanding understandings of whom scholarship is for and who gets to participate in peer review; they're *care-based*, modelling a kind of affectively charged vulnerability that shifts us away from a combative view of peer review towards a model of 'thinking with'; and they're *creative*, demonstrating knowledge creation as an ongoing process of thinking through doing, of thinking out loud and together. Podcasting might not be poised to save academia from itself, but we believe it *can* save scholarly knowledge creation for the twenty-first century by providing us with a vantage point from which we can step back and reconsider what's working and what isn't.

Interlude

Approaches to
Appreciative Review

FIGURE 6 *Appreciative peer-review approaches.*

4

Beyond Peer Review?

Picture this: Ian, Hannah and Lori are sitting in a bath together. We're all wearing 1920s-style full-length, woollen bathing costumes and have waterproof laptops, a Bluetooth speaker for podcast listening, separate bars of soap, but a communal ducky. We've also got an abundance of babies bobbing around in the bathwater with us (metaphorically speaking, of course). These babies are extremely cute and we just want to bite their tiny little toes and we also think they probably shouldn't be, you know, thrown out. But, unfortunately, the bath water has gotten filthy. No surprise, with all of us sharing it, and all of us so covered in the grime of a culture of prestige and metrics, capitalist scarcity and patriarchal, white supremacist notions of expertise. We definitely need to get this disgusting bathwater out of here, but can we throw it out without tossing all these beautiful bobbing babies along with it?

Why don't we start with what needs to go?

Things We Want to Throw Out
(aka The Bathwater)

Obviously, or at least we hope obviously, we want to throw out a lot of things from academia, like systemic racism, sexual abusers (and their supporters), tuition fees, high pay for top managers, paywalled scholarship, bullies, and professors who check their Facebook during student presentations, etc. etc. etc. (and far too many et ceteras). Aside from this, we have three potentially less obvious ideas as well.

Daft Measurements! (Throw out metrics! Throw out grades!)

Years ago, racist colonial scientists used to measure how clever different races were by measuring the size of their skulls. We now know this to be not only racist, but also nonsense. It was a way of upholding hierarchies between people from different parts of the world and with different skin colours and different-sized heads. Thank god we don't do that anymore.

Nowadays, we have university systems that measure students and academics not by the size of their skulls, but by their ability to write in a certain way as decided by a department or teacher and publish lots of times in the 'right' places, respectively. English-language higher education and English-language publishing not only dominate, but are also on the rise. All three of us are native English speakers and so have had massive advantages when it comes to our education and now our academic work. We are also all white (so people think we're cleverer than we are in academic settings) and one of us is even a man (jackpot!). Loads of research has shown how class, gender and ethnic bias have played into the assessment of academics and students.[1] Our new systems of ranking are every bit as biased as phrenology, or IQ after it, and every bit as lodged in our unthinking 'common sense' of how intelligence works. When you talk to a scholar anxious about grade inflation, it quickly becomes clear that they think grades are real, correlating to some measure in the world despite the fact that 'there is no consensus on what grades are in the first place' (Blum 2020, 5). Grade inflation is, in fact, grade *compression*, a phenomenon in which a smaller set of grades are being used to rank students; attempts to combat this compression are ultimately about maintaining grades' usefulness for distinguishing between, i.e., *ranking*, students (Blum 2020, 5).

---

[1]Gender and racial bias in student evaluations of faculty has been identified by, for example, Boring, Ottoboni and Stark (2016); Boring (2017); Chávez and Mitchell (2020); Heffernan (2022); MacNell, Driscoll and Hunt (2015); Mengel, Sauermann and Zölitz (2017); Spooren, Brockx and Mortelmans (2013). Gender and racial bias in teacher evaluations of students has been identified by Botelho, Madeira and Rangel (2015) and Malouff and Thorsteinsson (2016), among others. Bias among teachers with respect to socioeconomic status of students has been identified by Batruch et al. (2023); Doz (2023); and Hanna and Linden (2012); among others.

It's hard for many academics to wrap their heads around the problem with ranking, in part because most of us got to where we are by being well ranked. We're likely to be the ones who got As, or whatever your local equivalent is, who published in the right places and spoke at the right conferences and played the game the way it was intended to be played. And, as is so common for people who have come through a challenging system and succeeded, academics have a tendency to mistake correlation for causation, to believe that it was the terrible system that got us here, that made us who we are, that without grades and grants and metrics and artificially imposed scarcity, we would never have been pushed towards whatever greatness we might now claim. How else to explain that model of mentorship, still so pervasive in many disciplines, where academics put graduate students through the same set of inhumane and unjust practices they themselves may have endured, under the guise of professionalization or training?

But, of course, as we all know, correlation is *not* causation, and ending up at the top of an unjust ranking system doesn't suddenly make that ranking system okay. So let's throw it out. Let's try to persuade our departments, universities and students (!) that letter or number grades are problematic, and counter to the actual mission of education. This isn't a pipe dream: ungrading is an active concern. As Susan D. Blum summarizes in the introduction to *Ungrading: Why Rating Students Undermines Learning (and What to Do Instead)* (2020), a whole range of institutions, from kindergartens to medical schools, are throwing out traditional grades, 'emphasizing mastery rather than arbitrary deadlines and measures, learning rather than compliance' (4). So many of the metrics we rely on in academia are, ironically, not supported by evidence of the effectiveness of teaching or the impact of research. We might compare studies on the ineffectiveness of grading in encouraging learning to studies on the ineffectiveness of conventional peer review to identify errors in research. When we look into the histories of both practices, we find a whole bevy of social and institutional forces that have more to do with the creation of artificial scarcity than they do with the actual mission of the university, which is (or ought to be) producing and disseminating new knowledge through teaching and publishing.[2]

---

[2]Along with creating a socially just world.

Consider, for example, the practice of summarizing a career's worth of scholarly activity with a single number. Let's unpack what the 'lifetime summary' number at the top of one's CV – the number of articles published, the number of conference presentations given, the number of chapters written and so on – really tells us. For one, we can get a sense of how long this person has been an academic, with higher numbers presumably accumulating over time. We can also get a sense of how much funding is available to this person for flying around the world to present at conferences, as well as how easy it might be for them to travel without jumping through economic and bureaucratic hoops. (We know that for academics in many countries, travel can be fraught with lengthy and expensive visa application processes.) Publication numbers might give us a clue as to whether this person is skilled at writing and perhaps even how fast they can write – or of how big their grants are and how many grad students they can bring on to co-author papers with them. If we care to surmise more deeply, we might consider how the person with a high lifetime summary number probably enjoys a lifestyle in which systemic racism, sexism, burdens of child care or elder care, career hiatuses for parental leave or sick leave, disability and the like do not hinder their ability to constantly and consistently attend to their publishing obligations. These numbers, in other words, can tell us something about the privileges a particular academic has access to, and quite a bit less about the substance of their scholarly work. We'd argue that lifetime summary numbers are an insult to our work and the integrity of scholarship. They are meant only to lazily rank and categorize us, to sort supposed 'good' academics from supposed 'mediocre' ones with no more consideration than a quick glance, like a barcode tattooed on our forehead.

But what if podcasts and other forms of non-traditional scholarly output were to be counted in this number? Wouldn't that be a win? We're so glad you asked, if only because we love a quick 'NO'. Lori, for example, used to spend time arguing to ensure that her university would 'count' such things, participating in drafting policy that would hopefully result in scholars, particularly non-tenured or pre-tenure scholars, who engage in non-traditional scholarship being protected from bias when it came time to evaluate, grant tenure and promotion and so on. While her own media production department understood this mindset, at the university level, Deans and VPs of research and innovation often came from business, science and engineering backgrounds and simply could not (or would not) understand the concept of audiences or professional awards organizations as peer review, nor creative works or non-traditional works as scholarship. Eventually Lori stopped trying to convince them, which is fine for a tenured academic, but not a choice that precariously employed or non-tenured faculty have available to them. The point here is that in the university milieu, only certain very specifically structured things can be understood as legitimate scholarship. And if we work to make podcasting count among that, there is a very real risk that our institutions will create new norms that scholarly podcasting must adhere to, or more insidiously, that conceiving of our podcasts as scholarly will lead to us self-policing our own work to help make sure that it *counts*. In other words, we don't want the university to ruin podcasting for us by interpellating it into the status quo, turning it into another version of academic bean-counting.

If we don't set up ways of evaluating scholarly podcasting then we fear that someone else might set up a daft measurement, instead. As Tzlil Sharon argued in her spoken audio review of this chapter:

> [R]eally chasing after these numbers can actually get in the way of creativity and knowledge sharing. It's like, we're so focused on trying to win this game, that we forget why we got into academia in the first place. So definitely this reality has to change, there is no doubt about it. And yeah, we should be working together, pushing the boundaries of knowledge, not just competing with each other according to these distorted ranking systems. That being said, I don't think we should throw out measurements; measurements can still be important indicators of the impact and value of research. We just need to find a way to strike the balance between quantifiable metrics and the kind of open and collaborative academic culture that we want to see.

We understand and appreciate Tzlil's point here: a vanity-project podcast by, say, a university rector in which she uses the university's prestige and resources to produce a podcast for which she doesn't even write her own questions should not be compared to a scholarly podcast that requires research, planning, crafting and editing by individuals or small groups of scholars to advance knowledge in their field. The point is that they should not be compared at all: the act of comparison creates the type of ranking system that can be – and often is – gamed. Rather, podcasts should be evaluated openly and transparently by peers in a way that is meaningful for them in relation to the context of the field or discipline.

A fixation on conventional metrics and rankings detracts from the mission of the university – to educate, to create new knowledge, to address urgent contemporary issues. And so we say: *splash!* Out with that filthy water.

Scholarly Publishing Norms! (Throw Out Long Turnaround Times! Throw Out Unreasonable Expectations of Publishing Constantly! Throw Out Logocentrism!)

We had a really good idea, we hope, and we decided to write a book about it. Thank goodness we didn't write an article about it. It might have taken us less time to write, but possibly more time to publish. How does that work? Because journals have too many authors queuing up to publish in them because there is an academic arms race where everyone is trying to publish more than ever. Because many journals annoyingly[3] demand that the author guarantee their draft paper is not under consideration for publication anywhere else. Because the labour of editing journals and peer-reviewing scholarship is a vital service to the profession that is, nevertheless, both invisibilized and undervalued compared to the publishing itself, thus encouraging us to produce more scholarship without necessarily participating in the processes that bring that scholarship into the world.

And sometimes there are ideas that just don't fit into the temporalities of scholarly publishing, but that doesn't mean they

---

[3]The authors had some disagreement about this. On one hand, this demand is very annoying for scholars who would like a shot at having their work published in a timely manner, and would like to send it to several journals at once for consideration. On the other hand, this requirement is understandable from the point of view of the editors and peer reviewers, who don't want to do a load of free labour only to find out that the author will be publishing elsewhere.

are worthless or should never be voiced. As Stefan Partelow, co-host of the *In Common* podcast reflects,

> I think [podcasting] is a bit of a counter to academic knowledge sharing being a very slow process in terms of the projects that we work on. The [current] idea is you pick the projects that you think are good enough for you or feasible, and then you work on them for years and maybe you get a paper at the end of it. But in the meantime, you have so many ideas which come and go in your mind and you go, 'that could be a cool project, but I don't have time'. So the thought floats away. Or maybe you write it down for another day. And the podcast is, I think, a way to just have a quicker thought process and a sharing of ideas.

A sharing of ideas! That's a generous way of thinking about doing scholarship which runs counter to how norms currently function. Instead, it's just publish, publish, publish. But what is all this scholarship *for*? There are too many articles for any of us to read, too many journals for us to peer-review for, too much scrabbling for position and points and resources. And maybe that would be fine if we were having fun, if we felt that the writing of articles enhanced our teaching and vice versa, or if peer review consistently brought us generous and useful feedback that expanded our understanding. But for so many of us, that isn't the case. Publishing is either a desperate attempt to keep up with your institution's expectations of constant 'output' (a word that conjures up images of assembly lines or productivity charts), or even worse, a kind of hopeless hope labour, with thousands of precariously employed academics publishing on their own time without institutional support because they might one day land an increasingly rare secure position, while large journal publishers sell that work back to universities at increasingly outrageous rates that further cut into the budgets institutions *could* be using to, say, hire more faculty.

And all of this *has* to be done through writing, because writing sits at the top of the pyramid when it comes to what is considered 'proper scholarship'. Text has primacy; logocentrism is real. But scholarly works produced by modalities other than text can have equal merit, even if they are produced – and reviewed – in different ways than we're used to. Besides, if publishing in conventional journals is a bit of a scam, why not mess around and do something different? What's the worst that could happen? You might have fun.

The unmeasurable joy is one of the things that Ksenia Chmutina, co-host of *Disasters: Deconstructed*, likes about podcasting. As she explained to Ian:

> Very often this is the most enjoyable part of the week, you know, because we get to chat with all these amazing people and just discuss things instead of thinking, 'OK, I need to do this because, you know, my development review tells me so. Right? Or because I'll be measured on it.' To me, is that kind of part of the maybe lost academic freedom? . . . We don't really have enough of it any longer because we don't have time to discuss things anymore, because we're just so busy with everything else that we need to do. I don't want it to be measured. But equally, if it is, I think it needs to be acknowledged that not everyone is going to be able to do this and not everyone should. You know, if people have a good ability to communicate, then that's great. If they don't, then that's also fine, right? If we all of a sudden become great podcasters, then it'll be just information overload, like it happens for so many other things.

And there goes another bucketful of dirty bathwater. *Sploosh!*

Exclusivity! (Throw Out Current Admission Criteria! Throw Out 'The Canon'! Throw Out Precarious Labour Conditions!)

Why do we accept students in universities? Is it because they are clever when they apply? Or is it because they have the potential to learn and grow? What's gained by categorizing students at age eighteen (or whenever your country does it) based on how well they've managed to demonstrate their ability to pass tests or write papers? How is this a fair system when these children have gone to vastly different schools or had vastly different learning opportunities at home?

How do we accept articles and books to be published in certain journals? Is it their adherence to the canon? Do they have to show that they've read every-fucking-thing-written-since-1932 on a particular subject whether or not it's been subsequently found to be problematic so that we deem it to be 'good scholarship'? Or, rather, might our scholarly work be better if we are freer, if we can fly from the can(n)on in a superhero cape, hurtling into the sky towards who knows what destination? Does 'the canon' exist only because there are, indeed, seminal (yuck) thinkers in any field, or is it also true that situating new work in relation to the old work of rather old, rather white, and rather male people is a tool of exclusion? What if instead of a literature review that trots out all the same old texts, we have theoretical framings that dip in and out of foundational texts while leaving space for under-referenced scholars and our own original research?

Is job security something teachers should have to earn through years of unpaid labour for the same institutions that sold them a PhD as a promise of a career to come? Would we like teachers and researchers to be able to concentrate on their important work rather than worrying about whether they'll have a job next semester and what they're going to do over the summer when there's no academic work and they've already been fired from Tesco for unionizing after self-service tills took their colleagues' jobs?

Can we imagine an academia where we critically ask questions of the systems we work with and through, or do we have to accept the current situation as the right way to do things?

Surprise! We don't think the status quo is the only way! In fact, we think a lot of exciting things become possible when we imagine otherwise, but often imagining otherwise begins with unlearning what we have taken for granted. If you find yourself thinking 'yeah, but' . . . we encourage you to pause and interrogate that instinct. 'Yeah, but anonymous peer review is necessary to protect marginalized scholars from discrimination.' Insisting that marginalized scholars must hide their identities in order to make it in academia fails to move the needle on the white supremacy, ableism and patriarchy that structure our institutions, demanding, instead, that scholars need to write as though they are white men in order to succeed.[4] 'Yeah, but I need to publish

---

[4]Having said this, we recognize that it's not as straightforward as simply encouraging marginalized people to put themselves out there as pioneers in this space. We recognize the very real risks such scholars take in challenging the status quo in public.

conventional work if I want to be able to compete on the job market.' As Kathleen Fitzpatrick (2018) argues, academics are pitted against one another based on metrics that are framed as objective and meritocratic but that, in reality, are 'never neutral' (26). The 'competitive individualism' fostered by this metrics-based, neoliberal approach to knowledge creation 'makes all of us painfully aware that even our most collaborative efforts will be assessed individually' (27), an environment that Fitzpatrick links to a culture of critical cruelty and gatekeeping (129–30). 'Yeah, but we can't just let everyone into university.' Why not? What's stopping us? Availability of funding? Surely neoliberal defunding of education should be something we rail against, an externally imposed scarcity model that has very little to do with the actual work of education and scholarship.

University student admissions is the ultimate gatekeeper to academia, and thus the change we expect will make some scholars really worried. 'But how will we know who is a good student? How can we make sure we have the best?' A good start, we suggest, would be by paying attention to how current practices of admission have come into place, not least because this regulation of access reflects changing relationships between authority and different publics (Cantat 2022). A few hundred years ago universities were almost exclusively for elite white men in Europe and male children of elites in colonies. However, over time universities became sites of national interest, with states taking an active role in their regulation and attempting to harness their potential for the good of the nation (Neave 2001; Kwiek 2005). A massification of university study opened up university access for many in Europe and elsewhere in the decades following the Second World War. But this period of mass free education for many has been shifting since the 1980s with increasing fees and changing conceptions of whom and what a university is for. For instance, students from poorer backgrounds can be priced out of certain institutions due to tensions between individualized aspirations and cost (Baker 2019). Furthermore, individualizing neoliberal market logics now lead many to conceive of university as a private rather than a public good, tied to an individual's life project (Giroux 2016). Our point is that broad regulations around university access have never been neutral, but, rather, reflect differing governing rationales as they shift over time (Clancy and Goastellec 2007).

When it comes to university entrance, the social class of potential students' parents plays a large part in determining what type of higher education they can enrol in (Heiskala, Erola and Kilpi-Jakonen 2021), with those working-class students who choose not to go to university feeling as if only 'second rate' options are available to them due to their awareness of the hierarchies in higher education (Hutchings and Archer 2010). Moreover, once students enter the higher education system, social class differences are compounded (Bathmaker,[5] Ingram and Waller 2013). Which is to say, universities are not meritocracies, and the idea that the university takes the best students regardless of various intersectional marginalities is nonsense.

Currently, only particular forms and modes of students expressing knowledge are considered legible by assessors of their suitability for university: mostly written essays, written tests and interviews. As teachers, we have known students who are articulate critical thinkers when they feel they are in a space in which they are 'allowed' to express themselves and use a medium in which they feel most comfortable, but who may struggle with expectations for written essays in a certain style and formal interviews. Expectations around formal writing can exacerbate existing inequities by, for example, rewarding students with private school backgrounds who have received training in academic writing and interview techniques while punishing those who have not. The worth of potential students is measured within very strict contours: of whether they can pass state exams, write in a way that reads as legible for those who themselves have passed through a similar admissions system and, in some cases, interview well. Podcasting, if recognized as a legitimate mode of scholarly expression by researchers and teachers alike, can open up assessment of potential students; it's not about replacing writing, but recognizing that knowledge can be understood through a plurality of mediums when thinking about admissions.

There are lots of people who uphold the belief that 'real academics' are those with indefinite contracts (tenured in the North American context) with the rest being the 'not yet academics' or the 'never quite to become academics'. Strict boundary control is often a central tenet of homogeneous cultural formations that

---

[5]We didn't even make this up.

seek to reproduce themselves, so it is little wonder many academics behave in such a way. However, the result of this precariousness and boundary control is that middle-aged professionals with decades of expertise live an 'unfinished adulthood' as they seem to never fully arrive to the familial and domestic stability of others their age (Castellano 2023), and lots of brilliant research never gets published as brilliant working-class scholars drift away from academia because they never have time to publish amid the stresses of casual contracts that do not offer research time (Irving 2023). Much of what we love about academia (conversation, teaching, freedom) seems difficult when thinking about it in relation to precariousness. As Dylan Bird argued in his spoken audio peer review of this chapter:

> One additional aspect of academia that's frustrating us is the increasing casualization of the workforce. I know it's a massive issue in Australia and in many parts of the world. I think this actually makes some of those positive elements like conversation, collaboration more difficult because you're not spending as much time on campus. You're not getting to meet and interact with other students, other scholars from both your own discipline and other disciplines as well. And so I think there's a follow-on effect of making the experience not necessarily an enjoyable or fruitful one, while also being in a position of precarious employment.

We understand and empathize with this point of view – especially the one co-author of this book who does not have a permanent position in academia – however, one of our purposes in this book is to do some of the intellectual legwork needed for the creation of different systems, where things like collaborative scholarship and teaching are valued as important parts of creative scholarly lives. So we're throwing out the notion of exclusivity, with all its classed, gendered, racialized, geographic, able-bodied biases. *Splash!*

Things We Love (aka The Babies)

But if we throw out metrics, we hear you asking, *what will we put in their place?* The short answer is: nothing. This is the wisdom we have learned from ungrading: that grades don't *need* to be replaced with some other form of ranking or listing or imposing of artificial scarcity. Knowledge and learning are not enhanced by these systems; in fact, they are actively opposed to the collaborative practice of building meaning and understanding. We are clearly not suggesting there should be no systems of evaluation and review; we spent all of Chapter 3 detailing different possibilities for *how* such a review might take place. What we are opposed to is how existing systems of ranking (students, research, institutions) are detrimental to scholarship.

Audio in general and podcasting in particular have inspired us to get here: giving audio feedback to students or our peers; making podcast episodes that are reviews of scholarly work; reflecting on peer feedback we have received on podcasts we have made or been part of. Feedback can be better, scholarship can be better, publishing processes can all be better by thinking through the affordances of the audio form and what that might mean in terms of creating new and exciting forms of knowledge, and critical and curious forms of learning.

But if we throw out scholarly publishing norms, we hear you ask, *what will we put in their place?* Well, a whole myriad of new ways of creating and assessing publishing that are best suited to sub-disciplines and the mediums. We don't need one ring to rule them all and in the darkness bind them. We need a dynamic and reflexive system of knowledge creation that befits the complexity of the world.

But if we throw out exclusivity, we hear you cry, *what will we put in its place?* A complete rethinking of the way higher education currently decides who and what is deemed worthy.

Still, it is a daunting prospect to imagine being one of the first: one of the first teachers in your institution to stop grading your students, one of the first academics to stop trying to publish in traditional journals, one of the first universities to stop vying for a higher spot on the international charts. It feels a bit like being the canary in the coal mine, doesn't it? Maybe you'll show people that there's a problem, but you might not survive the demonstration. And yet, there are already teachers, researchers and universities starting to do this. Moreover, we're already losing the university as anything we might recognize as a place dedicated to knowledge and learning. So why not go out swinging?

Despite these fightin' words, we recognize that we don't have to throw everything out when we get rid of the dirty bathwater!

So let's take a closer look at the babies that remain. What do we love about academia and scholarship? Turns out, it's a lot of the same things that we love about podcasting: conversation, pedagogy and freedom.

Conversation

Academia is really about conversation. We are in conversation with our disciplines, with our colleagues and with the public. These conversations, whether literal or figurative, are the foundation of knowledge-building. Research – and peer review – is a conversation in which ideas are exchanged, suggestions are made and shaky ground is identified, building upon prior knowledge to take us somewhere new. Even traditional peer review is a form of conversation, albeit a fairly unwieldy one.

And maybe people who are not directly engaged in academia might think that conversation seems too fluffy to be research (and maybe academics who consider themselves free from fluff might think the same), but it's how a lot of complex ideas are worked out and worked through – whether it's mathematicians gathered around a blackboard or socially awkward sociology students gathered around a bottle of *pálinka*. As time is increasingly squeezed and fragmented within academia, there are fewer and fewer opportunities for conversations with colleagues about their or our work. As Dylan Bird pointed out to us, in his spoken audio peer review of this chapter:

> One thing that stands out to me immediately is the capacity to platform conversations that are sort of indeterminate, where you might have people from similar disciplines or very different disciplines engaging in some sort of thought experiments, having a chat, shooting the breeze, about things related to their area of expertise, which then could inspire further research projects or contribute to the greater sort of stock of knowledge – simply through having that conversation. A lot of academic culture can be quite safe and conservative I find, and there's a good reason for that. We want our insights, our statements to be based on peer reviewed research, to have a very solid stock of research and a foundation of knowledge behind it. But I think that can

sometimes lead to some of us being a bit reluctant to share our thoughts, to speculate on certain matters that might be beyond our direct area of expertise. And I actually think as humans, there's a lot to be gained from speculating, from sharing ideas, from sharing knowledge and seeing what comes from it.

For some, a one-off conversation with a fellow scholar, especially if you're being introduced to their ideas for the first time, is often not the place for deep engaged conversation. Sometimes it needs repeated conversations over many meetings, falling deeper and deeper into a topic, new contexts adding fresh layers of meaning to our ideas as we grow more and more willing to make ourselves vulnerable, to suggest outlandish possibilities, to go deep together.

And podcasting is a great reason for initiating a conversation with someone that you don't know. As Neil Fox, co-host of *The Cinematologists* told Ian:

Approaching a filmmaker, approaching a scholar, reading a thing, we do that all the time. We read a thing and we really get to talk to that person. We've got the podcast, you know. If I contacted Professor X and said, 'Can we just have a chat about your work?' Like, it's hard. Who's gonna make time for that? I wouldn't expect them to. We can do that with the podcast. We can say, look, 'we've got a podcast. We can put it out. These are our listeners. These are our partners.' And people are like, 'okay, sounds legit, let's talk about it.' And they're so rewarding, those conversations, you know? And in terms of what it brings to the scholarship: they inspire it and they fuel it.

Conversations can be so inspiring because they combine both depth and casualness, a feat that other mediums do not always manage. As Johanna Sebauer from *BredowCast* remarked:

It provides the necessary freedom to go deep into a topic. And there's no limit on time. You can talk for hours if you want. And sometimes that's necessary because scientific topics are so complex. And many media formats want you to reduce complexity, which is sometimes not possible and then it just doesn't make any sense to talk about science when you reduce complexity. We can let people have complexity, we don't need to make it unnecessarily simple, because there are people out there who really like to listen to complex stuff and really want to dive into it deeply. But at the same time, a podcast is also a very casual format. It's just a casual conversation between two people, a conversation that they would have at the pub after work. And so in those two aspects, they create a very nice environment to talk about science.

But conversations with colleagues aren't the only joyful forms of conversation, which leads us to our next true love: teaching.

Teaching

We love teaching: the performance of it, the conversation with students wherein we unpack our collective world and make sense of it through connections to our individual experiences and understandings, the satisfaction of finding out new things with new people with new (to us, at least) minds.

Not everyone loves teaching, for various reasons. Our methods for assessing teaching are as flawed as those for assessing research, with sites like *Rate My Professor* turning teaching into a popularity contest that studies show are consistently won by straight, white, able-bodied, English-speaking men (surprise surprise!).[6] It's hard to maintain a passion for teaching if you work in a climate where students are treated as units of tuition, and encouraged to think of their education as something they're buying rather than a transformative experience. Plus, taking teaching seriously in many institutions is a battle against the logics of merit and review processes, where research is what 'really' counts and teaching is treated as something you should try to earn/buy time off from so you can focus on your 'real' work.

But for those of us who love teaching, we want to reaffirm how brilliant it *can* be. Sure, sometimes our plans and ideas fall to pieces, we mess up our class prep and students are left thinking we're useless.[7] But when we step into the unknown with our

---

[6]See, for example, Baker (2019), Chalmers (2021), and Duggan and Bishop (2023).
[7]Some of us have had moments when we met students, years later, who told us which class within our course sucked and we're still anxious about that now. But we've

students, seeing where our co-learning takes us, we are reminded that knowledge is not a stable object, uncovered with a chisel like Michelangelo chipping away all the marble that isn't David; no, knowledge is *emergent and co-created*, coming into being through the very process of working through it. It is conversational and non-linear, characterized by false starts and failures, red herrings and dead ends, so many of which disappear in the forms of knowledge we present to the world. But those tangled processes are alive and well in the classroom, where we know that students don't learn by having facts implanted into their heads but by *doing things* with new ideas, testing them out and putting them into action. And we love putting ideas into action, too, which is why podcasting brings us such joy, and, we hope, makes us better teachers (see Turner, Schaefer and Lowe 2021).

All three of us love having our students make podcasts, even in classes when the topic is not podcasting. For instance, Ian once co-taught a media studies course for students who had experienced displacement as part of the Open Learning Initiative (OLIve). Invited guests came in each week to speak to the students, with one or two students then interviewing the speaker after the class for the *Voice Matters Podcast* series.[8] Hannah regularly encourages her students to make podcasts in her publishing studies courses in lieu of essays, often as part of helping them develop their own 'personal cyberinfrastructure' (Watters 2015). Kent Davies, a collaborator on the Manitoba Food History Project alongside Kimberley Moore and Janis Thiessen, spoke to Ian about what making podcasts with students can bring to scholarly work:

We have students working on podcasts because this is a very new experience for a lot of them, and they will take the story and produce things in new and exciting ways that we hadn't considered. And I think that's a really cool facet to all of this: whether they want to do more soundscapes, they want to do less narration, they want to do a lot of segmentation, they want to make it like a kind of funny, you know, a game show or

---

also had moments when we met students, years later, who told us how valuable something that happened in our classroom ended up being to them.
[8]Something he wrote about in a blog post for *Times Higher Education* (Cook 2018).

something to reflect the narrative that's going on in the story. They're doing all sorts of fun stuff with it that we didn't consider . . . And I think that that's one of the cool things about having classes tackle podcasting: you'll get different kinds of outcomes that you didn't expect.

For some academics, there isn't a lot of intersection between their research and their course curricula, but like Kent Davies lays out previously, we also love it when we can bring our research into the classroom and get our students excited about the things we're excited about and do podcasting at the same time.

There are also interesting ways in which podcasts can also be used as teaching. Robert Huish, the creator of the *The Global Development Primer* offers an interesting example of how it can work. He created a closed podcast series, which can only be accessed by students and that serve as an introduction to a topic, and an open public podcast series, which has interviews with researchers in the field of international development. As he explained to Ian:

> I don't advocate that podcasting is the ideal means or solution to all teaching requirements. In this case, it does very well for an introduction course that's designed to raise awareness. In International Development Studies, you see people come into the university without even knowing what those two words mean together. So there's a lot of awareness building that needs to occur. And [a podcast series] is something that can achieve that goal very easily, that is if it's about trying to raise awareness and sort of a cohesive baseline of what terms are and exposing [students to] the broader research community. And that's the goal of this operation.
>
> . . . You are right in the sense that there will be a lot of pushing from administration to try to do the massive online models with the idea that if people can just kind of passively listen to podcasts and then receive credit from it, people will see the dollar signs go up. But let's be really clear about what is going to be missed: it doesn't follow a model that's best for every subject at every stage. I would not argue that a third year, fourth year class should be done through podcasts. You have other skills that need to be developed, engagement skills, speaking skills, interpersonal skills that need to be achieved. So that wouldn't really work.

What's hopefully clear from these examples is that commitment to teaching as a site of collaboration and experimentation is not only an aspect of the university worth holding onto, but vital to our understanding of the work we do – and of the value that podcasting can bring into this work.

Freedom

Having ideas is brilliant, but having ideas and testing them out slowly, letting them float along with the detritus of academia until they are pulled into an eddy or whirl by a colleague or a student or in a trance while descaling your kettle, is even better. Then, in time, the idea can become a podcast (or a paper or a presentation) and the world comes alive not only for you or the people you're directly speaking to about it, but also for the wider world – the community who cares, or might care, about advancing research in the fields you're interested in.

Where and how do these ideas become alive? In labs and libraries, through failure and re-failure. Intellectual pursuit, when it's done best, is an ongoing experiment in and with the world, a never-ending process that understands that meaning is made and unmade again a thousand times, never stable, never complete. Lauren Berlant once said that scholars are always interrogating our objects (2011); by that they meant that we don't arrive at an idea or understanding and sit proudly on it like a hen trying to hatch a Fabergé egg. We keep working it until it doesn't work anymore, and then we try something new, or maybe even something old (because honestly, to hell with the fetishization of innovation in the university, too).

And sound-based scholarship, partly because it's not counted and peers don't really know how to categorize it, can offer some forms of freedom. For instance, Ian collaborated with seven audio diarists to publish a podcast a day about their experiences at the start of the coronavirus pandemic, and then reworked them as a cacophony of voices through embedded audio players (Cook et al. 2020). In a very different example of non-conventional scholarship, law Professor and *Ipse Dixit* co-host Brian L. Frye includes podcast episodes in his series by an incarcerated man who records them on a contraband mobile phone. Lori took quantitative data she'd gathered about diversity on commercial radio stations and hacked an old radio to become an interactive data visualization and sonification object through which users could physically explore the information.[9] These examples make use of freedom from institutions and scholarly publishing norms, inspired by the affordances of sound-based media, and create opportunities to do scholarship that advances knowledge *differently*.

Freedom to try out different forms of scholarship also entails a freedom to fail. In the 2022 keynote address for OTESSA (the Open/Technology in Education, Society, and Scholarship Association), scholar and teacher Brenna Clarke Gray argued that when academics tell stories of our failures, we cherry-pick the ones that ultimately ended in a success that turns the failure into a story of triumph over adversity. We don't tell stories of failures that were just . . . failures. Her example of an irreconcilable failure was her own experience of pregnancy loss, an often unspeakable but all too common experience.[10] Naming this failure, this loss, in a way that didn't offer a happy ending or reframe it as a surprise form of productivity was not just an act of courage: it was a modelling of a version of academia in which ideas are living things, emergent and unpredictable, interwoven with the messy complexities of our own lives. It's no coincidence that Gray is also a podcaster,[11] a scholar attentive to the pedagogical nature of public scholarship and to the wider stakes of how we think and talk about the ideas and experiences that deserve to be open and public.

To be allowed to fail, we need freedom not only from state interference into our research, but also from the market and the neoliberal managerial stranglehold it has academia in (Ivancheva 2022). Freedom from the academic market means the freedom to get things out quickly and informally – to write a blog post, post a Twitter thread or make a podcast episode – as well as the freedom to be slow. There's a slow food movement, and there's a slow academia movement as well (Allegra Lab 2013). Some good things

---

[9]A digital version can be found online at diversityonradio.ca.

[10]Alison Mountz's 'Women on the edge: Workplace stress at universities in North America' (2016) offers an ethnographic account of women academics' struggles with fertility and pregnancy loss.

[11]She makes *You Got This!*, a podcast about learning technology, and *Hazel & Katniss & Harry & Star*, a weekly podcast about young adult literature and its film adaptations.

take time, but too often we push our work out into the world too fast so as to meet the demands of the scholarly production machine, only to have it linger in peer-review limbo for months or even years. (That's not the kind of slow we're talking about.)

There is radical potential in work that pushes beyond the status quo of scholarly communication – one that can break down the walls between scholarly and non-scholarly knowledge, can engage communities in the work of universities and vice versa and can challenge the very notion of what expert knowledge looks or sounds like. This kind of work gestures towards the multiple ways in which knowledge might be created and shared. But there is also a risk here that we might only accelerate the crisis of the university by simply adding something new for it to demand from already over-taxed scholars. And while the destruction of the university as a whole would give us a lot more free time, that isn't quite the freedom we had in mind.

A Manifesto[12] from a Bath: Knowledge Creation for the 21st Century

Throughout this book we have turned to hypotheticals and imagined figures, but not because these figures don't exist. There are people working in academia today, across institutions and positions, who are striving to create more space for the things we love (and we've covered a lot of those in Chapter 3). But how to create more of what we love and less of what we loathe? How to keep our bathwater clean in spite of ourselves?

Here is our manifesto, written from a bath free from dirty water and with space for more babies.

Make Scholarship Pedagogical

Here's one place to begin: making our knowledge public, not as an afterthought, an experiment in knowledge mobilization or

---

[12]With thanks to peer reviewers Tzlil Sharon and Martin Spinelli for pushing us to have a manifesto and call it one.

dissemination or whatever buzzword your funder is using, but as the *first* thought, as the *sine qua non* for being an intellectual. That doesn't mean that everyone needs to be a podcaster or a media pundit, but it means thinking about whom knowledge can be in service to; it means thinking about the university as an institution that is intended to be of public service, a public good. What good can you do, then?

Of the many beneficial impacts of making knowledge public, one that stands out to us is the breaking down of the conventional boundaries between teaching, research and service – categories that are not only artificial but also hierarchized in a way that always privileges research. Scholars have found that public scholarship is often categorized as service, the bottom of the ladder, something we're all supposed to do but that doesn't really 'count' (Alperin et al. 2019). But public scholarship is both *of service* and inherently pedagogical (Ketchum 2022). Look at podcasting as an example (don't we always?): podcasts assume an audience of non-specialists, prompting podcasters to take the time to *explain*, often via conversation and anecdotal examples, thus opening their knowledge up to a wider audience. See? Pedagogical. And because teaching is one of the things we love about academia, why not extend teaching beyond the classroom and our immediate students to wider publics? Connecting research to pedagogy and pedagogy to research de-silos our work.

We certainly aren't the first ones to note the pedagogical roots of podcasting. For over a decade, institutions have been using the medium as a way to share lectures and events more broadly, such as the University of Oxford's podcast series. Howard-Sukhil, Wallace and Chakrabarti (2021) link podcasting to the larger project of the public humanities, a field that began as straightforward advocacy for humanities scholars to consider audiences beyond their immediate peers, but which has since developed into a robust field with its own areas of study, including challenges to established paradigms of how we produce expert knowledge (sound familiar?). As Juan Pablo Alperin explained in an interview with Stacey Copeland for the *Amplified* audioblog series, thinking about *how* we communicate our research is as central to making knowledge public as conversations about open access:

> I think in the earlier years, the conversations about scholarly communications focussed very much around open access

and about making research objects, particularly publications, available to a public. And that's where a lot of, sort of, the origins of much of my own involvement in the work of the Public Knowledge Project has been. But I think over time, as we, I think as a community, have grown, but also as the rest of the world has caught up to understanding the value of openness, there is a broadening out from that very narrow sort of focus of open access on the academic publications and to a definition of something of open science that looks not just at them giving access to the work that's happening within academia, but rather opening the doors of academia to the public and to a broader set of audiences. So to me, the part of open science that gets me excited is this idea that we can open up our processes and what we do, not just for transparency, which I think is important, and for giving people an opportunity to see what it is that we're doing, but rather to involve them and to have them be included in those processes and helping to shape questions and helping to participate in the work. (Copeland 2022)

Thinking seriously about our scholarship as a conversation with multiple possible publics is pedagogical at its core, and it's vital to the ideal mission of contemporary higher education. Public pedagogical scholarship links back to the dirty bathwater of admissions we threw out earlier, because when we make the effort to make our scholarship open to wider groups of publics, we make the idea of university study an idea open for more. Hannah has been making *Witch, Please* for long enough (since 2015!) that students who have completed whole degrees have reached out to say that they never would have considered the possibility without the demystification of academia and theory central to the podcast's project. As Freja Sørine Adler Berg pointed out in her audio spoken peer review of this chapter, podcasting in academia can be for 'people who prefer to listen or who learn by listening rather than reading, or who are slow readers or who are dyslexic'. It can be an equalizer of kinds.

But podcasting is also a form of service for many scholars, comparable to organizing a conference or editing a journal. The nature of podcasting as a conversation means academic podcast producers are naturally bringing together thinkers from within their discipline as well as from without, creating online space for asynchronous and ongoing conversations in similar ways to conference organizers or journal editors: service, teaching and research brought together in a neat little packet of zeros and ones distributed via RSS that fulfils some of the needs of the classroom, the research lab and the university – but that, by virtue of its boundary-crossing nature, remains so often uncountable. Which brings us to:

Make Podcasting Citable

There are a variety of reasons why scholars want their podcasts to be citable. For example, Mack Hagood, sound studies scholar and producer of the podcast *Phantom Power*, told Dario Llinares on *The Podcast Studies Podcast*:

> I'm in a place that I think maybe a lot of folks might be where I am trying to figure out what [producing a scholarly podcast] counts as on my CV. And hey, to be frank, it's also reaching way more people than any academic article I will ever write. And so, but what does that really mean? (Hagood in Beckstead and Llinares 2021)

There, we've just cited a podcast (as we have many times throughout this book). It's easy: every style guide has an entry for how to do it. But when we say 'make podcasting citable', we're really talking about assigning equal value to a citation of a scholarly podcast as we do to book or journal citations. We're also talking about increasing the visibility and discoverability of scholarly podcasts, as well as creating infrastructure to index and archive podcasts even after their active production is finished. We want podcasts to 'count' in the sense of recognizing their significance and value to scholarship and knowledge creation – but we want them to count without necessarily being counted.

Let's start with how we make podcasts count without counting them. 'Count' is, of course, operating in two registers here: determining the quantifiable value of something (giving it a number) and recognizing the significance or value of something. The conflation of these understandings of counting in academia – if something matters then it should be quantifiable, or if it *counts* we should be able to *count* it – is part of the problem. The creators of the

HuMetricsSSH project have proposed a set of core values: Equity, Openness, Collegiality, Quality, Community ('HuMetricsHSS: Our Values Framework' n.d.). This interest in openness and community complicates the question of counting, whether it's the question of how, or even whether, publicly engaged scholarship is counted or, perhaps more relevantly here, the question of how we measure the impact of a medium with its own logics of quantifiability.

The problem is that podcasts are fairly easy to count, at least in the sense of assigning them a quantifiable number. Download numbers are widely tracked, as they determine a show's ranking on charts and its ability to secure valuable advertising spots. Ad revenue for podcasts is generally determined based on CPM (cost per mille, or per thousand downloads) and general industry wisdom holds that a show doesn't start becoming marketable to advertisers until it reaches an average of 20,000 downloads per episode. Most scholars, as you might imagine, do not hit anywhere near those numbers. They are often making niche podcasts and do not expect their podcasts to generate income. Sometimes they podcast as part of a project, and for those with full-time permanent contracts, they produce podcasts as part of their regular scholarly activities. But in both instances, at some point they need to decide whether, and where, the podcast might appear on their CV. Vincent Racaniello, co-host of the podcast *This Week in Virology* (TWIV) and other podcasts, told Ian:

> I know some people who have been on TWIV have put it on their CV and I think that's quite interesting. And they even say, you know, I've been on TWIV five times as a way of saying, like, this is a badge. And I think that's good because it's an honour because not everyone is on . . . I think now they're recognizing the value of it. But we're still not at the point where it has any formal academic use because it's not peer reviewed.

What Racaniello suggests is that you might try your darnedest to count a podcast, but you can do all the counting in the world and it won't matter unless your institution recognizes it.

Academics invested in public and community-engaged scholarship (including, of course, podcasting) face a double bind. On the one hand, public and accessible scholarship satisfies the corporate logics of the modern university, demonstrating impact and value in ways that more conventional scholarly work cannot; at the end of the day, digital media like podcasts are just going to have more downloads than a journal article. On the other hand, in response to the recognition that public scholarship can easily become complicit with the neoliberal agenda of modern university governance, some scholars have doubled down on the value of traditional scholarly work, paywalled journals and projects that reject usefulness. We need to refuse the conflation of scholarly value with popularity; using the metrics of clicks or views or likes or social media shares has been the bane of much journalism and it will do the same to academic work.

Another way scholars have responded to the challenge of 'counting' their podcasts is to emphasize the amount of work that goes into a podcast. Different types of podcasts require different amounts of labour, including the often hidden labour of upskilling. Two academics turning on a recorder for a chat and uploading their wisdom unedited into the ether is a far stretch from a carefully crafted audio documentary series, which might take hundreds of hours to produce – labour that might be audible only to other radio and storytelling experts who have the skill to distinguish well-crafted audio from amateur work. We know that neither number of downloads nor hours of labour should simplistically determine the value of our work as scholars – hence our proposal of different, more appreciative models of peer review in Chapter 3 – but the urge many podcasters feel to somehow articulate the value of their work within the metric-fixated environment of the modern university is understandable.

Indeed, the desire to count podcasts at all betrays an ongoing attachment to the very concept of countability. Johnathan Bentley Singer writes about the exciting potential of 'podcasting as social scholarship', but goes on to argue that standards for evaluating podcasts need to be developed as well as production guidelines for faculty (2019). The need to standardize the evaluation and production of podcasts seems to be the next immediate thought for many when they think about the 'potential' of podcasting in academia. We're sure you've figured out by now that we really don't want to go down that road. Production guidelines for faculty? Standardized evaluation? No thanks.[13]

---

[13]But 'Yes, please!' to *support* for faculty in terms of resources such as technical infrastructure and guidance on how to use it, time, money . . .

Siobhan McMenemy, Senior Editor at Wilfrid Laurier University Press, discovered that we're not alone in our preference to avoid such regulation when she developed the first sets of peer-review questions for *Secret Feminist Agenda*. She incorporated some questions about what forms of existing scholarship the podcast might be comparable to:

If you were to assess the potential of a peer-reviewed podcast series to contribute new scholarship to a particular field, to which scholarly form would a podcast series be comparable: a monograph, an edited collection, a special issue of a journal article, a journal article, none of these? Why?

The response from the peer reviewers was clear: they were not interested in counting the work. As reviewer Cheryl E. Ball wrote: 'Ugh. I knew this question was coming. I hate it so much, and yet this is always the question people want to know because quantifiability is Sooooooo Stronnnnngg in academia (and so useless in the humanities)' (Ball 2018). Ball was ultimately less interested in how to *count* the podcast than in how to recognize that it was *done*, a structural challenge to an ongoing series. Reviewer Amanda L. French similarly struggled to quantify the work of an ongoing series: '[T]he serial form of the podcast makes it substantially different from those examples. If anything, maybe running this podcast series is comparable to founding and editing a scholarly journal or . . . founding and running a scholarly speaker series or conference or institute.' The sentiment across the reviews was clear: trying to count the podcast in any conventional way was missing the point.

A recurring question we encounter when discussing the possibility of using peer review to help legitimize podcasting as a form of scholarly activity is whether incorporating podcasting into the systems of university evaluation and quantification will ruin the radical potential of the medium. Our answer? *Maybe. Probably.* The university as an institution is extremely good at appropriating and interpellating activities and knowledges that appear to be resistant to its structures. Fred Moten and Stefano Harney (2004) write as much about the challenges of critiquing from within the institution, since the labour of critiquing the institution *is the labour of the institution*. We can see the same mechanisms at work in decolonization or anti-racism initiatives, what some critics have called the 'EDI industrial complex', in which the thinking and organizing of BIPOC students and scholars is interpellated by the university as a way of defanging that critique, rendering it institutional and thus a marker of the institution's own benevolence. No wonder, then, that some academics who turned to podcasting as a way of escaping the stifling, normalizing force of academia are deeply resistant to the idea of incorporating their podcasts right back into those systems. (In fact, Cheryl Ball noted what she considers such an interpellative force in her peer review of Season 3 of *Secret Feminist Agenda,* which she identified as having become normalized and even institutionalized in comparison to the unruly DIY feel of the first season.)

Scholarly podcasting, and the experimental peer review approaches that we have outlined, are, like ungrading, an opportunity to pry open the traditional structures of academia and ask: what if we did things differently? What else is possible if we don't take for granted that 'real' scholarship is written, anonymously reviewed, and sanded down until it looks like all other scholarship? What excites us about scholarly podcasting is its potential to imagine otherwise, to open up spaces for forms of resistance big and small. But lest we forget, the goal here is not to throw everything out or, as Hannah often puts it, *burn it all down.*[14] Let's go beyond sighing at our colleagues who proudly boast that their school is number 1 in the country for X, Y or Z and call them in, speak to them about how rankings are a game that devalues their work. Perhaps point them to the 2021 *UNESCO Recommendation on Open Science*, which calls for not only international collaboration on the development of open access publishing policies, but also a larger transformation of how we create, assess and disseminate research, including a shift away from conventional measures of research impact (23) and the promotion of open peer-review processes that include broader non-academic publics in the assessment of research and its impacts (30).

Hopefully at this point you'll believe us when we say we want podcasts to be citable *not* because we want to boost our citation count or h-index, but because we want podcasts to be incorporated into the rich and ongoing conversation that is knowledge creation at its best. One of the first steps towards making podcasting citable

---

[14]Although on some days, the idea of burning it all down is *quite* appealing.

is to increase the discoverability of podcasts for academics. Whether it's our library catalogues, disciplinary databases or Google Scholar, scholarship becomes discoverable via its inclusion in research databases, and that inclusion depends on scholarship being indexed (literally, brought together in a searchable list, like the index at the back of this book, except it's an enormous list of journals and books). Indexing has been central to the growth of open access publishing, helping to overcome old-fashioned biases towards paywalled and print-first journals by putting online journals on an equal playing field. Not too long ago, professional associations like the MLA were advising their members to take online journals as seriously as print ones (an intervention that now seems absurdly obvious), and indexing can similarly help scholarly podcasts to be accepted more generally into the world of scholarly publishing.

At the moment, it's really hard to know what's contained in different podcasts, and that can deter researchers and scholars from using them in our work. Keywords, show descriptions and episode notes give some idea of what's in an audio file, and web crawlers can easily index these texts so they can be surfaced by search engines. But audio isn't so easily indexed – at least not yet. And let's face it, the prospect of listening through minutes or hours of sound to find that particular point you want to cite, while potentially pleasurable, can be dauntingly time-consuming. So text-based transcripts are essential for making academic podcasts accessible to the widest range of users for the widest range of purposes, not least of which is to enable d/Deaf persons to participate in listening. However, this recursiveness – that is, that we must ultimately turn a podcast *back* into text – presents what Dario Llinares characterizes as 'a really interesting problem and a paradox, because that would suggest that podcasting still requires a root within a textual framework that an academic can go back to' (Fox and Llinares 2018, 36:53). At the time of writing, some podcast platforms have initiated auto-transcription of podcast audio in order to index it, but these transcriptions are not necessarily available to the public nor are they available across all podcasting platforms. Without text-based transcription, podcast audio is a bit of a black box. What we can look forward to, we hope, is the ability for keyword searches to surface specific clips of audio from within podcasts.

Furthermore, podcasts, like all forms of digital media, are vulnerable to disappearing. Jeremy Morris, founder of the podcast archiving project PodcastRE (short for Podcast Research), points out that podcast feeds may end abruptly or cease to be maintained, and often aren't saved or archived properly (n.d.). So ensuring that podcasts and podcasting are robust means of scholarly production and peer review will require an equally robust means of archiving and indexing them. Morris has begun this work; PodcastRE seeks to preserve podcasts and present an interface for researching them, because:

> [w]hat today's podcasters are producing will have value in the future, not just for its content, but for what it tells us about audio's longer history, about who has the right to communicate and by what means. We may be in a 'Golden Age' of podcasts but if we're not making efforts to preserve and analyze these resources now, we'll find ourselves in the same dilemma many radio, film or television historians now find themselves: writing, researching and thinking about a past they can't fully see or hear. (Morris n.d.)

The most robust means of archiving podcasts entails saving copies of the audio files themselves to a well-maintained server, which may not be possible for all podcasters because audio files are big and podcasts have lots of episodes and also who has a server lying around? You could just save the RSS files which point to the location of those audio files on a vast and dispersed network of servers, but if the files are removed from those servers – say, the podcaster decides to no longer pay the ongoing fees to host audio from their defunct podcast – the archived RSS feed becomes useless. While IT infrastructure and expertise are imperative here, they are not enough to ensure the ongoing viability of podcast scholarship. Lori recalls having done some creative pedagogy with podcasts as far back as 2003 (Beckstead 2005), but they've unfortunately been wiped from the face of history by random server purges done by IT personnel who didn't have a sense of the potential academic importance of such files. Similarly, it can be a challenge to convince IT departments not to place limits on file sizes, or to unexpectedly change domain names, or to otherwise create, unconsciously or not, a challenging milieu in which to experiment with podcasting.

This is where universities, and especially university libraries, can step in. Academic librarians have the skills, knowledge and (sometimes) the resources needed to house digital collections. This means that podcasting scholars and librarians need to work together. Back before the university Ian worked at was attacked by an authoritarian regime and, in response, its leadership decided to move it to a different country (Cantat and Dönmez 2021), he co-founded a podcast library: podcasts.ceu.edu. One of the motivations was to create a library where podcasts were categorized by type of podcast, creators, guests, places, chronological periods, topics, disciplines and unit. Researchers could subscribe to any of the items mentioned in the category by email or RSS feed (e.g., they could subscribe to all the podcasts about Glossop[15] or Gingers[16]). Podcasters were encouraged to add chapter markers and full transcripts. Another example comes from the Amplify Podcast Network, which has partnered with the Digital Humanities Innovation Lab at Simon Fraser University. They're developing a podcast preservation tool that will safeguard podcasts and their accompanying metadata (including Apple Podcast subject tags, transcripts, show notes, cover art, etc.) by allowing them to be deposited into institutional or disciplinary repositories. Amplify, as of the writing of this book, has yet to solve the problem of indexing, though partnering with the Public Knowledge Project's Open Journals System (OJS), with their rigorous indexing tools, may be one way forward. We want podcasts to pop up on Google Scholar when we do our searches; we want students to find them in library catalogues. This is not an insurmountable barrier, and, indeed, as multimedia scholarship grows in popularity and legitimacy, it's a problem we'll need to collectively solve sooner rather than later.

We know it's not impossible to index multimedia scholarship because, increasingly, journals are accepting multimedia submissions. Some journals – *BC Studies*, *The Journal of Interactive Technology and Pedagogy*, *Modernism/modernity* (via their Print Plus platform) and *electronic book review*, to name just a few – have begun to explicitly accept podcast episodes, soundworks and other kinds of digital media for submission. These journals, while

---

[15]A legendary town in a magical area of England, where very tall redheads are produced.
[16]Ian is a very tall redhead.

generally focused on publishing one-off episodes, demonstrate that all of the infrastructure for evaluating, publishing and indexing scholarly podcasts exists. What is needed is a shift in our collective understanding of what constitutes scholarly production – a shift this book is attempting to foment.

It's not enough to index scholarly podcasts, though. As Jonathan Sterne explains, we don't need just technical and institutional infrastructures to help us tag, index and preserve scholarly podcasts; we also need 'cultural infrastructures where people develop and sustain more advanced techniques of listening to scholarship, as well as to the world, and where we better support one another's intellectual forays into sound' (Sterne et al. 2018, 282). We need to develop methods for engaging with podcasts that are as rigorous as how we engage with textual scholarship, but that are also appropriate to the medium. *BC Studies*, for example, worked with Siobhan McMenemy at Wilfrid Laurier University Press to create specific review criteria for podcasts, demonstrating that podcasts can be evaluated as rigorously as written scholarship. They ask reviewers to think not only of the content of submitted podcasts, but also of the use of sound:

> How does the podcaster make use of the medium and genre? Have they done so effectively? Does the audio format contribute to the scholarship? Does the podcast offer something that text alone cannot? How does this podcast demonstrate the potential of the medium for scholarly dissemination? Does the author incorporate background noises, sounds, music, and prominent sounds? ('Peer Review: Scholarly Podcast Submissions')

If our peer-review standards for podcasts are going to attend to their use of the audio format, and their ability to do something that text-based scholarship alone cannot do, then our *use* of this scholarship needs to do the same. When we talk about making podcasts citable, we don't simply mean the mechanics of how to properly write out the citation in whatever format, but, rather, engaging with the scholarly ideas in podcasts in a way that doesn't either frame them as an object of study or reduce them to a transcript of words spoken. How do you properly cite, for example, part of a conversation that will need a lot of contextualization, or a scholarly podcast in which sound plays a significant role in the argument?

Technologically speaking, there's nothing stopping us from embedding a sound clip in an article, for example, or from making our own sound-based scholarship that cites the work of others via clips, a sound-specific model of citation. What's harder to solve is the incorporation of different genres of knowledge production into existing citation norms. For instance, if during a conversation someone coins a phrase in conversation, like 'the scholarly publishing machine', whom should the idea be attributed to? The person who said it? The host/producer of the podcast who set up the conversation?[17] All of those involved? Should a concept first coined in conversation be given the same weight as one that is embedded in argumentation, existing literature and disciplinary contexts? These are all good questions, and they do not apply only to scholarly podcasting. There are short texts with throwaway phrases that have thousands of citations, 'ghost articles' that are cited but never existed and citations for citation's sake (among many other issues). The problem here is not only finding fair ways to reference other scholars' work, but, rather, slowing down and rethinking how and why we cite to make it a more thoughtful and deliberate practice.

While we can imagine some concrete tools that would help scholarly podcasters, more important is a collective willingness to take podcasting seriously as a form of knowledge production, and to engage it on its own terms, for all of its rich sonic possibilities, rather than constantly attempting to make it fit into boxes created for text.

Make Scholarship Collaborative

We hate to do this *again*, but let's start with what we don't mean: collaboration is not the same as playing nicely with others, nor is collaboration synonymous with collegiality. 'Collegiality' is a complex term in academia, both a vital principle of how universities (ought to) work and yet another gatekeeping mechanism. Collegial governance is one of the core principles of universities as an institution, and at the heart of the preservation of academic freedom:

---

[17]Most style guides indicate that the name(s) of the host/producer should be used, making correct attribution rather fraught.

we are not managed by government or industry, but, rather, make our own decisions based on academic standards (Dea 2021). It's a pretty good sign of how important this value is that conservative governments are constantly seeking to undermine it, along with the collective bargaining power of academics. But the collegiality in collegial governance is not about *being* collegial:

> Collegial governance is so named because it is governance by the *collegium* of scholars. The first misconception is that collegial governance means polite or agreeable governance. We often refer to individual colleagues who are good-natured and pleasant as 'collegial.' Hence, some people misunderstand collegial governance likewise to connote governance characterized by 'good manners' and cooperativeness. (Dea 2021)

Expectations of collegiality in terms of 'good manners', like language around institutional 'culture' and 'fit', are a gatekeeping method that effectively delimits who is considered to be the right kind of academic (Dawsone et al. 2022). But collegiality in the sense of our collective membership in the *collegium* of scholars reminds us that collectivity and collaboration are at the heart of all that we do, at the heart of what makes a college a college, or a university a university.[18] Being pitted against each other by the prestige- and scarcity-based models of modern academia can lead us to forget that the whole *point* is collaboration, community and collectives. We make better knowledge when we make it together.

Collaboration can and should move in lots of different ways, the way sound does when it's emitted from a source – vibrating, reflecting, being absorbed. It should move sideways, into disciplines scholars didn't imagine pursuing; it should moves outwards, valuing knowledge originating in a wide range of contexts; it should move backwards and sideways at once, finding work that falls outside disciplinary canons; it should move forward as it opens itself up to new possibilities in a scholarly world characterized not by scarcity, but by endless generosity. Let's break those down a bit.

---

[18]College means 'body of colleagues' while 'university' suggests community and cooperation. Go read the OED entries on both these words, they're fascinating.

Collaborating sideways means trying out what it means to talk through ideas with scholars who think about the world in quite different ways than you do, but who often think about many of the same things. This could be simply having a conversation on a research topic you're both thinking about, but it could be more than this: it might mean committing to interrogating one another's research over a prolonged period of time in a way that pushes you both to think about something new. It might mean that if, say, you were a historian of ancient Chinese cities, and you met an anthropologist of contemporary urban China, you might commit to making a podcast in which you explore different aspects of urbanism by combining your different, yet complementary, disciplinary foci. As Jason von Meding, co-host of *Disasters: Deconstructed* told Ian:

> [It's] something that we believe strengthens science, you know, that kind of engagement with other ways of working, other methodologies, other theories. And it really makes you start to ask new questions and develop new processes. For me, the podcast is also like a weekly practice, which helps me to improve my own thinking. I think it's important to consider what this actually does when you're engaging with new people all the time, maybe challenging some of your own assumptions about what they do and asking new questions about the way you do things. So, I find that's really healthy in itself as a personal practice.

It also means stepping outside the micro fields in which scholars have become specialists to find out, understand, interrogate and be amazed by the work others close by are doing. As Art Woods, co-host of *Big Biology* explains:

> Going to conferences and not even understanding what the person, your intellectual next door neighbour is doing, that's what's been so fun about [podcasting], is it just kind of blows the doors off of that. And, you know, I like my own little micro field. I'm happy with it. I think the questions in the field are interesting, but I'm kind of tired of writing for and talking to an audience that's so small. And so this is a chance to just go way, way bigger.
>
> I think the thing, at the beginning, that took a lot of getting used to is feeling way out of your comfort zone, because there

you are talking to people about stuff that you really don't have any idea about. And you're trying to draw them out into a conversation that's interesting for them . . . it's been super fun to learn a bunch of biology that's way far away from what I normally do.

Collaborating outwards means embracing the public-facing affordances of scholarly podcasting to pull in different types of knowledge as well as people to discuss that knowledge, whom the scholars who uphold the status quo of academia tend to exclude. We think this is important for all the reasons people might expect us to say: that non-scholarly knowledge is also valuable, that academia is controlled by classist ideologues who exclude working-class, non-white, non-western/northern and feminist knowledge as inferior, that we need to get ourselves out of the sad shitshow that passes for theoretical innovation in a lot of our disciplines by stepping not only into other parts of academia, but outside it completely. But, we think it's important for another key reason: so that academia doesn't swallow podcasting. A lot of really nice, well-meaning people we know tell us, 'we're scared that academic podcasting, this cool, wonderful, free thing we've been doing, will be co-opted by the relentless machine of academia.' And, yes, this is a real concern, but only if academic podcasting becomes a dull reflection of scholarly publishing as it is today. And one of the key ways to avoid this outcome is for scholars who podcast to think beyond looking to only other scholars to talk about scholarship.

Collaborating backwards and sideways means challenging the current scholarly convention that, when writing a research article, 'the canon' is given its due reverence. It's kind of wonderful that there is not really the space for this in a podcast. It would certainly sound strange if one were to do a lit review in the middle of audio scholarship. What this opens up space for, we hope, is a feminist politics of citation[19] (Ahmed 2013) in which we acknowledge and

---

[19]Ahmed writes, 'Citation is feminist memory. Citation is how we acknowledge our debt to those who came before; those who helped us find our way when the way was obscured because we deviated from the paths we were told to follow. . . . Citations can be feminist bricks: they are the materials through which, from which, we create our dwellings' (2017, 15–16). A feminist politics of citation is important because 'We cannot conflate the history of ideas with white men, though if doing one leads to the

establish the feminist genealogies of our disciplinary knowledge with a view to creating more just forms of knowledge by looking beyond those same old voices to explore other histories we might trace and other voices we might draw in.

Collaborating forwards means not knowing where you're going when you start. It means embracing the unpredictability of collaboration, conversation and doing things differently. The fixation on metrics in contemporary academia discourages experimentation and failure because we don't want to waste our time doing anything that won't 'count'. This scarcity-based thinking makes us less adventurous, less bold, more fearful and, ultimately, conservative in terms of how we think. For instance, as Hannah Fitzpatrick from *State of the Theory* told Ian:

> [Podcasting]'s an avenue for me to practise ideas, to think things through, to get feedback. It's also an avenue for me to explore stuff that I wouldn't necessarily have time to write in a paper. So we can talk about live action Disney movies, for example, because I have really strong feelings about that, but I don't have to write about it because I'm not a scholar of animation and Disney!

Forms of exploitation can also be framed as 'collaboration' within hyper-individualized reward systems, such as those that govern grants in Europe and elsewhere. Principal Investigators (PIs, who usually have permanent contracts) win prestigious grants that allow them to hire PhD students and post-doctoral researchers to work on their projects. Even if the PI is extremely conscious of power dynamics and allows their students and postdocs as much opportunity as possible to flourish, the prestige of the 'big grant' is, nevertheless, accrued by the PI, which in turn will allow them to apply for further grants, while the PhD students and postdocs often do the majority of the work (Rajaram 2021). Sometimes the exploitation is more obvious, with PI's refusing to allow postdocs to work on anything other than work that falls strictly within 'their' project. Once again, we see the system of contemporary academia act as a limiter of scholarly creation. But in getting rid of exclusivity

---

other then we are being taught where ideas are assumed to originate. Seminal: how ideas are assumed to originate from male bodies' (2017, 16).

and daft measurements, we hope that this issue is ameliorated as much as possible.

* * *

So if you didn't have time to read that whole manifesto – and we know it's long; our fingers are shrivelling up – how about this:

We believe that scholarship can be fun. That fun and rigour are not opposed. That there is too much publishing and not enough conversation. That metrics will be the death of us. That playing the game of metrics is only hastening the demise of the university as we know it. That another way is possible, a way rooted in care, collaboration and community. That scholars need to take back how we define success, productivity, value and prestige. That the scarcity logics of capitalism have no place in the world of knowledge creation. That knowledge should be open, collaborative and accountable. That we can engage with one another's work appreciatively, not cruelly. That 'this is the way it's always been done' is no excuse to keep doing it that way. That the crisis of false news and conservative suspicion of expertise will not be addressed by doubling down on jargon and gatekeeping. That universities should serve the public. That scholarship should be public. That being public does not undermine or devalue scholarly work. That transparency and vulnerability engender trust. That scholarly knowledge should be conversational and pedagogical. That podcasting can be a form of scholarship. That videos and zines and music and graphic novels and tweet threads and Instagram selfies and group chats can all be forms of scholarship. That the expansion of forms will not dilute scholarship but, rather, set it free. And that within that freedom there is a possibility of saving knowledge creation from the steady march of the scholarly publishing machine!

The dirty bathwater has been thrown out (measurements, publishing norms, exclusivity), the babies have been saved (conversation, teaching, freedom), and the bath is now overflowing with our sog-free manifesto: a call for pedagogical scholarship, citable podcasts and collaboration. Before we argue about who is going to mop up, let's get out of this chapter (and out of this extended metaphor).[20]

---

[20]Yes, let's. My lips are turning blue. – Lori

Conclusion

Podcasting as a Means to Revitalize Knowledge Creation

A reminder of where we've been. In Chapter 1 we offered a brief history of peer review, highlighting how it's been used as a form of discipline, and also the ways in which it is currently unsound (from speed to meanness and more). We argued that scholarly podcasting is a form of podcasting that is potentially open to peer review, which means scholarly podcasts create new, accountable knowledge that can be interrogated, cited and revised in response to comments and critiques.

In Chapter 2 we moved on to interrogating the affordances of podcasting in general, and scholarly podcasting more specifically, arguing that it is a public and participatory sonic action built on the pillars of voice, conversation and digital publishing. Within each of these pillars are exciting possibilities for scholarship as well as potential pitfalls. Voice, for example, is a powerful medium for communication: it is intimate, relationship-building, embodied and affective. But it also can't be anonymized, and is plagued by ideological assumptions about voice rooted in conservative notions of authority and expertise. The conversational dimension of podcasting makes the process of knowledge creation more accessible, modelling how we arrive at understandings of complex topics discursively, but sound-based scholarship also lacks the precision of the written. And digital publishing opens out the affordances of seriality and interactivity while also potentially embedding podcasting in capitalist platforms and logics. At the intersection of these three pillars we identified other exciting affordances, from the expansion of the publics for scholarship to the rhythmic potential of creating scholarship that is ongoing rather than one-and-done. We concluded that the complexity of podcasting as a medium demands a similarly nuanced approach to peer review, one that is attentive to what makes podcasting distinctive and exciting.

With this in mind, Chapter 3 turned to the question of how sound might intervene into our peer review processes to shift how we go about it. The ideal model of peer review for podcasting, we argued, is one rooted in awareness of who the scholar is and how they're working with the medium, awareness that has the potential to morph into appreciation if done well. We suggested several potential approaches to appreciative review, and, in order to show that appreciation in action, we looked at a variety of examples of innovative peer review in and around sound-based scholarship, before outlining an approach to peer review rooted in creativity, community and care. Being creative means not only taking an interest in research creation, but also attending to scholarship that is open, generative, process-based and invested in learning through doing, by embracing those qualities in the very act of review. Being communal means reviewing rooted in trust, accountability and openness to peers beyond the university. And embracing care means valuing vulnerability, risk and openness to failure. The vulnerability of care, alongside the responsiveness built into creativity and the expansion of peer inherent in communal orientations, allows us to re-envision how scholarship is made and whom it is for.

Our concluding chapter moved beyond the practicalities of *how* we might peer-review podcasts into a more radical vision of how embracing podcasting as a medium, and communal, creative and care-based reviewing as a process, might help us to envision a version of academia that is more open, inclusive and community-engaged and less rigid and attached to metrics. We argued for a vision of the future university that throws out daft measurements, antiquated scholarly publishing norms and an image of rigour based in exclusivity, while holding onto the values of conversation, teaching and freedom. We concluded by calling for an approach to scholarship that is rooted in pedagogy, is deeply collaborative and supports making podcasts citable.

The vision of the university we offer might seem like a pipe dream, but this moment – when scholarly podcasting has begun to be taken seriously but hasn't yet been fully integrated into the logics of the modern university – is the perfect one in which to intervene and seize upon the radical potential of doing our scholarship differently.

Interlude

Can Podcasting Transform Academia?

Okay, so podcasting *might* be able to disrupt the academic status quo. Because it has not yet been fully incorporated into the existing logics of scholarly communication, it has the potential to evade the neoliberal metrics and box-ticking exercises that increasingly pervade every dimension of academic work. Is there a way to hold onto this subversive potential while also credentialing scholarly podcasting so that it will 'count'? Is there a way to make sure that it doesn't count more for those who are already disproportionately advantaged within existing academic structures – that podcasting doesn't become its own form of privilege for those whose voices are already perceived as authoritative, or for those with tenure (where it still exists) or enough seniority that they don't need to worry about taking risks? It's a tricky proposition, but one that we don't want to say 'no' to outright. So, instead, we offer a *maybe* alongside a potential way forward, rooted in practices of appreciative listening and reviewing that are caring, creative and communal. At the end of the day, anything we can do to make academia a more inclusive

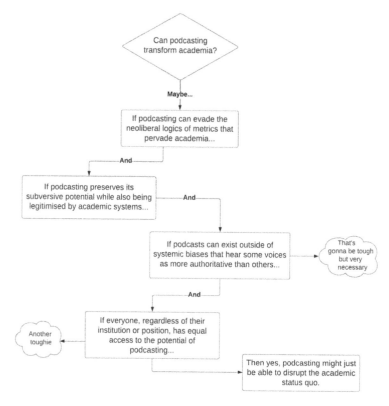

FIGURE 7 *Can podcasting transform academia?*

and collaborative place that values a greater diversity of voices is worth trying.

A Lift in Brazil (Alternate Reality Break No. 4)

Dr Gigi Grayson was running late for her panel. The conference was one of those godforsaken ones that sprawled across multiple hotels and multiple floors, leaving you racing from room to room with barely a moment to actually chat with colleagues – if you could find anyone you knew in the first place. She found herself longing for the cosy intimacy of a podcast conversation, where she could actually sit down with someone and dig into a topic. Plus, once it was released, she could be confident that more than five people would listen, which is more than she could say about most of the panels at this conference.

She dashed into the lift, just making it through as the doors closed. The person already in there had a name tag that read 'Dr Marina Makandar, University of North Northington'. Gigi had never heard of her, but that wasn't surprising considering how many subfields of history were represented at this conference. It was a shame most people didn't bother to attend panels outside their narrow specialties. She was just opening her conference programme to double-check that she had the room number right (she was *definitely* going to be late) when the lights in the lift flickered and then went out, the car slowly grinding to a halt.

Forty-seven minutes later, when the maintenance crew pried the lift doors open, Gigi and Marina were in the middle of an excited conversation about the unexpected intersections of their research areas.

'It's a shame we didn't record this conversation,' Gigi commented; 'It's probably the most interesting one I'm going to have this week.'

'Well if you're free next Tuesday afternoon,' Marina replied, 'I've been looking all year for a butterfly expert to come on my podcast, *Podonian Avatars!*'[1]

And both women laughed as they raced for the bathroom.

Podcast or Perish

Scholarly podcasting is already transforming how peer review can be done, and we need much, much more transformation and experimentation to revitalize scholarship and knowledge creation for the 21st century.

The sites of scholarly knowledge creation have become both ossified and inhumane, part of the larger systemization of academia

---

[1] As far as we know, there's no connection between the Pannonian Avars and butterflies. We made it up. This is an alternate reality, remember?

that seeks to make our work legible to neoliberal governments and corporate logics of productivity. The reality, however, is that knowledge creation is happening in a thousand rich, dialogic and informal ways, within and beyond the walls of academic institutions. The goal of peer-reviewing podcasts is not to bring podcasting into those dehumanizing systems, but to let scholarly podcasting (as a public and participatory sonic action) disrupt the status quo by opening up gaps within and between these static structures. Scholarly podcasting, like an unexpected lift conversation at a 5000-person conference, offers a liminal space where we might not necessarily be able to throw out all the constraining conventions we've been railing against in this book, but we may be able to set them aside for a moment and do something different.

And so we must leave you here, with this slim volume that took us longer than we expected to write, because we were so determined to make it match, in spirit and execution, the energies that excite us about scholarly podcasting. We spent hours in conversation, articulating to one another the sources of our knowledge and the tacit disciplinary conventions that weren't always translating from anthropology to sound studies to publishing studies. We invited one another into our lives in large ways and small, sharing childcare crises and family deaths, cat hijinx and health scares. As much as we could across three time zones and two continents, we tried to bring our whole selves into the writing process, making space for embodied and contextual knowledges, for conversations we'd had on Zoom from the back of taxis or thoughts that emerged while visiting an island populated by giraffes. We had multiple false starts, long rambling passages that went nowhere, hare-brained schemes that never ended up yielding fruit (to mix a metaphor). And along the way, we learned to *appreciate* one another, to understand where we were each coming from and how our differing perspectives might add up to something more than the sum of their parts. There's an old saying that co-authorship is twice the work for half the credit, but by now it should be clear that neither work nor credit is how we want to think about making knowledge. The *real* knowledge, you might say, is in the conversations we had along the way.

Afterword

Putting Our Money Where Our Mouths Are, or How We Had a Book About Peer Review Peer-Reviewed

This book went through a few different types of peer review. The authors decided to put our money where our mouths are and make our peer review open, collaborative, conversational, community accountable and public. In addition to the publisher's usual peer-review procedure (i.e., we received two written reviews of the draft book, one from series editor Martin Spinelli and one from an anonymous reviewer), we thought we'd open up reviews to a wider range of peers, using a variety of approaches.

For Chapter 1, in which we argued that scholarly publishing and peer review need to be reconsidered and revised, and that scholarly podcasting could afford new avenues for knowledge creation, we invited peers to comment on a publicly available draft of the chapter. (This is something Ian had already tried in his previous book [Cook 2023], and he liked it a lot!) We sent email invitations to various podcast and media studies-related listservs asking folks if they would kindly have a look at our draft and provide some comments. We provided a link to the chapter in the form of a Google Doc and asked reviewers to feel free to either comment anonymously or log into their Google account and make their identity known. Reviewers were encouraged to read and respond to each other's comments, making this review process an example of **conversational** review. Eighteen reviewers commented using their names and there were also comments left anonymously. Although it's impossible for us to tell whether the anonymous comments were left by the same person or by several anonymous commenters, we suspect it's likely the latter. In all there were a total of 151 comments and suggestions added to the document – and that was just for one chapter! Additionally, four reviewers wrote more general feedback; one appended several paragraphs of feedback to the end of the draft and three others (two anonymously and one using their name and institutional affiliation) answered the questions and prompts we provided via a survey.

We then sat with the comments for a while and considered what to do with them all. It was a little overwhelming to get so much feedback, from people we know professionally, from strangers with names and from anonymous people as well. Ian suggested it might be a system open to abuse as Hannah or Lori could log on as an anonymous user and leave comments to argue for something that Ian wanted taken out.[1] We then had conversations about what we thought were the big takeaways that called for substantial reworking and, after agreeing on our high-level revision priorities, went through the comments one by one, deciding which ones we would respond to and resolving points of contradiction. For instance, in Figure 8, commenters are candidly responding to our assertion in Chapter 1 that one of the reasons for peer review's delayed timelines is the depersonalization of anonymity; when it doesn't feel like the work we're reviewing was written by a real person, we feel less pressure to respond. In their responses, reviewers spoke to different experiences that we ultimately decided reinforced rather than undermined our point.

We're very happy to have gotten as much feedback on Chapter 1 as we did. The reviewers' thoughtful comments helped us sharpen our arguments, avoid the pitfall of setting up a false dichotomy between written and sound-based scholarship, and reorganize the chapter so our argument would be more obvious to the reader.

For Chapter 2, in which we theorized podcasting as three pillars – voice, conversation and digital publishing – built on a foundation of sound, we conducted a peer review by podcast. That is, we invited

---

[1]Hannah and Lori neither confirmed nor denied doing this.

FIGURE 8 *A conversation among peer reviewers in the comments.*

our series editor Martin Spinelli to have a conversation with Lori about the contents of the chapter.[2] As we mentioned earlier, Martin had already given us written feedback on the entire book, but speaking to him in person on a podcast provided an opportunity to explore some of that written feedback with more nuance. The episode begins with Lori giving a summary of the chapter – mainly for the potential listener's benefit (Martin was, of course, already familiar with the material). But as we have argued elsewhere in this book, presenting one's scholarly work on a podcast pushes the scholar to, among other things, simplify and summarize their own material as well as consider various potential listeners and what they might need in order to participate in this 'public and participatory sonic action'.

As is often the case with this approach to peer review (which we would classify as **public, conversational** and **media-adaptive**), we did not necessarily capture the syntactic and structural details one might

---

[2]You can hear that conversation here: https://oprpodcast.ca/2023/08/30/podcastor-perish/.

get to in a written review. However, we were able to talk through the strengths and weaknesses of the chapter, together and out loud, using the affordances of synchronous conversation to gain a much deeper understanding of the reviewer's intent and meaning. One of the primary bugaboos Martin had about the book overall was what he considered our overuse of transcripts of conversations. Just as we argue in this book that sound media have different affordances and limitations than print media, Martin suggested that using transcripts of sound-based media in a print book was a mistake, stating in his written review that he thought it was 'indulgent', 'lazy', 'unduly taxing' and even 'insulting' to the reader. Martin was right – we had transcripts of conversations in the draft that went on too long – but we admit the language of his written review raised our hackles. Speaking about it in person provided more context for this reaction: Martin doesn't like reading long quotations. In fact, Martin and Lori laughed while admitting that neither of them likes to read songs, poetry and, sometimes, even quotations that are inserted into a prose-based text. By the end of the conversation, Martin better understood our goal for including the transcripts and Lori better understood what needed to change. In response, we pared back the length and number of transcripts and added a note at the beginning of the manuscript telling readers to expect some transcribed conversations and explaining the theoretical underpinnings of our decision to include them (albeit in a reduced number).

During the conversation Martin responded to a question from Lori about how it felt to give feedback on a podcast:

> This is so much easier, and so much better and so much more fun. I mean, . . . I can look you in the eye, even though it's mediated by screen. And it's also . . . less taxing because . . . I don't have to worry about stringing my thoughts together perfectly. I don't have to worry about absolutely spot-on grammar. I can just kind of speak to you as a human being. And that's really good . . . . When you can hear the tone of my voice [and] inflection of my voice, and . . . we can have a kind of instantaneous dialogue and a back and forth and we can kick ideas around [it] feels . . . much more productive that way.

Because Chapter 3 focuses on case studies that model appreciate review, we chose a peer-review process that showed our appreciation to the creators of the case studies in question, following the principles of **community accountable** review. After gathering the contact information for all of the case study creators, we invited them to participate by reading the chapter, answering questions and optionally commenting on the chapter itself, which we shared via Google Docs. We invited twenty-seven authors, received positive responses from fifteen of them and, ultimately, received nine actual responses; we likely could have gotten a higher response rate if we hassled those six missing authors a little more, but given the richness of the responses we did receive we decided against it. In addition to answers to specific questions about the case studies and our arguments, we also received 128 comments or suggestions directly on the Google Doc itself.

As with the open review of the first chapter, we had a lot of feedback to work through – but because we had invited a select group of reviewers and requested specific feedback, that review was more focused and generally less contradictory, especially when it came to reviewers addressing their own projects that we had included as case studies. One of the key benefits to this approach was the inclusion of area experts who normally would not be invited to participate in a peer-review process – specifically editors, who have enormous experience in the actual implementation of peer-review practices – who flagged for us moments when we were being reductive or failing to understand nuances of the publishing process. Across the board, the Chapter 3 reviewers helped flesh out our case studies by highlighting details we might have missed from our outsider perspectives, whether that's the complexities of assessing public history projects or the way editors communicate with contributors at a particular journal.

When we asked them to reflect on this peer-review process, the case study creators expressed appreciation for being included – a valuable reminder of another affordance of community accountable review, which is the creation of community. In this case, we called into existence a community of scholars and editors engaged in nontraditional scholarly communication and chose to make ourselves accountable for how we engaged with and discussed their work. Offering the people you're writing about a chance to read what you've written and give feedback is, frankly, a bit intimidating, but it also invites incredible expertise and nuance while also reframing how we interact with our peers in terms of accountability rather than competition.

Chapter 4 is, at its heart, a declaration of our (utopian) views on how academia needs to change, and how new approaches to peer review via podcasting might enact that change. We chose to invite graduate students or recently graduated students from the field of podcast studies to peer-review this chapter because, as early career scholars, they are academic insiders whose fresh (possibly even not yet jaded) perspectives we wanted to hear. And we literally wanted to hear them: we invited them to record themselves 'thinking out loud' in reaction to the chapter, a sort of audio diary of their comments and reflections. We sent invitations to ten people and got four audio diaries in return.

Our experience of listening to their insightful feedback solidified our belief in the many ways that podcasting can produce appreciative peer review. The recordings were conversational (one student mentioned how it felt like she was talking to us even though she was just speaking to her recorder), embodied and contextual (we all fell in love with the gorgeous Australian birdsong that accompanied Dylan Bird's recordings), and for the most part felt very authentic (though, of course, there are power dynamics at play). It was feedback that we first listened to and only then auto-transcribed and read back. We included a lot of their thoughts directly into Chapter 4 as it felt as if they were in conversation with the text in a meaningful way.

In their reflections, these reviewers spoke to their emotional responses when reading and speaking about the chapter, whether it be letting off steam or worrying about the future out loud. Reflections on the medium were largely positive, but with caveats. Both the non-native English speakers spoke to their concerns about expressing themselves via audio. For instance, Freja Sørine Adler Berg told us:

> I think it was a hurdle for me that I'm not a natural English speaker. So I was afraid that I would forget key words . . . so I actually wrote a lot of words on the paper so I would not forget them. So in the end . . . it was not the stream of consciousness that I had wished it could be. But it was definitely much less time consuming than traditional written peer review. Because I only took these short, very fluffy notes and then I spoke from there. So it was fun, but if I was a natural English speaker, it would be more fluent I guess.

It's important to take such considerations into account and, while acknowledging non-native speaking bias also exists in written forms of scholarly communication, to be aware of the anxiety oral recording communication produces as well.

The reviewers of this chapter, possibly inspired by our own utopian bent, also reflected on this type of review and speaking and listening more broadly. For example, Dylan Bird said:

> One thing that excites me most about podcasting in the scholarly sector, is its role in the peer review process, which we're all participating in here. Having been through the peer review process, having had articles peer reviewed, it can be quite an isolating experience. And it's very easy when dealing just with text for meaning to get lost, or the precise sentiment behind a given suggestion for a change or statement about the quality or otherwise of an article to be lost in the textual exchange. I think the more that we can use human voice to share ideas, the more that we can have a more nuanced sense of where someone might be coming from, and perhaps pick up on hesitations or, or the force with which someone might be making a statement.

In a similar-ish vein Tzlil Sharon reflected on the need for listening to become a more central practice in academic work:

> I would argue that the precondition for making podcasting a legitimate scholarship is making listening a more central practice in our academic work. And I think this is something harder to convey. And I mean, it will take time until people learn how to listen. And until we have the criteria to know what this listening actually means and how we want people to listen to us.
>
> [The idea of conversation as being how scholarship is done] goes hand in hand with podcasting, because . . . one moment, it's here and the next it's gone. So you always have to be straining forward towards a possible meaning. And I like this position. I think podcasts and conversations situate us in the mode of listening and, like, waiting to respond. And that's what research is all about in a sense.

Conversing with, listening with and thinking with the reviewers of all the chapters has, we believe, made for a much stronger book.

It pushed us to define what we meant by 'scholarly podcasting', to radically restructure one chapter, and change the way we presented arguments in another. Editors often say that finding reviewers is one of their more difficult tasks. We asked reviewers to be part of our book in a way that we hope was intellectually meaningful, respectful and which valued their critical insights. We were overwhelmed by the response as more than thirty people volunteered their time to join us in conversation about what podcasting can do for peer review. Their generosity, we believe, is not only testament to the wonderful people that they surely are (we don't know most of them!) but also to what happens when you try to create the conditions for appreciative review: peer review can become engaging and rewarding for reviewee and reviewer alike.

Gratitude

The authors would like to thank the following Creative, Collaborative and Caring peer reviewers. We Appreciate you!

Freja Sørine Adler Berg
Anonymous (who contains multitudes)
Ebrahim Bagheri
Erin Kathleen Bahl
Richard Berry
Dylan Bird
Robert Cassanello
Sara Jo Cohen
Erin Conlin
Stacey Copeland
Cecile Farnum
Kim Fox
Christine Geraghty
Felix Girke
Jennifer Guiliano
Calvin Hillis
Dyfrig Jones
Berenike Jung
Emily Katharina

Gordon Katic
Anja Krieger
Megan Lyons
Jessica McDonald
Siobhan McHugh
Siobhan McMenemy
Alexandra Mogyoros
Ashika Prajnya Paramita
Tarja Rautiainen-Keskustalo
Tom Sayers
Karen Sebesta
Tzlil Sharon
Martin Spinelli (series editor)
Kylie Sturgess

WORKS CITED

AAUW (2020) 'Fast Facts: Women Working in Academia', *American Association of Academic Women*. Available at: https://www.aauw.org/resources/article/fast-facts-academia/ (Accessed 3 June 2023).

'About' (2016) *Somatic Podcast*, 21 April. Available at: https://somaticpodcast.com/about/ (Accessed 2 June 2022).

'About Reviews in Digital Humanities' (no date) *Reviews in Digital Humanities*. Available at https://reviewsindh.pubpub.org/about (Accessed 14 February 2022).

About this Network | H-Podcast | H-Net (no date) Available at: https://networks.h-net.org/ZZ-about-podcast-ZZ (Accessed 4 July 2022).

Abraham, N. (1995) *Rhythms: On the Work, Translation, and Psychoanalysis*. Stanford: Stanford University Press.

Ahmed, S. (2013) 'Making Feminist Points', *feministkilljoys*, 11 September. Available at: https://feministkilljoys.com/2013/09/11/making-feminist-points/ (Accessed 15 July 2022).

Ahmed, S. (2017) *Living a Feminist Life*. Durham: Duke University Press. Available at: http://ebookcentral.proquest.com/lib/ryerson/detail.action?docID=4769414 (Accessed 1 May 2023).

Alperin, J. P., Nieves, C. M., Schimanski, L. A., Fischman, G. E., Niles, M. T. and McKiernan, E. C. (2019) 'Meta-Research: How Significant are the Public Dimensions of Faculty Work in Review, Promotion and Tenure Documents?' *eLife*, 8, p. e42254. Available at: https://doi.org/10.7554/eLife.42254 (Accessed 8 June 2022).

Allegra Lab (2013) 'Academic Slow Food Manifesto', *Allegra Lab*, April. Available at: https://allegralaboratory.net/academic-slow-food-manifesto/ (Accessed 2 May 2023).

An Editor's Guide to the Peer Review Process | Taylor and Francis Group (no date) Available at: https://editorresources.taylorandfrancis.com/managing-peer-review-process/ (Accessed 24 April 2023).

Association of University Presses (no date) *Preamble: Why Peer Review is Important, Best Practices for Peer Review*. Available at: https://peerreview.up.hcommons.org/preamble/ (Accessed 14 February 2022).

Auer, P. (2009) 'On-line syntax: Thoughts on the temporality of spoken language', Language Sciences, 31(1), pp. 1–13. Available at: https://doi.org/10.1016/j.langsci.2007.10.004.

Austin, T. (2016) 'Interiority, Identity and the Limits of Knowledge in Documentary Film', *Screen*, 57(4), pp. 414–30. Available at: https://doi .org/10.1093/screen/hjw044 (Accessed 17 April 2022).

Australian Research Council (2015) *Introduction: Definition of Research, State of Australian University Research 2015–16*. Available at: https:// www.arc.gov.au/sites/default/files/minisite/static/4551/ERA2015/intro -3_define-research.html (Accessed 27 June 2022).

Australian Research Council (2017) 'ERA 2018 National Report', Australian Government. Available at: https://dataportal.arc.gov.au/ ERA/NationalReport/2018/ (Accessed 31 May 2022).

Bacevic, J. (2019) 'With or Without U? Assemblage Theory and (de) Territorialising the University', *Globalisation, Societies and Education*, 17(1), pp. 78–91. Available at: https://doi.org/10.1080/14767724.2018 .1498323 (Accessed 28 May 2023).

Baker, C. A. (2019) 'A QuantCrit Approach: Using Critical Race Theory as a Means to Evaluate if Rate My Professor Assessments Are Racially Biased', *Journal of Underrepresented & Minority Progress*, 3(1), pp. 1–22. Available at: https://doi.org/10.32674/jump.v3i1.1012 (Accessed 17 April 2022).

Baker, Z. (2019) 'Priced Out: The Renegotiation of Aspirations and Individualized HE "Choices" in England', *International Studies in Sociology of Education*, 28(3–4), pp. 299–325. Available at: https://doi .org/10.1080/09620214.2019.1619471 (Accessed 17 July 2022).

Baldwin, M. (2018) 'Scientific Autonomy, Public Accountability, and the Rise of "Peer Review" in the Cold War United States', *Isis*, 109(3), pp. 538–58. Available at: https://doi.org/10.1086/700070 (Accessed 14 February 2022).

Ball, C. E. (2018) *Review by Cheryl E. Ball*. Waterloo: Wilfrid Laurier University Press. Available at: https://www.wlupress.wlu.ca/Scholarly -Podcasting-Open-Peer-Review/Secret-Feminist-Agenda/Season-1/ Scholarly-Reviews-of-the-Secret-Feminist-Agenda-Podcast/Review-by -Cheryl-E.-Ball (Accessed 2 June 2022).

Ball, C. E. and Eyman, D. (2015) 'Editorial Workflows for Multimedia-Rich Scholarship', *The Journal of Electronic Publishing*, 18(4). Available at: https://doi.org/10.3998/3336451.0018.406 (Accessed 17 June 2022).

Bastian, H. (2015) 'Weighing Up Anonymity and Openness in Publication Peer Review', *PLOS Blogs: Absolutely Maybe*, 13 May. Available at: https://absolutelymaybe.plos.org/2015/05/13/weighing-up-anonymity -and-openness-in-publication-peer-review/ (Accessed 19 July 2022).

Basu, S. (no date) *The Delightful World of Super-Niche Podcasts | WNYC | New York Public Radio, Podcasts, Live Streaming Radio, News, WNYC*. Available at: https://www.wnyc.org/story/super-niche -podcasts/ (Accessed 19 May 2022).

Bathmaker, A.-M., Ingram, N. and Waller, R. (2013) 'Higher Education, Social Class and the Mobilisation of Capitals: Recognising and Playing the Game', *British Journal of Sociology of Education*, 34(5–6), pp. 723–43. Available at: https://doi.org/10.1080/01425692.2013 .816041 (Accessed 17 July 2022).

Batruch, A., *et al.* (2023) 'Are tracking recommendations biased? A review of teachers' role in the creation of inequalities in tracking decisions', Teaching and Teacher Education, 123, p. 103985. Available at: https:// doi.org/10.1016/j.tate.2022.103985.

Baugh, J. (2000) 'Racial Identification by Speech', *American Speech*, 75(4), pp. 362–4.

Beckstead, L. (2005) 'The Bouncing Story Project: International Online Radio Drama Collaborations in the Classroom', *Radio in the World: Papers from the 2005 Melbourne Radio Conference*, Melbourne, Victoria, p. 505.

Beckstead, L. (forthcoming) 'Context is King: Podcast Packaging and Paratexts', in L. Beckstead and D. Llinares (eds) *Podcast Studies: Practice into Theory*. Waterloo: Wilfrid Laurier University Press.

Beckstead, L. and Llinares, D. (2021) *Mack Hagood of Phantom Power: Sound Studies and Scholarly Podcasting*. [Podcast], 17 December. Available at: https://www.podpage.com/podcaststudiespodcast/mack -hagood-of-phantom-power-sound-studies-scholarly-podcasting/ (Accessed 29 April 2023).

Berlant, L. (2011) *Cruel Optimism*. Durham: Duke University Press.

Bhaskar, M. (2019) 'Curation in Publishing', in *The Oxford Handbook of Publishing*. Oxford: Oxford University Press. Available at: https:// doi.org/10.1093/oxfordhb/9780198794202.013.6 (Accessed 30 June 2022).

Biagioli, M. (2002) 'From Book Censorship to Academic Peer Review', *Emergences: Journal for the Study of Media & Composite Cultures*, 12(1), pp. 11–45. Available at: https://doi.org/10.1080 /1045722022000003435 (Accessed 14 February 2022).

Björk, B.-C. and Solomon, D. (2013) 'The Publishing Delay in Scholarly Peer-Reviewed Journals', *Journal of Informetrics*, 7(4), pp. 914–23. Available at: https://doi.org/10.1016/j.joi.2013.09.001 (Accessed 2 May 2022).

Blagojević, M. and Yair, G. (2010) 'The Catch 22 Syndrome of Social Scientists in the Semiperiphery: Exploratory Sociological Observations', *Sociologija*, 52. Available at: https://doi.org/10.2298/ SOC1004337B (Accessed 14 May 2023).

Blum, S. D. (2020) 'Why Ungrade? Why Grade?' in Susan D. Blum (ed.) *Ungrading: Why Rating Students Undermines Learning (and What to Do Instead)*, 1–22. Morgantown: West Virginia University Press.

Bone, K. D. (2021) 'Cruel Optimism and Precarious Employment: The Crisis Ordinariness of Academic Work', *Journal of Business Ethics*, 174, pp. 275–90. Available at: https://doi.org/10.1007/s10551-020-04605-2.

Boring, A. (2017) 'Gender Biases in Student Evaluations of Teaching', *Journal of Public Economics*, 145, pp. 27–41. Available at: https://doi.org/10.1016/j.jpubeco.2016.11.006 (Accessed 20 June 2022).

Boring, A., Ottoboni, K. and Stark, P. B. (2016) 'Student Evaluations of Teaching are not only Unreliable, they are Significantly Biased against Female Instructors', *Impact of Social Sciences Blog*.

Botelho, F., Madeira, R. A. and Rangel, M. A. (2015) 'Racial Discrimination in Grading: Evidence from Brazil', *American Economic Journal: Applied Economics*, 7(4), pp. 37–52. Available at: https://doi.org/10.1257/app.20140352 (Accessed 26 March 2023).

Brinson, N. and Lemon, L. (2022) 'Investigating the Effects of Host Trust, Credibility, and Authenticity in Podcast Advertising', *Journal of Marketing Communications*, pp. 1–19. Available at: https://doi.org/10.1080/13527266.2022.2054017 (Accessed 19 May 2022).

Brković, Č. (2022) '"Thinking With" When Peer Reviewing: Introduction to the PoLAR Online Emergent Conversation on Peer Review', *PoLAR: Political and Legal Anthropology Review*, 45(1), pp. 112–18. Available at: https://doi.org/10.1111/plar.12482 (Accessed 28 April 2023).

Brown, S., Clements, P., Grundy, I., Ruecker, S., Antoniuk, J. and Balazs, S. (2009) 'Published Yet Never Done: The Tension between Projection and Completion in Digital Humanities Research'. Available at: https://dspace.library.uvic.ca/handle/1828/8120 (Accessed 4 July 2022).

Buckler, E. (2020) 'First Peer-Reviewed Rap Album Published with U-M Press', 2 November, University of Michigan Library. Available at: https://www.lib.umich.edu/about-us/news/first-peer-reviewed-rap-album-published-u-m-press (Accessed 13 July 2022).

Bunn, M. and Bennett, A. (2020) 'Making Futures: Equity and Social Justice in Higher Education Timescapes', *Teaching in Higher Education*, 25, pp. 698–708. Available at: https://doi.org/10.1080/13562517.2020.1776247 (Accessed 19 July 2022).

Burnard, P., Mackinlay, E., Rousell, D. and Dragovic, T., eds (2022) *Doing Rebellious Research: In and beyond the Academy*. Leiden, Netherlands: Brill (Critical Issues in the Future of Learning and Teaching).

Butler, J. (2012) 'Precarious Life, Vulnerability, and the Ethics of Cohabitation', *The Journal of Speculative Philosophy*, 26(2), pp. 134–51. Available at: https://doi.org/10.5325/jspecphil.26.2.0134 (Accessed 20 June 2022).

Butterwick, S. and Dawson, J. (2005) 'Undone Business: Examining the Production of Academic Labour', *Women's Studies International*

Forum, 28(1), pp. 51–65. Available at: https://doi.org/10.1016/j.wsif
.2005.02.004 (Accessed 30 May 2022).

Canadian Press, T. (2019) *Funding for Ontario Colleges and Universities
to be Tied to 'Performance Outcomes'* | *CBC News, CBC*. Available
at: https://www.cbc.ca/news/canada/toronto/ontario-colleges
-university-performance-funding-budget-1.5094751 (Accessed
20 June 2022).

Cantat, C. (2022) 'The Politics of University Access and Refugee Higher
Education Programmes: Can the Contemporary University Be
Opened?' in C. Cantat, I. M. Cook and P. K. Rajaram (eds) *Opening
Up the University: Teaching and Learning with Refugees*. New York
and Oxford: Berghahn Books, pp. 89–110. Available at: https://
www.berghahnbooks.com/downloads/OpenAccess/CantatOpening/
(Accessed 17 July 2022).

Cantat, C. and Dönmez, P. E. (2021) 'Authoritarian and Neoliberal
Attacks on Higher Education in Hungary', *Radical Philosophy*, 210,
pp. 55–64.

Carey, K. (2020) 'The Bleak Job Landscape of Adjunctopia for Ph.D.s',
New York Times, 5 March. Available at: https://www.nytimes.com
/2020/03/05/upshot/academic-job-crisis-phd.html (Accessed 20 June
2022).

Cariou, W. (2020) 'On Critical Humility', *Studies in American Indian
Literatures*, 32(3), pp. 1–12. Available at: https://doi.org/10.1353/ail
.2020.0015 (Accessed 9 September 2021).

Castellano, V. (2023) 'Unfinished Adulthood: Discontinuous Precarities as
Epistemic Opportunities', *Allegra Lab*, May. https://allegralaboratory
.net/unfinished-adulthood-discontinuous-precarities-as-epistemic
-opportunities/.

Chalmers, J. K. (2021) 'Perceptions of Women in Authority Positions: The
Role of Warmth and Competence', Master's Thesis, University of Kent.
Available at: https://doi.org/10.22024/UniKent/01.02.88012 (Accessed
19 May 2022).

Chávez, K. and Mitchell, K. (2020) 'Exploring Bias in Student
Evaluations: Gender, Race, and Ethnicity', *PS: Political Science &
Politics*, 53(2), pp. 270–4. Available at: https://doi.org/10.1017/
S1049096519001744 (Accessed 20 April 2023).

Chion, M. (1994) *Audio-Vision: Sound on Screen*. Translated by
C. Gorbman. New York: Columbia University Press.

Chua, L. and Mathur, N., eds (2018) *Who Are 'We'?* Oxford and
New York: Berghahn Books. Available at: https://doi.org/10.3167
/9781785338885 (Accessed 26 July 2022).

Chugh, R., Grose, R. and Macht, S. (2021) 'Social Media usage by Higher
Education Academics: A Scoping Review of the Literature', *Education*

and Information Technologies, 26. Available at: https://doi.org/10 .1007/s10639-020-10288-z (Accessed 17 April 2023).

Clancy, P. and Goastellec, G. (2007) 'Exploring Access and Equity in Higher Education: Policy and Performance in a Comparative Perspective', *Higher Education Quarterly*, 61(2), pp. 136–54.

Clevenger, S. (forthcoming) 'On Idleness and Podcasting', in L. Beckstead and D. Llinares (eds) *Podcast Studies: Practice into Theory*. Waterloo: Wilfrid Laurier University Press.

Clevenger, S. and Oliver, R. (2016) 'Philosophy', *Somatic Podcast*, 22 June. Available at: https://somaticpodcast.com/philosophy/ (Accessed 16 July 2022).

Clevenger, S. and Rick, O. (2021) 'The Uses of Imperfections: Communicating Affect through the lo fi Podcast', *Journal of Audience Reception Studies* 18, pp. 323–38.

Cook, I. M. (2018) 'How Podcasting can Help us Rethink Higher Education', *Times Higher Education (THE)*, 12 November. Available at: https://www.timeshighereducation.com/blog/how-podcasting-can -help-us-rethink-higher-education (Accessed 20 July 2022).

Cook, I. M. (2022) 'Fuck Prestige', in C. Cantat, I. M. Cook and P. K. Rajaram (eds) *Opening Up the University: Teaching and Learning with Refugees*. New York and Oxford: Berghahn Books, pp. 209–19.

Cook, I. M. (2023) *Scholarly Podcasting: Why, What, How*. Routledge. Available at: https://www.routledge.com/Scholarly-Podcasting-Why -What-How/Cook/p/book/9780367439446 (Accessed 4 July 2022).

Cook, I. M., Krishna, P., Adi, Kotsila P. and Ådahl, S. (2020) 'The Corona Diaries', *Allegra Lab*, April. Available at: https://allegralaboratory.net/ the-corona-diaries/ (Accessed 17 July 2022).

Copeland, S. (2022) 'What is Open Science? ft. Dr. Juan Pablo Alperin', *Amplified*, 24 May. Available at: https://amplifypodcastnetwork.ca /2022/05/24/what-is-open-science-ft-dr-juan-pablo-alperin/ (Accessed 20 July 2022).

Copeland, S. and McGregor, H. (2021) *A Guide to Academic Podcasting*. Waterloo: WLU Press. Available at: https://scholars.wlu.ca/books/2 (Accessed 1 September 2021).

Copeland, S. and McGregor, H. (2023) 'Why Podcast?: Podcasting as Publishing, Sound-Based Scholarship, and Making Podcasts Count', *Kairos: A Journal of Rhetoric, Technology, and Pedagogy*, 27(1). Available at: https://kairos.technorhetoric.net/27.1/topoi/mcgregor -copeland/index.html (Accessed 29 August 2023).

Crowe, K. (2019) *Why does it Cost Millions to Access Publicly Funded Research Papers? Blame the Paywall | CBC News, CBC*. Available at: https://www.cbc.ca/news/health/research-public-funding-academic -journal-subscriptions-elsevier-librarians-university-of-california-1 .5049597 (Accessed 13 June 2022).

Dawson, D. (DeDe), Morales, E., McKiernan, E. C., Schimanski, L. A., Niles, M. T. and Alperin, J. A. (2022) 'The Role of Collegiality in Academic Review, Promotion, and Tenure', 17(4), p. e0265506. Available at: https://doi.org/10.1371/journal.pone.0265506 (Accessed 22 July 2022).

Dea, S. (no date) 'Two Misconceptions about "Collegial Governance"', *University Affairs*. Available at: https://www.universityaffairs.ca/opinion/dispatches-academic-freedom/two-misconceptions-about-collegial-governance/ (Accessed 6 June 2022).

Desson, C. and Evans, K. (2022) 'It's Pronounced Why?' Available at: https://www.cbc.ca/player/play/2021935171559 (Accessed 15 April 2022).

Docot, D. (2022) 'Dispirited Away: The Peer Review Process', *PoLAR: Political and Legal Anthropology Review*, 45(1), pp. 124–8. Available at: https://doi.org/10.1111/plar.12479 (Accessed 4 July 2022).

DORA (2013) *The Declaration on Research Assessment (DORA)*, *DORA*. Available at: https://sfdora.org/read/ (Accessed 4 April 2023).

Douglas, S. J. (2013) *Listening In: Radio and the American Imagination*. Minneapolis: University of Minnesota Press.

Doz, D. (2023) 'Factors Influencing Teachers' Grading Standards in Mathematics', *Oxford Review of Education*, 0(0), pp. 1–19. Available at: https://doi.org/10.1080/03054985.2023.2185217 (Accessed 28 April 2023).

Duggan, M. and Bishop, C. (2023). '"Our Teaching Is Rocking Their Ontological Security": Exploring the Emotional Labour of Transformative Criminal Justice Pedagogy', *Social Sciences*, 12(3). Available at: https://doi.org/10.3390/socsci12030162 (Accessed 15 May 2023).

Durrani, M., Gotkin, K. and Laughlin, C. (2015) 'Serial, Seriality, and the Possibilities for the Podcast Format', *American Anthropologist*, 117(3), pp. 1–4. Available at: https://doi.org/10.1111/aman.12302 (Accessed 12 May 2021).

Edison Research (2022) 'Super Listeners 2021 from Edison Research and Ad Results Media', *Edison Research*, 16 February. Available at: https://www.edisonresearch.com/super-listeners-2021-from-edison-research-and-ad-results-media/ (Accessed 18 May 2022).

'Editorial Board and Review Process' (no date) *Kairos: A Journal of Rhetoric, Technology, and Pedagogy*. Kairos: A Journal of Rhetoric, Technology, and Pedagogy. Available at: https://kairos.technorhetoric.net/board.html#review (Accessed 5 April 2022).

Ehrick, C. (2022) 'Ethereal Gender: Thoughts on the History of Radio and Women's Voices', in M. Lindgren and J. Loviglio (eds) *The Routledge Companion to Radio and Podcast Studies*. London: Taylor & Francis, pp. 144–51.

Eidsheim, N. (2012) 'Voice as Action: Toward a Model for Analyzing the Dynamic Construction of Racialized Voice', *Current Musicology*, 93, pp. 9–33, 152.

Eisenlohr, P. (2007) *Little India: Diaspora, Time, and Ethnolinguistic Belonging in Hindu Mauritius*. Berkeley: University of California Press.

Else, H. (2020) 'How a Torrent of COVID Science Changed Research Publishing – In Seven Charts', *Nature*, 588(7839), p. 553. Available at: https://doi.org/10.1038/d41586-020-03564-y (Accessed 13 June 2022).

Estermann, T., Pruvot, E. B., Kupriyanova, V. and Stoyanova, H. (2020) *The Impact of the Covid-19 Crisis on University Funding in Europe: Lessons Learnt from the 2008 Global Financial Crisis*. European University Association. Available at: https://eua.eu/downloads/publications/eua%20briefing_the%20impact%20of%20the%20covid-19%20crisis%20on%20university%20funding%20in%20europe.pdf (Accessed 7 July 2022).

Euritt, A. (2020) 'Within the Wires' Intimate Fan-based Publics', *Gender Forum: An Internet Journal for Gender Studies*, 77, pp. 34–50.

Feldman, Z. and Sandoval, M. (2018) 'Metric Power and the Academic Self: Neoliberalism, Knowledge and Resistance in the British University', *tripleC: Communication, Capitalism & Critique*, 16(1), pp. 214–33. Available at: https://doi.org/10.31269/triplec.v16i1.899 (Accessed 14 February 2022).

Felsenstein, F. and Connolly, J. J. (2015) *What Middletown Read: Print Culture in an American Small City*. Amherst: University of Massachusetts Press.

Fire, M. and Guestrin, C. (2019) 'Over-optimization of Academic Publishing Metrics: Observing Goodhart's Law in Action', *GigaScience*, 8. Available at: https://doi.org/10.1093/gigascience/giz053 (Accessed 19 July 2022).

Fitzpatrick, K. (2011) *Planned Obsolescence: Publishing, Technology, and the Future of the Academy*. New York: New York University Press. Available at: http://ebookcentral.proquest.com/lib/sfu-ebooks/detail.action?docID=865470 (Accessed 13 June 2022).

Fitzpatrick, K. (2018) *Generous Thinking: A Radical Approach to Saving the University*. Baltimore: Johns Hopkins University Press.

Flaherty, C. (2020) *Scholarly Rap, Inside Higher Ed*. Available at: https://www.insidehighered.com/news/2020/10/05/university-michigan-press-releases-first-rap-album-academic-publisher (Accessed 13 July 2022).

Fox, N. and Llinares, D. (2018) 'Cinematologists: Knowing Sounds', *Media Practice and Education*, 19(1), pp. 48–51. Available at: https://doi.org/10.1080/14682753.2017.1362170 (Accessed 11 March 2022).

Fyfe, A., Coate, K., Curry, S., Lawson, S., Moxham, N. and Røstvik, C. M. (2017) 'Untangling Academic Publishing: A History of the Relationship between Commercial Interests, Academic Prestige and the Circulation of Research'. Discussion Paper. University of St Andrews. Available at: https://eprints.bbk.ac.uk/id/eprint/19148/ (Accessed 2 June 2022).

Garcia-Marin, D. and Aparici, R. (2020) 'Domesticated Voices and False Participation: Anatomy of Interaction on Transmedia Podcasting', *Comunicar*, 28(63), pp. 97–107. Available at: https://doi.org/10.3916/C63-2020-09 (Accessed 21 July 2022).

Giroux, H. A. (2016) 'Writing the Public Good Back into Education: Reclaiming the Role of the Public Intellectual', in J. R. Di Leo and P. Hitchcock (eds) *The New Public Intellectual*. New York: Palgrave Macmillan, pp. 3–28.

Glass, I. (no date) 'If You Don't Have Anything Nice to Say, SAY IT IN ALL CAPS', This American Life. Available at: https://www.thisamericanlife.org/545/if-you-dont-have-anything-nice-to-say-say-it-in-all-caps/act-two-0 (Accessed 13 February 2022).

Goodale, G. (2011) *Sonic Persuasion: Reading Sound in the Recorded Age*. Baltimore: University of Illinois Press. Available at: http://ebookcentral.proquest.com/lib/ryerson/detail.action?docID=3413865 (Accessed 15 April 2022).

Gray, B. C. (2022) 'Things Unsaid: Exploring the Margins and Limits of Open', Congress of the Humanities and Social Sciences, 19 May.

Groth, S. K. and Samson, K. (2016a) 'Audio Papers – A Manifesto | Seismograf', *Seismograf*, 16. Available at: https://seismograf.org/fokus/fluid-sounds/audio_paper_manifesto (Accessed 4 July 2022).

Groth, S. K. and Samson, K. (2016b) 'Fluid Sounds', *Seismograf*, 16. Available at: https://seismograf.org/fokus/fluid-sounds (Accessed 5 July 2022).

Guidelines for Reviewing Podcasts and Podcast Series | H-Podcast | H-Net (no date) Available at: https://networks.h-net.org/node/59220/pages/6227737/guidelines-reviewing-podcasts-and-podcast-series (Accessed 5 July 2022).

Hagood, M. (2021) 'The Scholarly Podcast: Form and Function in Audio Academia', in J. W. Morris and E. Hoyt (eds) *Saving New Sounds*. Ann Arbor: University of Michigan Press (Podcast Preservation and Historiography), pp. 181–94. Available at: https://www.jstor.org/stable/10.3998/mpub.11435021.14 (Accessed 15 June 2022).

Hagve, M. (2020) 'The Money behind Academic Publishing', *Tidsskrift for Den norske legeforening*. Available at: https://doi.org/10.4045/tidsskr.20.0118 (Accessed 13 April 2022).

Hammersley, B. (2004) 'Audible Revolution', *The Guardian*, 12 February. Available at: https://www.theguardian.com/media/2004/feb/12/broadcasting.digitalmedia (Accessed 11 May 2023).

Hanna, R. N. and Linden, L. L. (2012) 'Discrimination in Grading', *American Economic Journal: Economic Policy*, 4(4), pp. 146–68.

Heffernan, T. (2022) 'Sexism, Racism, Prejudice, and Bias: A Literature Review and Synthesis of Research Surrounding Student Evaluations of Courses and Teaching', *Assessment & Evaluation in Higher Education*, 47(1), pp. 144–54. Available at: https://doi.org/10.1080/02602938 .2021.1888075 (Accessed 20 April 2023).

Heiskala, L., Erola, J. and Kilpi-Jakonen, E. (2021) 'Compensatory and Multiplicative Advantages: Social Origin, School Performance, and Stratified Higher Education Enrolment in Finland', *European Sociological Review*, 37(2), pp. 171–85. Available at: https://doi.org/10 .1093/esr/jcaa046 (Accessed 17 July 2022).

Howard-Sukhil, C., Wallace, S. and Chakrabarti, A. (2021) 'Developing Research through Podcasts: Circulating Spaces, A Case Study', *Digital Humanities Quarterly*, 015(3).

'HuMetricsHSS: Our Values Framework' (no date) *HuMetricsHSS*. Available at: https://humetricshss.org/our-work/values/ (Accessed 15 June 2022).

Hutchings, M. and Archer, L. (2010) '"Higher than Einstein": Constructions of Going to University among Working-Class Non-participants', *Research Papers in Education*, 16(1), pp. 69–91. Available at: https://doi.org/10.1080/02671520010011879 (Accessed 17 July 2022).

Ingold, T. (2011) *Being Alive: Essays on Movement, Knowledge and Description*. 1st edn. London: Taylor & Francis. Available at: https:// www.routledge.com/Being-Alive-Essays-on-Movement-Knowledge-and -Description/Ingold/p/book/9781032052311 (Accessed 21 June 2022).

Irving, E. (2023) 'Oxford University's Other Diversity Crisis' 1843 Magazine', *The Economist*, 1 March. Available at: https://www .economist.com/1843/2023/03/01/oxford-universitys-other-diversity -crisis (Accessed 15 April 2022).

Ivancheva, M. P. (2022) 'The Double Bind of Academic Freedom', in C. Cantat, I. M. Cook and P. K. Rajaram (eds) *Opening Up the University: Teaching and Learning with Refugees*. New York and Oxford: Berghahn Books, pp. 51–68. Available at: https://www .berghahnbooks.com/downloads/OpenAccess/CantatOpening/ (Accessed 17 July 2022).

Jajdelska, E. (2007) *Silent Reading and the Birth of the Narrator*. Toronto: University of Toronto Press.

Jakobson, R. (1981) *Selected Writings Volume III: Poetry of Grammar and Grammar of Poetry*. Berlin: De Gruyter Mouton. Available at: https://doi.org/10.1515/9783110802122 (Accessed 9 July 2022).

Jefferson, T., Rudin, M., Brodney Folse, S. and Davidoff, F. (2006) 'Editorial Peer Review for Improving the Quality of Reports of Biomedical Studies', *Cochrane Database of Systematic Reviews*, 1.

Available at: https://doi.org/10.1002/14651858.MR000016.pub2
(Accessed 20 July 2022).

Jenkins, H. (2006) *Convergence Culture: Where Old and New Media Collide*. New York: New York University Press.

Kairos: A Journal of Rhetoric, Technology, and Pedagogy (no date)
Available at: https://kairos.technorhetoric.net/board.html (Accessed
20 April 2022).

Kane, B. (2014) *Sound Unseen: Acousmatic Sound in Theory and Practice*. Oxford and New York: Oxford University Press.

Karpf, A. (2007) *The Human Voice: The Story of a Remarkable Talent*. London and New York: Bloomsbury.

Kaur, J. (2021) 'Towards an Anthropology of Coups', *Allegra Lab*.
Available at: https://allegralaboratory.net/towards-an-anthropology-of
-coups/ (Accessed 19 July 2022).

Kell, G. and Berkeley, U. C. (2021) *UC's Deal with Elsevier: What It Took, What It Means, Why It Matters*. Los Angeles: University of California Press. Available at: https://www.universityofcalifornia.edu
/news/uc-s-deal-elsevier-what-it-took-what-it-means-why-it-matters
(Accessed 14 February 2022).

Keohane-Burbridge, E. (2023) 'Review: *Dig*', *Reviews in Digital Humanities*, IV(1/2). Available at: https://doi.org/10.21428/3e88f64f
.84da360f (Accessed 24 August 2023).

Ketchum, Alex D. (2020) 'Report on the State of Resources Provided to Support Scholars Against Harassment, Trolling, and Doxxing While Doing Public Media Work', *Medium*, 14 July. Available at: https://
medium.com/@alexandraketchum/report-on-the-state-of-resources
-provided-to-support-scholars-against-harassment-trolling-and
-401bed8cfbf1 (Accessed 13 May 2023).

Ketchum, Alex D. (2022) *Engage in Public Scholarship! A Guidebook on Feminist and Accessible Communication*. Montreal: Concordia University Press.

Kezar, A., DePaola, T. and Scott, D. T. (2019) *The Gig Academy: Mapping Labor in the Neoliberal University*. Baltimore: Johns Hopkins University Press. Available at: http://ebookcentral.proquest.com/lib/
ryerson/detail.action?docID=5899753 (Accessed 20 June 2022).

Kezar, A. and Maxy, D. (2013) 'The Changing Academic Workforce', *Trusteeship*, 21(3). Available at: https://agb.org/trusteeship-article/the
-changing-academic-workforce/ (Accessed 20 June 2022).

Kinkaid, E., Emard, K. and Senanayake, N. (2020) 'The Podcast-as-Method?: Critical Reflections on Using Podcasts to Produce Geographic Knowledge', *Geographical Review*, 110(1–2), pp. 78–91.
Available at: https://doi.org/10.1111/gere.12354 (Accessed 6 April
2022).

Krause, M. W. (2017) 'Voice-Only Communication Enhances Empathic Accuracy', *American Psychologist*, 72(7), pp. 644–54. Available at: http://dx.doi.org/10.1037/amp0000147 (Accessed 25 April 2022).

Kunreuther, L. (2010) 'Transparent Media: Radio, Voice, and Ideologies of Directness in Postdemocratic Nepal', *Journal of Linguistic Anthropology*, 20(2), pp. 334–51. Available at: https://doi.org/10.1111/j.1548-1395.2010.01073.x (Accessed 26 July 2023).

Kunreuther, L. (2014) *Voicing Subjects: Public Intimacy and Mediation in Kathmandu*. Los Angeles: University of California Press. Available at: https://www.ucpress.edu/book/9780520270701/voicing-subjects (Accessed 24 April 2022).

Kwiek, M. (2005) 'The University and the State in a Global Age: Renegotiating the Traditional Social Contract?' *European Educational Research Journal*, 4(4), pp. 324–41.

LaBelle, B. (2021) *Acoustic Justice: Listening, Performativity, and the Work of Reorientation*. London and New York: Bloomsbury Academic.

Lawy, J. R. (2017) 'Theorizing Voice: Performativity, Politics and Listening', *Anthropological Theory*, 17(2), pp. 192–215. Available at: https://doi.org/10.1177/1463499617713138 (Accessed 1 March 2022).

Leggo, C., Paré, A. and Riecken, T. (2014) 'Peer-Reviewer Round Table Response to Ted Riecken's Scholarly Podcast, "Mapping the Fit between Research and Multimedia: A Podcast Exploration of the Place of Multimedia within / as Scholarship"', *McGill Journal of Education / Revue des sciences de l'éducation de McGill*, 49(3). Available at: https://mje.mcgill.ca/article/view/9242 (Accessed 15 February 2022).

Levay, M. (2018) 'On the Uses of Seriality for Modern Periodical Studies: An Introduction', *The Journal of Modern Periodical Studies*, 9(1), pp. v–xix.

Lieberman, A., Schroeder, J. and Amir, O. (2022) 'A Voice Inside My Head: The Psychological and Behavioral Consequences of Auditory Technologies', *Organizational Behavior and Human Decision Processes*, 170, p. 104133. Available at: https://doi.org/10.1016/j.obhdp.2022.104133 (Accessed 16 April 2022).

Llinares, D., Fox, N. and Berry, R., eds (2018) *Podcasting: New Aural Cultures and Digital Media*. Cham: Springer International Publishing. Available at: https://doi.org/10.1007/978-3-319-90056-8.

Lowe, R., Turner, M. and Schaefer, M. (2021) 'Dialogic Research Engagement through Podcasting as a Step towards Action Research: A Collaborative Autoethnography of Teachers Exploring their Knowledge and Practice', *Educational Action Research*, 29(3), pp. 429–46. Available at: https://doi.org/10.1080/09650792.2021 .1908905 (Accessed 18 May 2023).

Lynch, K. and Ivancheva, M. (2015) 'Academic Freedom and the Commercialisation of Universities: A Critical Ethical Analysis', *Ethics in Science and Environmental Politics*, 15(1), pp. 71–85. Available at: https://doi.org/10.3354/esep00160 (Accessed 1 March 2022).

MacNell, L., Driscoll, A. and Hunt, A. N. (2015) 'What's in a Name: Exposing Gender Bias in Student Ratings of Teaching', *Innovative Higher Education*, 40(4), pp. 291–303.

Malouff, J. M. and Thorsteinsson, E. B. (2016) 'Bias in Grading: A Meta-Analysis of Experimental Research Findings', *Australian Journal of Education*, 60(3), pp. 245–56. Available at: https://doi.org/10.1177 /0004944116664618 (Accessed 26 April 2023).

Mayer, R. (2017) 'In the Nick of Time? Detective Film Serials, Temporality, and Contingency Management, 1919–1926', *The Velvet Light Trap*, 79, pp. 21–35. Available at: https://doi.org/10.7560/ VLT7903 (Accessed 30 June 2022).

McEnaney, T. (2019) 'This American Voice: The Odd Timbre of a New Standard in Public Radio', in N. S. Eidsheim and K. Meizel (eds) *The Oxford Handbook of Voice Studies*. Available at: https://doi.org/10 .1093/oxfordhb/9780199982295.013.12 (Accessed 20 June 2022).

McGregor, H. (2018) *Response by podcast creator Hannah McGregor*. Wilfrid Laurier University Press. Available at: https://www.wlupress .wlu.ca/Scholarly-Podcasting-Open-Peer-Review/Secret-Feminist -Agenda/Season-1/Scholarly-Reviews-of-the-Secret-Feminist-Agenda -Podcast/Response-to-Reviews-From-Podcast-Host-Hannah-McGregor -PhD (Accessed 22 August 2023).

McGregor, H. (2019) 'Yer A Reader, Harry: HP Reread Podcasts as Digital Reading Communities', *Participations*, 16(1), pp. 366–89.

McGregor, H. (2022a) 'Podcast Studies', *Oxford Research Encyclopedia of Literature*. Available at: https://doi.org/10.1093/acrefore /9780190201098.013.1338 (Accessed 8 July 2022).

McGregor, H. (2022b) *A Sentimental Education*. Waterloo: Wilfrid Laurier University Press.

McHugh, Siobhan (2019) 'Beyond Journal Articles: Navigating the NTRO (Non-Traditional Research Outcome)', *Flow: A Critical Forum on Media and Culture*, 27 April. Available at: https://www.flowjournal .org/2019/04/beyond-journal-articles/ (Accessed 18 August 2021).

McKittrick, K. (2020) *Dear Science and Other Stories*. Durham: Duke University Press.

McMenemy, S. (no date) *Scholarly Podcasting Open Peer Review*. Waterloo: Wilfrid Laurier University Press. Available at: https://www.wlupress.wlu .ca/Scholarly-Podcasting-Open-Peer-Review (Accessed 2 June 2022).

Mengel, F., Sauermann, J. and Zölitz, U. (2017) *Gender Bias in Teaching Evaluations*. ROA. ROA Research Memoranda No. 007. Available at: https://doi.org/10.26481/umaror.2017007 (Accessed 20 June 2022).

Menzies, H. and Newson, J. (2007) 'No Time to Think: Academics' Life in the Globally Wired University', *Time & Society*, 16(1), pp. 83–98. Available at: https://doi.org/10.1177/0961463X07074103 (Accessed 19 July 2022).

Meserko, V. M. (2014) 'Going Mental: Podcasting, Authenticity, and Artist–Fan Identification on Paul Gilmartin's Mental Illness Happy Hour', *Journal of Broadcasting & Electronic Media*, 58(3), pp. 456–69. Available at: https://doi.org/10.1080/08838151.2014.935848 (Accessed 27 June 2022).

Mewburn, I. and Thomson, P. (2013) 'Why do Academics Blog? An Analysis of Audiences, Purposes and Challenges', *Studies in Higher Education*, 38(8), pp. 1105–19. Available at: https://doi.org/10.1080/03075079.2013.835624 (Accessed 3 April 2022).

Mishra, S., Lunner, T., Stenfelt, S., Rönnberg, J. and Rudner, M. (2013) 'Seeing the Talker's Face Supports Executive Processing of Speech in Steady State Noise', *Frontiers in Systems Neuroscience*, 7, p. 96. Available at: https://doi.org/10.3389/fnsys.2013.00096 (Accessed 13 February 2022).

Morris, J. (no date) 'PodcastRE: About', *PodcastRE*. Available at: https://podcastre.org/about (Accessed 31 May 2022).

Morris, S. M., Rai, L. and Littleton, K., eds (2021) *Voices of Practice: Narrative Scholarship from the Margins*. Hybrid Pedagogy Inc. Available at: https://voicesofpractice.pressbooks.com/ (Accessed 28 December 2021).

Moten, F. and Harney, S. (2004) 'The University and the Undercommons: Seven Theses', *Social Text*, 22(2), pp. 101–15.

Mountz, A. (2016) 'Women on the Edge: Workplace Stress at Universities in North America', *The Canadian Geographer / Le Géographe canadien*, 60(2), pp. 205–18. Available at: https://doi.org/10.1111/cag.12277 (Accessed 1 June 2022).

Mussell, J. (2015) 'Repetition: Or, "In Our Last"', *Victorian Periodicals Review*, 48(3), pp. 343–58.

Neave, G. (2001) 'The European Dimension in Higher Education: An Excursion into the Modern Use of Historical Analogues', in J. Huisman, P. Maassen and G. Neave (eds) *Higher Education and the Nation-State*. Oxford: Pergamon, pp. 13–73.

Newman, K. (2014) 'Book Publishing, Not Fact-Checking', *The Atlantic*. Available at: https://www.theatlantic.com/entertainment/archive/2014/09/why-books-still-arent-fact-checked/378789/ (Accessed 13 April 2022).

Nimmo, Jamie (2023) 'Party's over at Spotify as Celebrity Podcast Deals Fall Flat', *The Times*, Saturday 28 January 2023. https://www.thetimes.co.uk/article/partys-over-at-spotify-as-celebrity-podcast-deals-fall-flat-prks60lg2?utm (Accessed 16 April 2023).

OECD (2021) 'Reducing the Precarity of Academic Research Careers'. Available at: https://www.oecd-ilibrary.org/content/paper/0f8bd468-en (Accessed 20 June 2022).

O'Regan, J. P. and Gray, J. (2018) 'The Bureaucratic Distortion of Academic Work: A Transdisciplinary Analysis of the UK Research Excellence Framework in the Age of Neoliberalism', *Language and Intercultural Communication*, 18(5), pp. 533–48. Available at: https://doi.org/10.1080/14708477.2018.1501847 (Accessed 14 January 2022).

Outram, D. (2006) *Panorama of the Enlightenment*. Getty Publications.

Patten, D. (2022) 'Joe Rogan Backs Down, A Bit; Promises To "Do Better" in Response to Covid Vaccine Dust-Up With Neil Young, Joni Mitchell', *Deadline*, 30 January. Available at: https://deadline.com/2022/01/joe-rogan-spotify-covid-controversy-neil-young-joni-mitchell-1234922830/ (Accessed 2 June 2023).

Pavlovic, V., Weissgerber, T., Stanisavljevic, D., Pekmezovic, T., Garovic, V. and Milic, N. (2020) 'How Accurate Are Citations of Frequently Cited Papers in Biomedical Literature?' bioRxiv, p. 2020.12.10.419424. Available at: https://doi.org/10.1101/2020.12.10.419424 (Accessed 21 June 2022).

'Peer Review: Scholarly Podcast Submissions' (no date) *BC Studies*. Available at: https://bcstudies.arts.ubc.ca/submissions/scholarly-podcast-submissions/ (Accessed 8 June 2022).

Rajaram, Prem Kumar (2021) 'The Moral Economy of Precarity', *Focaal* Blog, 9 February. Available at: http://www.focaalblog.com/2021/02/09/prem-kumar-rajaram-the-moral-economy-of-precarity/ (Accessed 2 June 2023).

Rak, J. (2013) *Boom! Manufacturing Memoir for the Popular Market*. Waterloo: Wilfrid Laurier University Press.

Rawls, A. W. and Garfinkel, H. (2002) *Ethnomethodology's Program: Working Out Durkheim's Aphorism*. Boston: Rowman & Littlefield.

Reay, D. (2004) 'Cultural Capitalists and Academic Habitus: Classed and Gendered Labour in UK Higher Education', *Women's Studies International Forum*, 27(1), pp. 31–9. Available at: https://doi.org/10.1016/j.wsif.2003.12.006 (Accessed 1 March 2022).

Reay, D., Crozier, G. and Clayton, J. (2009) '"Strangers in Paradise"?: Working-class Students in Elite Universities', *Sociology*, 43(6), pp. 1103–21. Available at: https://doi.org/10.1177/0038038509345700 (Accessed 1 March 2022).

Riecken, T. (2014) 'Mapping the Fit between Research and Multimedia: A Podcast Exploration of the Place of Multimedia Within / As Scholarship', *McGill Journal of Education / Revue des sciences de l'éducation de McGill*, 49(3). Available at: https://mje.mcgill.ca/article/view/9061 (Accessed 18 August 2021).

Ross-Hellauer, T. (2017) 'What is Open Peer Review? A Systematic Review'. F1000Research. Available at: https://doi.org/10.12688/f1000research.11369.2 (Accessed 14 February 2022).

Royston, R. A. (2021) 'Podcasts and New Orality in the African Mediascape', *New Media & Society*, p. 14614448211021032. Available at: https://doi.org/10.1177/14614448211021032 (Accessed 19 April 2022).

Saenger, P. (1997) *Space between Words: The Origins of Silent Reading*. Redwood City: Stanford University Press.

Salvati, A. J. (2015) 'Podcasting the Past: Hardcore History, Fandom, and DIY Histories', *Journal of Radio & Audio Media*, 22(2), pp. 231–9. Available at: https://doi.org/10.1080/19376529.2015.1083375 (Accessed 27 June 2022).

Savit, L. (2020) 'Examining the Fan Labor of Episodic TV Podcast Hosts', *Transformative Works and Cultures*, 34. Available at: https://doi.org/10.3983/twc.2020.1721 (Accessed 27 June 2022).

Schafer, R. M. (1977) *The Soundscape: Our Sonic Environment and the Tuning of the World*. New York: Alfred A. Knopf.

Schroter, S., Black, N., Evans, S., Godlee, F., Osorio, L. and Smith, R. (2008) 'What Errors do Peer Reviewers Detect, and does Training Improve their Ability to Detect Them?' *Journal of the Royal Society of Medicine*, 101(10), pp. 507–14. Available at: https://doi.org/10.1258/jrsm.2008.080062 (Accessed 20 July 2022).

Scriven, R. (2022) 'Making a Podcast: Reflecting on Creating a Place-Based Podcast', *Area* 54(2), pp. 260–7.

Seismograf Peer (no date) *Seismograf*. Available at: https://seismograf.org/peer (Accessed 5 July 2022).

Shahjahan, R. A. (2015) 'Being "Lazy" and Slowing Down: Toward Decolonizing Time, Our Body, and Pedagogy', *Educational Philosophy and Theory*, 47(5), pp. 488–501. Available at: https://doi.org/10.1080/00131857.2014.880645 (Accessed 19 July 2022).

Shahjahan, R. A. (2020) 'On "Being for Others": Time and Shame in the Neoliberal Academy', *Journal of Education Policy*, 35(6), pp. 785–811. Available at: https://doi.org/10.1080/02680939.2019.1629027 (Accessed 19 July 2022).

Singer, J. B. (2019) 'Podcasting as Social Scholarship: A Tool to Increase the Public Impact of Scholarship and Research', *Journal of the Society for Social Work and Research*, 10(4), pp. 571–90. Available at: https://doi.org/10.1086/706600 (Accessed 12 July 2021).

Small, C. (1999) 'Musicking – The Meanings of Performing and Listening. A Lecture', *Music Education Research*, 1(1), pp. 9–22. Available at: https://doi.org/10.1080/1461380990010102 (Accessed 27 April 2022).

Smith, J. (2019) 'ESC: Sonic Adventure in the Anthropocene'. Available at: https://doi.org/10.3998/mpub.10120795 (Accessed July 3 2021).

Smith, J. (2021) 'Lightning Birds'. Available at: https://www.press.umich .edu/11714652/lightning_birds (Accessed 26 July 2023).

Smith, R. (2006) 'Peer Review: A Flawed Process at the Heart of Science and Journals', *Journal of the Royal Society of Medicine*, 99(4), pp. 178–82. Available at: https://doi.org/10.1177 /014107680609900414 (Accessed 20 June 2022).

Smith, S. (2015) 'Multiple Temporalities of Knowing in Academic Research', *Social Science Information*, 54(2), pp. 149–76. Available at: https://doi.org/10.1177/0539018414566421 (Accessed 20 July 2022).

SMT-Pod: The Society for Music Theory Podcast (2021) *SMT-Pod*. Available at: smt-pod.org (Accessed 4 July 2022).

Sommers, M. S. and Phelps, D. (2016) 'Listening Effort in Younger and Older Adults: A Comparison of Auditory-Only and Auditory-Visual Presentations', *Ear and Hearing*, 37(Suppl 1), pp. 62S–8S. Available at: https://doi.org/10.1097/AUD.0000000000000322 (Accessed 13 February 2022).

Souleles, D. (2021) 'The Only Lesson is that there Aren't Enough Jobs', *Allegra Lab*, October. Available at: https://allegralaboratory.net/ the-only-lesson-is-that-there-arent-enough-jobs/ (Accessed 3 July 2022).

Spinelli, M. and Dann, L. (2019) *Podcasting: The Audio Media Revolution*. London and New York: Bloomsbury Publishing USA.

Spooren, P., Brockx, B. and Mortelmans, D. (2013) 'On the Validity of Student Evaluation of Teaching: The State of the Art', *Review of Educational Research*, 83(4), pp. 598–642. Available at: https://doi.org /10.3102/0034654313496870 (Accessed 20 June 2022).

Statistics Canada (2022) *The Daily – Trends in Private and Public Funding in Canadian Colleges, 2019/2020*. Available at: https:// www150.statcan.gc.ca/n1/daily-quotidien/220120/dq220120c-eng.htm (Accessed 7 July 2022).

Sterne, J., Lingold, M. C., Mueller, D. and Trettien, W. (2018) 'Demands of Duration: The Futures of Digital Sound Scholarship', in M. C. Lingold, D. Mueller and W. Trettien (eds) *Digital Sound Studies*. Durham and London: Duke University Press, pp. 267–84. Available at: https:// library.oapen.org/handle/20.500.12657/25765 (Accessed 22 September 2021).

Stoever, J. L. (2016) 'Introduction: The Sonic Color Line and the Listening Ear', in *The Sonic Color Line*. New York University Press (Race and the Cultural Politics of Listening), pp. 1–28. Available at: https://doi .org/10.2307/j.ctt1bj4s55.4 (Accessed 17 February 2021).

Sullivan, J. L. (2019) 'The Platforms of Podcasting: Past and Present', *Social Media + Society*, 5(4), p. 2056305119880002. Available at: https://doi .org/10.1177/2056305119880002 (Accessed 3 February 2022).

Sullivan, R. (2022) *The Betrayal of Anne Frank: A Cold Case Investigation*. New York: HarperCollins.

Taylor and Francis (no date) 'Understanding the Peer Review Process: What is Peer Review? A Guide for Authors'. Available at: https:// authorservices.taylorandfrancis.com/publishing-your-research/peer -review/ (Accessed 20 April 2023).

Tenenboim-Weinblatt, K. and Neiger, M. (2018) 'Temporal Affordances in the News', *Journalism*, 19(1), pp. 37–55. Available at: https://doi.org /10.1177/1464884916689152 (Accessed 29 June 2022).

Tennant, J. P. et al. (2017) 'A Multi-disciplinary Perspective on Emergent and Future Innovations in Peer Review'. F1000Research. Available at: https://doi.org/10.12688/f1000research.12037.3 (Accessed 14 February 2022).

The Public Historian (no date) Los Angeles: University of California Press. Available at: https://online.ucpress.edu (Accessed 20 April 2022).

Thorn, J. [@jessethorn] (2020) 'The #JJGo Drinking Game Is Here. If You're a @MaxFunHQ member, go to the BoCo page to Download this Year's Episode and Play along with me, @Jordan_Morris and Special Guest @BenjaminAhr as We Get WAY too Drunk and High to Drive. https://maximumfun.org/boco/[Tweet]', Twitter, 4 April. Available at: https://twitter.com/JesseThorn/status /1246623951272341504?s=20 (Accessed 29 April 2022).

Tobin, S. J. and Guadagno, R. E. (2022) 'Why People Listen: Motivations and Outcomes of Podcast Listening', *PLoS One*, 17(4), p. e0265806. Available at: http://dx.doi.org/10.1371/journal.pone.0265806 (Accessed March 16 2022).

Turner, M. W., Schaefer, M. Y. and Lowe, R. J. (2021). 'Teacher Development through Podcast Engagement', in P. Clements, R. Derrah and P. Ferguson (eds) *Communities of Teachers & Learners*. JALT. Available at: https://doi.org/10.37546/JALTPCP2020-07 (Accessed 10 May 2022).

Types of Peer Review (no date) Wiley. Available at: https://authorservices .wiley.com/Reviewers/journal-reviewers/what-is-peer-review/types-of -peer-review.html (Accessed 14 February 2022).

UNESCO (2021) 'Recommendation on Open Science', *UNESCO Digital Library*. Available at: https://unesdoc.unesco.org/ark:/48223/ pf0000379949.locale=en (Accessed 20 June 2022).

Vitali, F. (2016) 'Teaching with Stories as the Content and Context for Learning', *Global Education Review*, 3(1), pp. 27–44.

Vostal, F., Benda, L. and Virtová, T. (2019) 'Against Reductionism: On the Complexity of Scientific Temporality', *Time & Society*, 28(2), pp. 783–803. Available at: https://doi.org/10.1177/0961463X17752281 (Accessed 19 July 2022).

Ware, M. and Mabe, M. (2015) *The STM Report: An Overview of Scientific and Scholarly Journal Publishing*. International Association of Scientific, Technical and Medical Publishers. Available at: https://www.stm-assoc.org/2015_02_20_STM_Report_2015.pdf (Accessed 19 July 2022).

Warner, M. (2002) 'Publics and Counterpublics', *Public Culture*, 14(1), pp. 49–90.

Watters, A. (2015) 'The Web We Need To Give Students', *BRIGHT Magazine*, 25 June. Available at: https://brightthemag.com/the-web-we-need-to-give-students-311d97713713 (Accessed 20 July 2022).

Weidman, A. (2014) 'Anthropology and Voice', *Annual Review of Anthropology*, 43(1), pp. 37–51. Available at: https://doi.org/10.1146/annurev-anthro-102313-030050 (Accessed 7 February 2019).

Weiner, J. (2014) 'Toward a Critical Theory of Podcasting', *Slate Magazine*. Available at: http://www.slate.com/articles/arts/ten_years_in_your_ears/2014/12/what_makes_podcasts_so_addictive_and_pleasurable.html (Accessed 16 April 2022).

Welch, A. (2016) 'Audit Culture and Academic Production', *Higher Education Policy*, 29(4), pp. 511–38. Available at: https://doi.org/10.1057/s41307-016-0022-8 (Accessed 17 September 2021).

Weldon, G. (2018) 'It's All in Your Head: The One-Way Intimacy of Podcast Listening', *NPR*, 2 February. Available at: https://www.npr.org/2018/02/02/582105045/its-all-in-your-head-the-one-way-intimacy-of-podcast-listening (Accessed 27 April 2022).

White, D. (2021) 'Incitement! Incremental Theory for an Imminent Fascism', *Allegra Lab*. Available at: https://allegralaboratory.net/incitement-incremental-theory-for-an-imminent-fascism/ (Accessed 19 July 2022).

Whitford, E. (2020) 'Public Higher Ed Funding Still Has Not Recovered From 2008 Recession', *Inside Higher Ed*. Available at: https://www.insidehighered.com/news/2020/05/05/public-higher-education-worse-spot-ever-heading-recession (Accessed 7 July 2022).

Woodrow, R. (2016) *NTRO: A Model for Change, Non | Traditional Research Outcomes*. Available at: https://nitro.edu.au/articles/edition-2/ntro-a-model-for-change (Accessed 22 September 2021).

Wrather, K. (2016) 'Making "Maximum Fun" for Fans: Examining Podcast Listener Participation Online', *Radio Journal: International Studies in Broadcast & Audio Media*, 14(1), pp. 43–63. Available at: https://doi.org/10.1386/rjao.14.1.43_1 (Accessed 27 June 2022).

Wright, S. and Shore, C. (2017) *Death of the Public University?: Uncertain Futures for Higher Education in the Knowledge Economy.* New York and Oxford: Berghahn Books.

Yeates, R. (2018) 'Serial Fiction Podcasting and Participatory Culture: Fan Influence and Representation in the Adventure Zone', *European Journal of Cultural Studies*, 23(2), pp. 223–43. Available at: https://doi.org/10.1177/1367549418786420 (Accessed 27 June 2022).

Ylijoki, O.-H. and Mäntylä, H. (2003) 'Conflicting Time Perspectives in Academic Work', *Time & Society*, 12(1), pp. 55–78. Available at: https://doi.org/10.1177/0961463X03012001364 (Accessed 19 July 2022).

PODCASTS MENTIONED

We want you to listen to All. The. Podcasts., especially the ones experimenting with scholarship and peer review. To make that easier we've provided this list of all the podcasts we've mentioned in the book, along with a quick description of what they're about. We'd like to give you a link so you can find them easily but, well, a system for citing podcasts reliably with links that are permanent doesn't exist yet (see Chapter 4).

One other note: we *hate* it when Works Cited lists leave out podcasts and put them in their own separate list like they don't belong there among all the 'legitimate' scholarship. So where we've actually cited content from a podcast, you'll find that citation above in the Works Cited list, but you'll also find them listed below among all of the podcasts we mentioned anywhere in the book. So you can find all of these podcasts easily. Happy listening!

Amplified

> *Amplified* is an audio interview blog series created by Stacey Copeland for the Amplify Podcast Network.

The Annex Sociology Podcast

> *The Annex Sociology Podcast* is a show for academic sociologists. We discuss ideas, news and research of interest to the academic sociology community.

Archive Fever

> *Archive Fever* is a new Australian history podcast featuring intimate conversations with writers, artists, curators, fellow

historians and other victims of the research bug. On each episode, co-hosts Clare Wright and Yves Rees talk to archive addicts about what kind of archives they use, how often they use them, when they got their first hit. Join us as we ask: what madness is this?

Big Biology

Scientists talking to scientists, but accessible to anyone. We are living in a golden age of biology research. *Big Biology* is a podcast that tells the stories of scientists tackling some of the biggest unanswered questions in biology.

BredowCast

BredowCast is the podcast of the Leibniz Institute for Media Research | Hans Bredow Institute. Once a month, the hostess Johanna Sebauer discusses current topics from the perspective of communication science and media law with researchers.

Brexit Brits Abroad

This is a podcast all about what Brexit means to and for British citizens living in the EU27. Hosted by Dr Michaela Benson, it focuses on Brexit as it takes place in the context of real lives, busting myths about this forgotten population, and engages with questions about migration, identity, citizenship and belonging (with a few pondering on how to do sociological research about Brexit thrown in for good measure).

The Cinematologists

A podcast and film club that aims to bring fans, filmmakers, critics and academics together to watch, discuss and engage with cinema of all forms, genres and eras, hosted and produced by Dr Dario Llinares and Dr Neil Fox.

Disasters: Deconstructed

Ksenia Chmutina and Jason von Meding reflect on human society from diverse disciplinary and ideological perspectives to understand the root causes of disasters.

The Familiar Strange

A podcast about doing anthropology: that is, about listening, looking, trying out and being with, in pursuit of uncommon knowledge about humans and culture. Brought to you by your familiar strangers Ian Pollock, Jodie-Lee Trembath, Julia Brown, Simon Theobald and Kylie Wong Dolan, and produced by Deanna Catto and Matthew Phung.

Ganatantra

The *Ganatantra* podcast is about politics in India, but steering clear of intrigue and personalities, and the everyday news cycle.

GDP – The Global Development Primer

Dr Bob Huish covers a wide range of issues in International Development, while featuring the work of researchers and practitioners from around the world.

Harry & Katniss & Hazel & Starr

Brenna Clarke Gray and Joe Lipsett bring you a weekly podcast about young adult literature, their film and television adaptations and everything in between.

Heart of Artness

Heart of Artness is a journey into the labyrinthine workings of Australia's Aboriginal art world. We hear from artists and the non-Indigenous folk who interact with them to produce cutting-edge contemporary art. *Heart of Artness* is a University of Wollongong research project devised, produced and co-hosted by Siobhan McHugh with co-host Margo Neale, Senior Indigenous Curator at the National Museum of Australia, in association with art historian Ian McLean. It is funded by the Australian Research Council.

A History of Central Florida

A 50-episode podcast that examines the history of central Florida through local area objects found in museums, historical organizations and other places. By Robert Cassanello.

History of the World in 100 Objects

Director of the British Museum Neil MacGregor narrates 100 programmes that retell humanity's history through the objects we have made.

How to Build a Stock Exchange

Dr Philip Roscoe asks: What makes financial markets work? What is in a price, and why does it matter? How did finance become so important? And who invented unicorns? We will see that stock markets have places, and histories and politics, and come to understand just how influential stock markets are in our everyday lives. Can we fashion a finance that's fit for purpose and can contribute to a world worth living in?

In Common

A weekly podcast featuring interviews on human–environment relationships, featuring engaging stories, research findings and experiences from academics and practitioners.

Ipse Dixit

Ipse Dixit is a podcast on legal scholarship and features several special series including 'From the Archives' (historical recordings of interest to legal scholars and lawyers); 'The Homicide Squad' (investigations of the true stories behind different murder ballads); and 'The Day Antitrust Died?' (oral histories of the 1974 Airlie House Conference on antitrust law).

Island Crime

Each season of *Island Crime* focuses on one crime story based on Vancouver Island. Season 1: 'Where is Lisa?' digs into the disappearance of twenty-one-year-old Lisa Marie Young. Season 2: 'Gone Boys' follows the mystery of men who have gone missing in recent years on Vancouver Island. Season 3: 'Missing Michael' is the story of Michael Dunahee, a little boy from Victoria, BC, who vanished from a playground in 1991 at the age of four.

Marrying Out

Just two generations ago, before the term 'multiculturalism' became the norm, Australian society was polarized between two main groups: Protestants and Catholics. Irish Catholics were an underclass – Australia's first ethnic minority. When a Catholic married a Protestant, conflict and family fatwas often ensued. In Part One, mixed marriage couples describe how they bridged the gap, despite conflict with family and church authorities. In Part Two, children who grew up in a mixed marriage recall a hybrid world of divided loyalties. ABC Radio National, Hindsight.

The Maxwell Institute Podcast

Where faith and scholarship have a nice conversation over lunch. Scholars from the Latter-day Saint tradition and beyond talk about faith, history, scripture, philosophy, theology and more.

Mundaréu

Mundaréu, podcast de Antropologia produzido em parceria entre o Labjor/Unicamp e o Departamento de Antropologia da UnB. [Translation: Mundaréu, an anthropology podcast produced in partnership between Labjor/Unicamp and the Department of Anthropology at UnB]

My Dad Wrote a Porno

Imagine if your Dad wrote a dirty book. Most people would try to ignore it and pretend it had never happened – but not Jamie Morton. Instead, he's decided to read it to the world in this award-winning comedy podcast. With the help of his friends, James Cooper and Alice Levine, Jamie will be reading a chapter on each episode and discovering more about his father than he had ever bargained for.

My Favorite Theorem

Kevin Knudson and Evelyn Lamb speak with mathematics professionals about their favourite result. And since the best things in life come in pairs, guests explain what they think pairs best with their theorem.

New Books Network

Interviews with Authors about their New Books.

Open Peer Review Podcast

The aim of the *Open Peer Review Podcast* is to demonstrate how a podcast might be used by scholars and researchers as part of the pathway to a peer-reviewed research output, such as a published journal paper. Each episode focuses on one particular research project. A peer reviewer — an expert in the same field — joins the researcher to discuss the project in progress. Produced by Lori Beckstead along with Valentina Passos-Gastaldo and Anna Ashitey.

The People's Scientist

A weekly podcast covering the latest scientific findings on Neuroscience, Physiology and Nutrition. Dr Stephanie Caligiuri provides scientific evidence on important topics pertaining to our brain, body and nutrition.

Phantom Power

Mack Hagood explores how sound works in the arts, music and culture. Deep but accessible, each episode features the sounds and ideas of a contemporary artist, musician or sound scholar. Detailed production makes these more than just interviews – they're movies for your mind.

PhDivas

A podcast about academia, culture and social justice across the STEM/humanities divide. Dr Liz Wayne and Dr Christine 'Xine Yao are two women of colour, Ivy League PhDs navigating higher education. Biomedical engineer meets literary critic. Both fans of lipstick.

The Podcast Studies Podcast (formerly *New Aural Cultures*)

Examining podcasting as a practice, a technology and a medium, through an academic lens. Produced and hosted by Dario Llinares and Lori Beckstead.

Podlog

Moritz Klenk's daily podcast log. I jot down questions of my day, speaking of self-imposed chores (like daily podcasting), the torments and joys of a liberal arts dissertation, texts read and unread, friends, acquaintances and strangers, observations along the way, or nowhere in particular . . . 'Just this – that, various things'. (Translated from the original German)

Podonian Avatars

This podcast isn't real, but if it was, it would probably be a monthly discussion of new research on the Pannonian Avars, a mediaeval nomadic people probably of Mongolian origin who lived in Central and Eastern Europe, hosted by Dr Marina Makandar.

Preserves: A Manitoba Food History Project

A food history podcast hosted by Kent Davies and Janis Thiessen. From the packing table to the dinner table, from restaurant specials to grandma's secret recipes, we consider the cultural, social and commercial aspects of Manitoba food and what it means to us.

ResonanceCast

ResonanceCast is a new multimodal series that seeks to tease out timely shared concerns. After their articles have been published on Allegra Lab, we invite two authors to come together to discuss each other's texts and the wider-ranging issues both speak to. Their conversation is moderated by someone from the Allegra Lab editorial collective.

Secret Feminist Agenda

Secret Feminist Agenda is a podcast by Hannah McGregor about the insidious, nefarious, insurgent and mundane ways we enact our feminism in our daily lives.

Serial

Hosted by Sarah Koenig, *Serial* unfolds one story – a true story – over the course of a whole season. The show follows the plot and characters wherever they lead, through many surprising twists and turns.

Sexuality and Gender in Turkey Podcast (Mert Kocak)

In this podcast series, I interview young academics fresh from fieldwork, or still in the field researching sexuality and gender in Turkey.

SMT-Pod

SMT-Pod is a creative venue for timely conversations about music, with episodes chosen through an open, collaborative peer-review process. The variety of episode topics reflect the diversity of the scholars and their scholarship in the field, making *SMT-Pod* an invaluable publication for music analysts at any stage.

Somatic Podcast

Sam Clevenger and Oliver Rick explore topics concerning everyday experiences, spaces, cultures, practices and communities related to our bodies in motion. The podcast is intended to be a digital vehicle for collaboration, through which interested contributors can explore a topic of interest through the methodology of digital audio.

The Sources of the Nile

A podcast about media, science and water diplomacy in the Nile basin, exploring the role that media and scientific communication play in shaping transboundary conflicts and cooperation. Featuring journalists and researchers from different Nile countries who discuss the media coverage of hot topics like the Grand Ethiopian Renaissance Dam.

SRB Podcast

To many, Russia, and the wider Eurasia, are a riddle, wrapped in a mystery, inside an enigma. But it doesn't have to be. Sean Guillory dispels the stereotypes and myths about the region with lively and informative interviews on Eurasia's complex past, present and future, featuring an eclectic mix of topics from punk rock to Putin and everything in between.

State of the Theory

Politics. Power. Popular Culture. A mash-up of Serious Academic Questions and the most topical news and trends in pop culture, taking a new topic each week and colliding it with 'critical theory'.

Teaching in Higher Ed

A podcast exploring the art and science of being more effective at facilitating learning. Bonni Stachowiak also shares ways to increase personal productivity, so we can have more peace in our lives and be even more present for our students.

This American Life

A weekly public radio show and podcast hosted by Ira Glass. Each week they pick a different theme and put together different stories around it.

This Week in Virology

TWiV is a podcast about viruses – the kind that make you sick. With Vincent Racaniello.

The Vocal Fries

A podcast about linguistic discrimination. Carrie Gillon and Megan Figueroa teach you how not to be an asshole about language.

What the If?

Spencer Wirth-Davis and Ryan Kopperud ask strange, hilarious, paranormal, tough and mysterious questions – then laugh our way to the best answers we can muster.

Who do we think we are?

From Brexit and the COVID-19 pandemic to the Windrush deportation scandal, citizenship and the responsibilities of the

UK government to the people of Hong Kong, it seems that citizenship and migration in Britain are never far from the headlines. Professor Michaela Benson and her guests debunk taken-for-granted understandings of who is a citizen and who is a migrant in Britain today.

Witch, Please

A fortnightly podcast about the Wizarding World of Harry Potter hosted by Hannah McGregor and Marcelle Kosman.

You Got This!

A weekly podcast about teaching, learning and pivoting to digital from the Learning Technology and Innovation team at Thompson Rivers University.

INDEX

www.ingramcontent.com/pod-product-compliance
Ingram Content Group UK Ltd.
Pitfield, Milton Keynes, MK11 3LW, UK
UKHW020733280225
455688UK00012B/634